Breath of Africa

J. L. Bwye

Elfrida -
It is great to meet you
here, and thankyou for your
lovely hospitality.
Jane Bwye
June 2014 EAWL.

CROOKED
CAT

Discover us online:
www.crookedcatpublishing.com

Contact us:
enquiries@crookedcatpublishing.com

This book is dedicated
to the people of Kenya

BREATH OF AFRICA is a contemporary novel which draws on my experience of over half a century living in Kenya.

Its forty year gestation period led to long periods of support from many people; first and foremost my six children, whose upbringing was responsible for the protracted birth; and my husband Roy, who in the latter stages made sure I would not be distracted by household chores; with special mention to my daughter Heather Parsons whose painting inspired the cover.

I owe a big debt of gratitude to John Sibi-Okumu for his enthusiastic and valuable authentication of Charles, and the late Michael Legat got me thinking constructively about a plot. Then Richard Herkes provided thoughtful endorsement, which boosted my self-confidence. But without the support, encouragement and practical guidance from the on-line Authonomy community, this book would still be languishing in obscurity.

When I was about to abandon all hope and go the self-publishing route, along came Steph Patterson, the mother cat of Crooked Cat Publishing. Her enthusiasm, and the commitment of editor Maureen Vincent-Northam, has made the homeward stretch quite painless.

As they say in Kenya – *Asante sana* – Thank you very much.

Jane Bwye
Eastbourne, March 2013

Breath of Africa

PART I

1954 – 1960

A State of Emergency existed in Kenya between the years 1952 – 1959, declared by the Government as a result of terrorism, which was politically fuelled by conflict over land, between Mau Mau members of the Kikuyu tribe and British settlers.

CHAPTER 1

Kenya Highlands

"Watch out, someone's there!" Caroline Bond bent a blind away to peer out of the school's dining room window. In the bright moonlight she could see the silvery leaves and orange flowers of the grevillea trees lining the avenue to the school entrance.

A dark figure strode up the driveway, paused and looked towards the boundary, then disappeared behind the other side of the building.

Caroline brushed aside the blonde curls bobbing over her eyes. She consulted the watch she'd recently received for her fourteenth birthday, and turned to her friend who crouched beside her.

"Quick, Teresa, we've got five minutes to get out!"

She wrenched open the window. Its warped frame groaned loudly against the sill. Did the noise wake anyone? She waited for what seemed an hour as Teresa climbed through. Her friend's silky hair was caught into the collar of her dressing gown. Caroline reached forward to release the long black locks. But Teresa had frozen for a moment, unable to move, stuck midway in and out of the window.

A heavy crunch of footsteps rounded the corner of the building. Teresa glanced back, eyes stricken with panic, and Caroline gave her a mighty shove before sliding through herself.

The lower edge of the window was stuck against the frame. She closed it as much as she dared, but an extra shadow was visible to the discerning eye.

Caroline held her breath and looked at her best friend, who stared back, eyes wide, and gripped her closely behind a stone pillar.

***

Ondiek paused, turned his back and scrutinised the lines of gum trees that marked the boundary. He studied every yard, from the main road to the corner of the cemetery, where his gaze lingered. The girls often crept out to hide behind the single headstone of the nun's grave, which was nestled among the self-sown seedlings, but they were not his immediate problem.

He ignored the broken shadow of the pillar outside the dining room and continued his beat, then whipped off his greatcoat to bundle it beneath a bush. He needed to be free of impediment.

***

With her dressing gown flying open, and a piece of carrot bumping in her pocket, Caroline ran after Teresa through the sentinel row of trees and down the border track towards the main road. A strip of tarmac on a camber of dirt between grassy fields stretched before them. They jogged together along the footpath, ducking into the ditch twice as glaring headlights swept by.

Caroline wondered what old Boney, her stepfather, would think if he saw her now. She knew that the Mau Mau Emergency was in full swing and the farmers of the White Highlands, engrossed with fending off the freedom fighters, thought their children safer at school than in vulnerable homesteads isolated on vast estates. A curfew was in force, and there was no danger of meeting anyone on foot, but she slowed down and looked over her shoulder, anyway.

She could have sworn there was a half-naked figure, gliding through the grass behind them, but perhaps it was her imagination.

The forest loomed ahead, and a trail wound among the wattle trees, leading into open fields.

"Race you to the wheat field!" Teresa suggested.

Caroline accepted the challenge, even though Teresa, two years her senior and at least three inches taller, was the fastest runner in school. Her heels drummed along the track as she hurtled through the shadows.

Emerging from the trees, she stopped to draw breath and saw Teresa sitting on a clump of grass, emptying sand from her shoes. Fine, thought Caroline, you've beaten me this time, but wait till we get on the horses.

The wind shivered the wheatears in waves across the field. The tip of a nearby pine swayed as an owl hooted and leapt from its perch, its ponderous wings beating the air as it swung upwards. She breathed deeply and followed Teresa, walking with springy steps beside the field, feasting her senses on the scene, storing it in her mind until the next time she could escape the confines of the school.

Caroline crossed the main road, watching Teresa's shadow mingle with ghostly gum trees. Dozens of neglected gravestones loomed at different angles above the silvery swathes of grass near the race course. Caroline's footsteps quickened. A direct path to their destination lay through the graveyard.

"Let's not go that way," she said, as Teresa made for the short cut.

"Okay."

Caroline exchanged an understanding smile with her friend, then peered back through the trees. A fleeting shadow turned into the cemetery behind them. If someone meant to harm them, wouldn't he have attacked them by now? She decided not to tell Teresa, who would probably laugh at her, anyway. But she had to say something.

"Isn't it strange how we're frightened of this place, and yet don't mind the nun's grave?"

"Ssh…hurry up, Caroline, and keep quiet!"

They emerged from the trees and picked up the path, which led out onto the freshly mown expanse of the racecourse.

A loud crashing sound shattered the peace. It came from the forest a few yards away. Caroline darted towards the centre of the racetrack and stopped, her heart thumping wildly. The crashing also stopped, followed by a chill and heavy silence.

***

Ondiek held still among the trees. Warily, he stood over the creature, scarcely recognisable as a man, sprawling at his feet. His lips curled in distaste. The figure, glistening with filth, was naked but for a tattered piece of cloth around the groin. The wild, crinkled hair spread in mud-caked locks against a bed of leaves. The eyes, wide with hatred, glittered at him in the moonlight.

With a twist of his spear Ondiek pulled it free, tearing the barb against flesh, creating a jagged open wound in his victim's thigh. The eyes glazed. He took up his *rungu* and gave a sharp tap to the head.

***

Heavy steps blundered through the undergrowth, the menacing cracks becoming fainter in retreat. Several long moments passed.

Caroline recovered first. "That was a near thing. The steps are too heavy for a duiker, and I know there aren't any big animals in this part of the country. Do you think it was a Mau Mau?"

"Ssh..." Teresa put a finger to her lips, and then took to her heels.

Caroline fled along the racetrack behind her friend until the welcome sight of a hurdle loomed ahead. She dived behind, and peeped over to study the forest edge. At the level of the treetops, the moon slipped behind a cloud.

It felt safer in the dark afterglow, and she settled in the shelter of the hurdle to share a packet of cream biscuits she had stolen from the school tuck shop. She fingered the piece of carrot in her pocket. Her nerves were still jangling.

"Are we going to get the horses for our race?" Her voice came out in a tentative quiver.

Throughout the week, she'd been waiting for this moment. The last time they'd come here, to gallop bareback down the straight, she had coped better than Teresa with the slippery feel of the horse between her knees. She wanted to prove that her victory was not a fluke. But what if she fell off near the forest?

Teresa shook her head. "I've had enough excitement for tonight. I think the horses can do without their treat. Let's get back."

With mixed feelings, Caroline stood up to shake the crumbs from her dressing gown.

"I'm going to say hello to Domino anyway," she said, ducking under the rails. She glanced back, relieved to see Teresa following her to the stables.

The horses nickered, and Caroline fondled the ears of her big grey gelding, breathing gently into his nostrils and enjoying the tickle of his hairs as he nuzzled intimately against her neck. She palmed the piece of carrot, which he took delicately into his mouth and then scrunched it with his teeth.

He blew his nose loudly, snorting droplets directly into her face, making her step back laughing as she wiped the drizzle away with her sleeve. She opened the stable door, taking a head collar off its hook and tying the loose end of the rope to the opposite side of the noseband to make improvised reins.

"Are you coming, Teresa?"

Caroline took off her dressing gown and led the horse to a mounting block, hitching up her pyjama bottoms before throwing her leg over his back.

"We can walk them along the track as close as we dare to the forest, then turn and race back."

The feel of Domino's coat was warm against her bare thighs. His skin rippled as the large shoulder muscles moved in front of her. The horses jogged as they turned onto the track, but were obedient to the pull on the head collars. Caroline settled her body into the new motion, keeping Domino steady, waiting for Teresa.

The darkness of the forest loomed ahead, until Caroline felt they were close enough. Teresa wobbled uncomfortably half a length ahead of her. Caroline felt Domino tense his muscles in anticipation. She grabbed a large piece of mane in one hand and neck reined him round.

"Let's goooo!"

A thunderous rush of air took her breath away and hair whipped over her face to stream behind. Powerful muscles moved beneath her, thrusting her from side to side. She abandoned the rope and leaned along Domino's neck, clinging onto the coarse hairs of his long flowing mane.

Teresa's horse matched strides beside her. She closed her thighs, urging Domino on and called to him. An ear flicked back in acknowledgement and his gallop quickened. The whole world was rocking, swaying, thundering, but she drew ahead and the winning post flashed by.

"Wheeee!"

Her victory cry rang out and the horse beneath her swerved. Caroline let herself tumble off, rolling over on the springy turf to land flat on her back. She gazed up at the black star-pricked sky while regaining her breath, and then dusted herself off, casting a triumphant glance at Teresa who had fallen ten yards away.

The horses were cropping hungrily at the grass near the exit from the racecourse. It was only after determined tugging that Domino allowed himself to be led back into the confinement of his stable.

It was uncomfortable crouching behind the nun's tombstone, waiting for the guard. Five long minutes ticked by, and still no sign of him.

"I think he must have gone to sleep," whispered Caroline. But Teresa made her wait five more minutes before creeping down the path and climbing onto the veranda.

Caroline wrenched the window open with relief. Thank goodness a prowling nun hadn't discovered it and locked them out. She peered into the dining room.

"All's clear."

She bundled through and forced the window shut, but Teresa froze beside her.

"What is it?"

"Look."

The guard, his back turned, stood by the graveyard, as though studying it. Then he strode past the window, his unbuttoned overcoat billowing behind him, and disappeared down the drive.

"Do you think he's been there all the time, Teresa?"

"Of course not, silly. But let's get to bed quickly."

"Goodnight," Caroline whispered, then turned into her dormitory.

She never slept after these night forays. She huddled under her blanket with a torch, cramming a little red notebook with the story of her adventure, using a secret code.

The Mau Mau Emergency made life more exciting than school, with its lessons, games and prep.

But the thrashing in the forest preyed on her mind. It could only have been a man, possibly the same one who had stalked them along the road.

11

Her shoulders gave an involuntary shudder and she buried her face in her pillow.

CHAPTER 2

Kenya Highlands

Twenty miles to the south, the moon gleamed over a wood and iron farm cottage, its roof carpeted with creepers. The arc of a security light curved over the lawn, and a Rhodesian Ridgeback lay on the veranda steps, head on its paws.

Its ears cocked as a rapid burst of fire broke the silence.

The dog bounded down the drive, drowning the sound with full-throated barks.

Charles Omari, son of Ondiek, stirred uneasily in the staff quarters. He rose from his slatted bed to peer through a crack in the boarded window.

There it was again, a recurrent sound of gunfire in the night.

He secured the bolt on his door and hesitated, then dragged a table against it and piled two chairs on top. He heard no movement from Mwangi the driver in the next-door room. Charles shivered back to bed and folded the blanket over his head. If anything happened, he would call the spirits to witness that he had not heard a sound.

A fist crashed against his door, and the rough brogue of Dudley Myers called out.

"Open up, boy! I need you to drive the truck. Come on – it's an emergency!"

"*Ndio*, Bwana." Yes, sir.

Charles groaned back his answer and grabbed his trousers. He'd been temporarily employed to keep milk records while his cousin was on leave. Why had he boasted to the bwana that he could drive? It wasn't his job to get up in the middle of the night because of an emergency. Where was Mwangi anyway?

He heaved down the furniture he had stacked against the door, and followed Myers to the garage, where the memsahib waited.

The dog bounded towards them.

"Lie down, Simba! Guard the house."

It cowered back to the veranda.

The staccato sound of the party line telephone filled the empty house behind them.

Short…short…long…short…short…long…

A goose hissed.

And then again the telephone pealed out the code.

Charles drove past the stables, and turned left onto a feeder road.

"The shots came from Boney's farm next door," said Myers. "But first we must take the memsahib to the emergency meeting point."

After a twenty-minute drive, Charles swung the car off the main road. Four pairs of headlights probed the darkness ahead of him. Women and children gathered inside the farmhouse to brew coffee and huddle together through the waiting period, while their men conferred on the lawn. One man remained on guard over their families, while the rest prepared to confront the elusive enemy terrifying the agriculturally rich White Highlands.

Charles was detailed to drive a truckload of armed farmers towards the source of the disturbance.

He stopped by a wheat field, and several men jumped off to fan out in a crouching line facing the source of the shots. The labour lines where the workers lived lay some distance beyond.

Dudley Myers detached himself, flare in hand. A renewed burst of firing rent the air and the burly Irishman hurled his flare into the sky, bathing the huts in an eerie glow. Men dodged and weaved through the waist-high crop and entered the compound, firing salvoes into the air.

"You! Take us to the farmhouse."

Charles winced at the broken Kiswahili, and the haughty attitude of the Kenya Police Reservist who addressed him, but he reversed out of the field.

When would the white men realise that most Africans could understand English perfectly, despite the occasional difficulty with pronunciation? Once he returned from Oxford, he would refuse to talk to them in Kiswahili. But Charles knew he must be patient. His time would come. First he had to go to Nairobi to pass the entrance exam, and then find the funding. But God would help him get there.

The officer opened the garden gate at the end of an avenue of gum trees, which led away from the wheat field. He beckoned Charles to follow. A light burned in one of the windows.

The wooden floor of the veranda creaked under their feet. A narrow slit of light flickered onto the boards. Charles peered through a gap in the curtains. A hurricane lamp stood on a table beside an armchair, where a white-haired form hunched with his back to them.

"Check the doors and windows."

At the whispered order, Charles moved away, every nerve straining as he fumbled in the shadows, looking for evidence of a break-in. He prowled among the bushes which encircled the house. A twig scraped against a window and he ducked for cover. Nothing else moved, and he reported back.

"The shots can't have been a diversion, then, but we'd better make sure."

The officer rapped at the front door.

The figure in the armchair stirred and grunted, the telephone falling from his hand.

"Who's that?"

"It's the KPR. Are you all right, Boney?"

15

"Huh."

The old man corded up his dressing gown and shuffled to the door. He drew back the rusty iron bolts.

"There's some shooting in your labour lines, and we're making sure there's no funny business up here."

"So you heard it too, did you? I've been trying to get hold of young Myers, but there's no reply."

"Dudley's out there this minute, old chap, defending your property."

"Well, that's fine then. Come along in and have a drop of the hard stuff; leave the excitement to the young 'uns. Can't say I approve of this messing about with guns anyway. I trust my boys, despite the Emergency."

The officer declined. "I must get back to see what's going on. Are you alone?"

"My wife is in Nairobi on a shopping spree. I didn't go this time; it's all too energetic for me."

As Charles drew the truck up beside the line of farmers, a fusillade of shots burst over them. He scanned the shadows. Nothing stirred. Then he noticed a large store behind the huts.

An orange glow danced behind the slatted bamboo, and flames licked at the rafters. Another prolonged burst of shots filled the night, and he saw Myers staggering backwards.

An uncanny, high-pitched cry emanated from the farmer.

"Look, you bunch of bums! It's the bamboo which is expanding and bursting in the flames, not the Mau Mau shooting at us – it's the bamboo…the bamboo…"

He stumbled towards them, his inane laugh rising above the confused murmur of the farmers.

Charles joined the men to form a chain to the nearest water tap. They stripped to the waist before passing buckets between them. Then he realised there were no other black men present. Where were the workers? He stopped to rest, detaching himself. The labour lines were uncannily quiet. For the first time, he noticed the doors of the huts were ajar.

By morning, Mwangi still had not appeared, so Charles drove Myers back to the scene.

"You did well last night. Would you like to join the Home Guard when your cousin returns from leave? I can put in a good word for you."

Charles had no desire to become one of the loyalist troops.

"No thank you, Bwana; I'll be studying for my university entrance exam."

"Oh, you're one of those, are you?"

"Yes, Bwana; I'm going to Oxford."

"And what makes you think you'll get in?"

"I have a brother who is even now studying palaeontology there."

Charles knew that palaeontology had something to do with his tribal ancestors, but Myers changed the subject, and he suspected the farmer did not wish to show his ignorance.

"How old are you?"

"Twenty-two."

The farmers surveyed the damage, kicking among the ashes. Only two stone stools and some charred bamboo remained of the building. Boney stooped to pick up an object wedged under a stool and put it in his pocket.

A slow gathering of workers joined them as Boney and his Headman conversed in pidgin Swahili.

"How did the fire start?"

The Headman shuffled his feet and looked down.

"*Sijui.*" I don't know.

"You know that fires are forbidden in that store."

The man remained silent.

"Answer my question." Boney's voice was controlled.

"*Ndio,* Bwana."

"Who made the fire?"

The Headman's eyes slid back to the ground, and the crowd shuffled closer.

Boney gave up. He mustered the men and detailed their chores for the day. Myers hovered in the background, a revolver holstered prominently round his waist.

"You're not going to leave it at that, are you, Boney? What have you picked up?"

Boney showed it to him. "Looks like a bone from a very young animal."

Myers held out his hand. "I'll see to it."

"What are you going to do?"

"It's time you agreed to have your men screened by the police, Boney. There's obviously been some sort of oathing ceremony here. You can't get away from it."

Myers beckoned to Charles. "You can take me home now."

Charles shuddered. Everyone knew that the Mau Mau were holding secret rituals in the forests. He'd read stories in the newspapers about the Kikuyu people being forced to eat repulsive animal body parts, binding them with oaths to kill the white farmers who had taken the best land. Thank goodness his tribe was not involved.

When he had completed the milk records, Charles left the office to watch the herd disperse into a nearby field. Myers called him back.

"I didn't know Swara had calved down?"

He traced his finger down the paper, looking for the cow with the name of an antelope.

"No, Bwana, she hasn't."

"What's this, then?" Myers pointed at a scribble below the typewritten names of the milking cows. Charles hadn't noticed it. Someone must have come in during his absence from the office.

"How can she give milk this morning, when she's not had her calf? Did you write this?"

"No, Bwana."

"Who did?"

"*Sijui.*"

"What do you mean, 'I don't know'? Where's Mwangi?"

Charles shrugged. "I haven't seen him, Bwana."

"He tried to report sick this morning, had to have his leg bandaged, said he'd fallen over a fence. I don't believe him." Myers went to the door and shouted.

The driver limped round a corner of the stables, a dirty fez askew on his head. He passed Charles with a look of pure hatred in his eyes.

"Bring Swara to me."

Mwangi turned to call to one of the milkers.

"No – you!" The farmer stabbed a finger at Mwangi's chest. "Now!"

Mwangi ducked through the fence into the twenty-acre field.

The milkers were talking in low tones behind them, and Myers silenced them sharply.

"When you've cleared up this muck," he gestured towards the cowpats, "I want you to break up the concrete. We're going to lay new cement."

He motioned to Charles to unlock the door of a nearby store, and the men sullenly took an implement each. It would take them many hours.

The cattle grazed at the far end of the field. Charles watched as a cow bounded away from the herd, then doubled back. Mwangi, waving his arms, limped to cut her off. The cow hesitated, then charged at her tormentor. Mwangi fell, his hat toppling into the grass, to reveal lengths of wiry hair sticking up above his head.

The workers chuckled, and Myers motioned three of them to help bring the cow in, while Mwangi scrambled for his fez.

The animal had been forcefully induced.

After the evening milking, Myers beckoned Charles towards the garage.

"I want you to take me to Boney's farm again. I need to give this back."

He dug into his pocket and produced the charred piece of bone, shaped like a tiny hoof.

"It's a wonder that poor cow survived."

Charles looked meaningfully at his watch.

"As soon as Mwangi is fit enough to drive," Myers said in a rare moment of generosity, "I'll give you a couple of days' leave."

Charles and Myers stood by while Boney showed his Headman the evidence.

"We both know what this means," he said. "An oathing ceremony happened last night – didn't it?"

"Bwana…"

But Boney stopped him. "This is getting too big for us. It's time for you Kikuyus to go."

"Bwana," the Headman gabbled urgently, "I couldn't help what happened last night. We had to do it. If we'd refused we'd all be dead now. I don't mean you any harm. Please, it is those other white men—"

"And to the Mau Mau I'm just another white man to be got rid of. No – it's finished."

"But, Bwana, the police will beat our brains out."

"I'm sorry. I can do nothing about the police, but you could always turn informer."

The Headman's face hardened.

"Go back to work," said Boney. "Once you've all gone, I don't know how I'm going to manage."

Charles's cousin returned from leave, but Mwangi was still off work, and Myers asked him to remain as driver.

"You said I could have leave to visit my family."

"I did. You may go at the weekend, but only for three days. And don't be late back."

Five mudded huts nestled inside a barricade of thorns surrounding the family homestead. Its boundary had moved ten yards out from its position since his last visit. There was a new hut in the clearing.

Charles, son of the fourth wife of *Mzee* Ondiek, the wizened guard at the school, stepped gingerly across a patchwork of cracks in the bare earth between chicken droppings and cowpats.

As he approached the main hut, a stooped figure appeared bending under a load of firewood, which strained against the band round her forehead. Simaloi, the tribal sorceress and his father's first wife, had gained more wrinkles than he remembered. She was too old for child bearing but once she had unburdened herself of the firewood, she stood tall and proud, her features betraying her Masai ancestry. Charles had listened as a child to tales of raids against that nomadic tribe, which wandered at will over the south of the country. Simaloi was his father's most prized spoil of war. She had been captured as a young girl and had borne him many children, the eldest of whom, Jackson Ondiek, even now studied in Oxford.

Charles waited.

She greeted him by spitting at his feet to ward off evil. He smiled.

But she did not smile back.

"Your father's in trouble," she said. "I saw it in the signs last week. And he has taken another wife." She jutted her chin towards the new hut near the entrance to the compound.

Charles could not resist voicing his thoughts. "They are not connected – the trouble and the new wife?"

Simaloi's lips twitched. "No, but the trouble is serious."

His youngest half-sister emerged from the hut and squatted

on a stone stool beside them; she would inherit the secrets of her mother's skills when the old woman retired to the tribal cave at the end of her life. Only Jackson knew the location of the cave. Charles suspected that his brother's studies were connected to the secret it held.

"It's a very strong *thahu*," she said. "We're trying to find a way against it. We need to know who cursed him."

Mzee Ondiek appeared from the dark confines of the largest hut in the *boma,* bearing a large *sufuria* of *chang'aa,* and Charles rose to greet his father. He took the proffered tin mug and dipped it into the fierce home-brewed liquid, which seared his throat. He squatted on his heels beside the old man. By evening, the effects of the alcohol had loosened his father's tongue, and the tale he told was unlike any other Charles had heard.

"Once the girls were inside the building, I checked the window was closed."

"Is that all?"

"Yes, my son. My job is to guard the school from a Mau Mau attack."

"I know, *Mzee*," Charles addressed the old man with respect.

"Nothing was said in my instructions about anybody coming out of the building, but I know the students are my responsibility."

"Is this *thahu* connected with the man you speared in the forest?"

Mzee jutted his chin towards Simaloi. "She says so."

"Why didn't you kill him?"

"I couldn't wait; the forest was thick, and dark. And it would have frightened the girls even more. He made no sound when I took my spear from his leg, and there was much blood. Perhaps he did die?"

"You know he didn't."

A prickle of fear crept up Charles's spine, and he shivered it away. Bad things were happening; the country was in turmoil.

His pastoral Kisii ancestors had occupied these highlands for generations, moving their livestock wherever the grass was greenest, becoming more constrained for space as the white farmers staked their claims.

But the Kikuyu workers living as squatters on designated sections of the farms were claiming the land as theirs. It was the Kikuyu and the white men who were embroiled in this politically fuelled conflict. How could their curse harm his father?

"You'd better stay here, *Mzee*," said Charles, "until we find an answer to the curse."

Ondiek emitted a long drawn-out sigh. "I might do that. My strength is leaving me."

Charles turned to prepare for the night, but the old man touched his arm.

"One of the girls the Mau Mau stalked – Teresa – I've known from a little girl."

"Teresa? You mean Teresa Myers from our farm?" asked Charles.

"Yes, and her friend Caroline."

Charles thought of Caroline who often came to stay with Teresa, a quiet girl with softly moulding jodhpurs scarcely hiding her budding figure. But he preferred the tomboyish Teresa. He knew her better and admired her vivacity and reckless courage. Her olive skin and profuse black hair, which wound into tight curls when wet, excited him. The girls rode round the farm on their horses, innocently leaving in their wake groups of mocking *totos*, who would imitate their motion of rising to the trot amid roars of raucous laughter.

He needed to warn Teresa against further night escapades. It would give him an excuse to see her.

CHAPTER 3

Kenya Highlands

Caroline drew rein after a long gallop across the stubble, and waited for Teresa to catch up. The Christmas holidays were nearly over and she'd spent most of the time, as usual, on the Myers' farm. She preferred it here, to the old-fashioned gloominess of Boney's house. She still thought of it as Boney's place even though she'd lived here with her mother for nearly half her life. The way those two carried on together caused her to feel superfluous, and Boney being old enough to be her grandfather, made it ridiculous.

It wouldn't have been like this if her father were alive. But Caroline dismissed the thought of his vague figure from her distant past. She had no difficulty deciding between the wide open spaces of Africa and the crowds of smoggy London. If she wanted to stay here, she told herself, she'd have to put up with being ignored.

The horses cooled off while they walked through a stand of wattle trees and emerged onto a hill overlooking the dairy.

Teresa would be a senior this year, and there were Higher School Certificate exams for her to face.

"I know you want to go on one last midnight ride before I leave school, Caroline, but as a prefect I have to set a good example, and it was rather frightening last time."

"I suppose so…"

"And Charles has warned me off," she continued. "Apparently that crashing we heard in the forest might have

24

been something to do with the Mau Mau."

"So you've told him our secret?"

"He seemed to know it already."

Caroline saw Charles emerge from the dairy, and wave to them. Teresa waved back and took up the reins to urge her horse down the slope.

By the time Caroline had walked Domino to the stables, Teresa had gone back up the hill hand in hand with Charles. Caroline watched them disappear into the bushes. She led the horse into his stable and rubbed him down. The *syce* hovered nearby, but she waved him away.

"We'll have to be content with our own company again, won't we?" She mumbled against Domino's neck as she slipped on the head collar to lead him to the paddock. The *syce* followed with Teresa's chestnut, and Caroline leaned against the gate, watching the horses gallop away, bucking, rearing, and revelling in their freedom.

The sun warmed the back of her neck, and she took off her riding cap to shake out her hair. She gazed at the gleaming lines of Domino's toned muscles, comparing him with the chestnut, and envying the contented way they cropped the grass side by side, with not a care in the world. Domino swished his tail, stamped his feet, and quivered the skin at his withers to shrug off the flies. He turned his head, mouth dripping with half-chewed grass, to nudge away the persistent insects from his flanks leaving a dark stain on his coat.

Puffs of cloud floated over the gum trees on the horizon, and the intensity of blue turned into lighter shades as she craned her neck to look directly overhead. Filled with peace, she turned her head towards the stables.

Dudley Myers stood outside the dairy, watching her. How long had he been there?

"Where's Charles?"

She glanced back up the slope. "I'm not sure..."

A figure rounded the corner of the office to stop beside

Dudley.

"I know where he is, Bwana. Do you want me to fetch him?"

"Yes, Mwangi. I need to talk to him."

Helplessly, Caroline watched the man run up the hill. She gestured towards the grazing horses.

"A pretty sight, aren't they?"

But Dudley's eyes were on the hill.

"I'm going to need a driver when the police take all the *Kukes* away for screening," he muttered. "The other tribes are not nearly as intelligent or hard-working. But that young chap would be better than nothing."

Caroline saw Charles emerge from the brow of the hill and run down the slope, brushing at his clothes. A couple of twigs were sticking from his close-cropped head.

"Been spending your tea break having a nap, have you?" Dudley motioned Charles into the office. "I'll have to find more for you to do in future. I want you to drive the truck to the Nairobi Races tomorrow. Mwangi will show you what needs to be done. And you must call the *watu* for a meeting this evening."

Caroline went to the tack room. She took down Domino's bridle from its hook and looked for the saddle soap, and then she heard the office door slam. Dudley's car accelerated up the drive, and a few minutes later Teresa walked in.

"My, that was close! Did Daddy suspect anything?"

"You're very lucky – he was only looking for Charles."

"Thanks, Caroline. I don't know what we'd do without you."

But Caroline was angry. "That doesn't mean I don't disapprove of you both," she said. "Do you really know what you're doing? What if something happens?"

"What do you mean?"

"You know…" Caroline faced Teresa in exasperation. They'd learned their biology at school; surely Teresa knew what she was referring to. "It's not that I don't like Charles…"

26

Teresa threw her head back. "Oh, Caroline, you do make me laugh – you wait until you fall in love!"

"But isn't it risky, being alone so often with him? And you'll have to confess, won't you?"

Caroline had often seen Teresa queuing to go to confession on Fridays when the priest came to the convent, and sometimes wished she, too, could escape the monotony of study.

Teresa tossed her head. "Nothing's *happened*." She looked away. "And anyway, Charles knows what he's doing, I can rely on him. His people know how to enjoy sex without going too far. He told me they have to, because if a girl loses her virginity before marriage she is ruined."

Caroline started rubbing vigorously at her saddle. Teresa took a bridle apart and prepared to clean it.

"That man Mwangi gives me the creeps. He stole up on us so quietly. I was glad when he followed Charles down. The way he was looking at me made me feel as if somebody had walked over my grave. Do you think it might have been him in the forest that night we broke out of school?"

"You don't have to worry about him, Teresa. I've just heard that he's being sent away with all the rest of the Kikuyus. They're going into detention until the Emergency is over."

***

That evening Myers addressed the gathering of workers, using his Headman as interpreter.

"The police are going to take away all the Kikuyus and ask about the Mau Mau. But you needn't worry if you've only taken the first oath… If you confess, you won't go into detention. But you won't be allowed back here to work. You will have to go to the reserve."

There was uproar.

"We've lived on the farm for years, and we don't have any

shambas in the reserve," they shouted.

"Anybody who does not confess…" Myers bellowed over the clamour, "…and who is found telling an untruth, will be detained in prison!"

A stunned silence descended on the crowd. The people broke into groups and murmured together. Finally, they pushed the Headman forward.

"We want Mwangi to buy some things for us when you go to Nairobi. We won't have anything when we get to the reserve. We will pay him."

The men rummaged in their pockets and their *bibis* reached hands deep into their cleavages to unfold filthy pieces of cloth. They drew out stained bank notes tattered with use and, one by one, approached Mwangi. He noted down their requirements. Most asked for blankets, kettles, and farm implements, and some entrusted a whole month's wages to the driver.

***

Caroline hung over the stable door watching in the half-light as Domino pulled at his hay net. Behind the off-cuts of the stable wall, she heard a scuffle and a whisper.

A pair of headlights swung up the drive, and she coughed.

"My parents have arrived, Teresa. See you tomorrow!"

Teresa caught up with her as she walked towards the farmhouse.

"I'd better not stay with Charles when you're not there to keep watch."

"I don't know why I'm doing this for you. It's bound to come out one day. If you went out with one of our neighbours, it would be so much less complicated."

"Caroline! You of all people…"

"I don't disapprove of Charles. You know I don't, Teresa. But I dread to think what your father would do if he found out.

Why don't you come to Scottish dancing anymore? We're getting out of touch, and I'm sure people must be beginning to suspect something."

"Why? Have you been saying anything?"

"Of course not!"

Teresa tossed her head.

"Those club parties are boring, and none of the boys are half as interesting as Charles."

"But at least if you act like a normal girl, you won't attract attention."

"Tell you what, Caroline – why don't you come with us to the Nairobi races tomorrow? Daddy and I are following the horses in the car this time, so there'll be plenty of room for you. And then I promise I'll go with you to the club."

***

Charles wrestled the heavy horse transporter round the hairpin bends of the Great Rift Valley escarpment. The lorry creaked and groaned up the steep gradient, and he could hear the horses stamping in an effort to keep their footing on the wooden floor behind him.

A succession of sharp sounds was followed by an urgent banging on the back panel of the cab.

"You'd better stop," said Mwangi beside him.

He drew the ponderous vehicle to a halt. The *syces* were struggling with a horse on its knees. They stopped it from falling onto its side by pulling at the head collar and shouting at it to get up. Mwangi sneered, but the head *syce* reassured Charles.

"It's not your fault. That horse was trying to fight with the one next to him."

"He might be lame when we arrive," Mwangi said. "It's happened to me before. I think that was the one expected to win tomorrow."

Charles ignored the hint of malicious hope in the man's voice, but he reluctantly found himself in agreement with the tirades against their employer which followed. Bwana Myers was a harsh master, and offensive in his treatment of the workers.

"And you'd better watch your behaviour with that white girl," Mwangi threatened. "Your family won't like it; you'll get into trouble with the boss and lose your job."

Charles didn't bother to tell him that his job wasn't important. He'd already received his results from the Oxford entrance exam.

"You'll be sorry; I have my eye on that girl. She escaped me once, but I'll get her in the end and then that man Myers will suffer the full power of my oath. Anybody who stands in my way will pay for it." Mwangi's voice turned heavy with menace. "How is your father?"

Charles stared through the windscreen, his mind racing. So, it *was* Mwangi who had been stalking the girls. He could now tell Simaloi, who would have a name against which to base her defence. He shifted in his seat, ashamed at himself for the thought. He was an educated Christian, above such superstitions, but he knew they were real enough for his family. He feared for them, and he feared for Teresa, but he refused to react, and they drove the rest of the journey in silence.

The horses were off-loaded and trotted out before being led to their stables. They were all sound.

Myers summoned Mwangi.

"I won't need you this weekend, but you must buy those things for the *watu* and make sure you're back here early on Monday morning."

He turned to Charles.

"I want you to take the two memsahibs in my car to Muthaiga Club and drop Mwangi off at River Road on your way. Then come back here."

Caroline and Teresa climbed into the back seat, allowing Mwangi to sit in the front beside Charles. They drove past the immaculate lawns and gardens of the Nairobi suburbs. Near the city centre, Mwangi directed them down a hill onto an enormous roundabout and they branched off into River Road.

Charles stopped to let Mwangi out, while Teresa transferred to the passenger seat. People crowded the pavements, spilling out onto the narrow street. Cars were parked haphazardly on both sides. Cyclists swept forward whenever a space appeared. Caroline screwed her nose at the blocked drains spewing with rotten fruit, torn paper, and odorous sludge. There was not a white face in sight.

"Have you locked your doors?"

Charles reached across Teresa to push the knob on her window down, and Caroline made the back doors secure.

The crowd took Mwangi with them along the pavement.

"He's looking into the window of that clothes shop," said Caroline. "Now he's gone in."

The car inched forward, and Mwangi emerged wearing a long black overcoat. He stuffed some notes into a wallet, and then placed the money in an inner pocket before looking behind him, and walking on.

"I bet it isn't his money he spent on that coat!"

"Of course not, Teresa," said Charles. "He would consider his friends owe him for the trouble he is about to take on their behalf."

They continued down the street in stops and starts, watching Mwangi dive into shops. He had a large *kikapu* in his hand, which bulged out further each time he emerged. A road branched off to the right and Charles swung the wheel to accelerate up a steep hill. Caroline looked back.

"He's stopping at a canteen now," she announced.

"I wouldn't be surprised if he spent the rest of the evening drinking away what's left of that money," said Teresa as she directed Charles towards Muthaiga.

They passed the Mathare slums on the outskirts of the city.

"I'm sorry you're not allowed into the club, Charles, or we could have tea together – their doughnuts are delicious."

Charles pulled a face.

"I wouldn't want to go in a place like that, anyway," he said. "Doughnuts, or no doughnuts. But one day, when Kenya is independent and I am rich and famous, I will come back and demand respect from those snobbish colonialists."

"You know, the club even has a room where women are forbidden to go," said Teresa. "Their rules are so archaic, it's laughable. And they aren't the only club in Nairobi like that, so you needn't be too offended."

Charles smiled. "But I agree that women should be made to know their place. That is an essential part of our culture."

The gates of the exclusive club appeared, and they pulled up under the porch of the low pink building, overhung with golden shower creeper. Charles took out the luggage, depositing the bags in the foyer. Their hands brushed together, as Teresa thanked him.

Myers waited on the steps of the Members' enclosure, as Charles arrived back at the racecourse.

"Where have you been?"

"The traffic was bad, Bwana."

"Well, hurry up and give me the keys. I'm late for dinner."

Charles hovered near the rear door of the car.

"You'll have to find somewhere to sleep. Ask one of the *syces*. Do you want some money?"

"Yes, Bwana."

Myers handed him two shillings.

Charles stepped back to avoid the loose gravel as the car wheels spun, and watched it race away. The place was deserted. The pool of light from a single globe on the steps only served to increase the inkiness of the forest on the other side of the road. He turned towards the car park, his steps quickening. He found the lorry, and spent the night curled under a blanket against a bale of hay in the back.

In the morning, he bought himself a mug of tea at a kiosk and listened to the touts asking the *syces* which horses were likely to win. From a distance, he watched Teresa enter the gate, a trainer's badge on the lapel of her jacket. She wore a navy blue suit and court shoes, and he noticed her trying to avoid digging her heels into the soft turf. He strained his neck at the rails for glimpses of the horses as they thundered past at each race, and then he had another night in the back of the lorry. This time a brawl developed near the vehicle, people banged against its sides, and drunken shouts kept him awake until morning.

When he emerged to buy tea, Charles saw Mwangi hovering near the kiosk, with no sign of the overcoat or the *kikapu*.

"Give me one."

Without a word, Charles dug into his pocket for another coin, deposited it on the counter, and turned away. He did not begrudge Mwangi a mug of tea with the bwana's money, but had no desire to talk to him.

"You have to move the lorry, and get ready for loading the horses," Mwangi said.

Teresa supervised the loading, and then Myers checked that the bolt on the back was secure. Charles climbed into the cab.

Myers looked round. "Come on, Mwangi!" he shouted. "What's the matter with you?"

The man came reluctantly closer.

"I'm not coming with you, Bwana."

"Of course you are. Get in."

"I have nothing left."

"Why? What do you mean?"

"I met a friend, Bwana, who promised to help me buy everything from a cheap place. I don't remember going to bed, but when I woke up this morning, I was alone, and my jacket with the money had gone."

"Your jacket?"

"The one I bought."

"You bought a jacket, with the workers' money?" Myers' voice rose a pitch.

Mwangi nodded miserably.

"Serves you right! Get in."

"I can't go back, Bwana."

But Myers prevailed, and Caroline and Teresa hid their smiles.

At home, the workers were summoned and Mwangi had to tell them how he had lost their money. He tried to defend himself with excuses and dire threats.

Silence. An old woman wearing a faded headscarf started to shake. Deep gurgles emanated from her ample frame and glistening tears rolled down her cheeks. The young girl next to her started to giggle, and the crowd surged forward, surrounding Mwangi. They carried him with them, chuckling over the story of the driver trying to do business in the big city.

***

"I think their sense of humour is amazing," Caroline said. "They make the best of what happens, however disastrous it is. If it were a crowd of whites, they'd be baying for Mwangi's blood."

She sat with Teresa and Charles at the top of the hill above the stables. A cloud covered the sun, and a sharp breeze swept up the slope, blowing her hair into her eyes.

"Make no mistake, you can be sure they haven't forgotten what he owed them and he'll never live it down," said Charles. "Nor will he forget that we were witnesses to his shame."

CHAPTER 4

Kenya Highlands

Domino stumbled, and Caroline pulled him up sharply. They had worn a circular track in the grass, but it tilted downhill on one side. She'd thought of making some jumps on the lower level but Teresa had stopped her; it would draw attention to the place. Her chestnut, hitched to a tree in the nearby gum plantation, swished his tail at the myriad of flies clouding his body. Caroline didn't have to look further to know that Teresa and Charles were somewhere among the trees, oblivious to everything but themselves.

She let out the rein for the horse to stretch, and scanned the track on the Myers' side of the border. The glint of a white-topped cab appeared above the long grass and a puff of dust rose above it. She shouted a warning, and then returned to her reverie.

Sunday lunch parties round farm swimming pools were good fun, and she loved the energetic abandon of the reels at the Scottish dancing sessions at the local golf club. But the boys seemed so immature compared to Charles. Teresa had come with her once, but it hadn't been a success.

Caroline remembered how Ian Clayton, a childhood friend, had led her onto the floor for the Gay Gordons.

"I'd think twice about going round with her," he'd mumbled into her ear as he twirled her under his arm. "There's been a dirty rumour..."

Caroline recoiled. How had their secret got out?

But Ian whispered into her ear. "It's amazing, especially with that gun-toting father of hers. If it's true she's carrying on with their new driver, I don't envy her when he finds out!"

The music stopped, and she allowed herself to be led away for a drink. She had felt a twinge of shame at the time, for not standing up for Teresa.

The car went out of sight over the brow of a hill, but they had heard her call. Charles gave Teresa a leg up, and then he disappeared into the trees.

"There's Scottish dancing tonight at the Claytons'," Caroline said as she urged Domino up alongside the chestnut. "Shall we go? Mum has offered to take us."

"Oh, I don't know. I'd just as soon stay here."

"I hear their eldest son Brian is on holiday from London. Have you met him yet, Teresa?"

"No, I haven't."

Caroline telephoned her mother.

"What a pity you won't meet Brian. I think you'd like each other..."

Caroline smiled to herself. She wasn't the only one whose parents tried to match-make.

"...but thanks for letting me know," her mother continued. "I'll go to Nairobi instead. A friend has asked me to join her on safari. Can you ask Dudley to take you back to school on Monday?"

"Don't worry, Mum, we'll arrange it. Have fun!"

Caroline wished she could go on safari too. The nearest she had been to big game was on their annual holidays to the coast, when they sometimes passed an elephant on the road through the Tsavo game park.

She had a summons from Mother Superior.

"Your stepfather is here to see you."

Boney hadn't come alone before, and he looked troubled.

She moved forward to accept his usual brief hug, and he held her close. The Head left them together.

"Where's Mum?"

"I don't know how to say this, my dear," Boney stopped, and Caroline waited, wondering. "Your mother is – gone."

"Gone? Where?"

Caroline caught her breath, and a vision passed through her mind of her mother disappearing into the blue, perhaps being captured by Somali bandits.

"No – not gone away… She had an accident." He looked at her. "She's – no longer…"

His voice ended in a little choke. He sat down, and Caroline couldn't speak. She could see the truth in his eyes. Every part of her strained against the knowledge; this wasn't real. But she had to say something.

"What happened?"

"A car accident last night, a few miles outside Nairobi." He forced out every word. "They were returning home after their safari…"

He faltered, but Caroline's mind was numb; she could feel nothing. In the silence, she knew that Boney needed comforting. She went to kneel at his feet, burying her head in his lap.

He took a deep breath, and his voice grew stronger as he described the scene, all the while stroking her head and trying to comfort her. She should be grieving, but felt strangely detached. She rose and sat beside him, reaching her arms round his shoulders, head close to his.

As he spoke, she pictured the dusk giving way to inky night. This time of year low cloud would envelope the hills above Nairobi, reducing visibility to a few yards on the road, which meandered between the smallholdings of the Kikuyu reserve. Caroline imagined the dull orbs of light from approaching vehicles as they crept past each other. In her mind's eye she saw her mother straining to see the grass verge and use it as a guide as she drove.

Why hadn't they stopped and waited for the fog to lift?

"A lorry with no lights was approaching on their side of the road. They had no chance."

Boney said the last four words with heavy finality.

Something died inside her. A tearing, silent scream choked at her throat as nature's umbilical cord fractured, leaving an abysmal emptiness. Caroline's mind tried to recall tender times and scenes, and then tears welled from the depths of her soul, flooding the cavity of her loss.

The sound of rosary beads clacked outside the door. She stood up automatically as Mother Superior appeared. The nun put an arm round her shoulders and addressed Boney.

"I expect you want to take her home." She turned to Caroline. "Go and pack a suitcase, my dear, while I get your father a cup of tea."

Home, at dawn, she wandered into the garden where her mother had spent many tender hours ministering to the flowers, creating a colourful world of wonder. The roses, amazingly, were in full bloom, drinking the soft morning dew. She bent over a deep red blossom, drawing in the sweet scent of its nectar. The golden shower creeper covering Windmill Cottage caught the sun's rays shining through the trunks of a nearby gum plantation. Above the brightening glow, the cast iron construction of a windmill rose in stark lines against the streaks of dawn. Boney had built it to draw the borehole water up into the roof tank. It creaked now, in response to a waft of breeze, a harsh mechanical sound to match the cawing of a crow perched on a bough above. Caroline looked up. One for sorrow.

And her eyes watered again. *Mum – you've left me. Where are you? Do you know what I'm feeling?* No answer. Absolute nothingness. Only memories.

To stop the flow, she shook herself and her body shuddered,

releasing the sobs. Drained, she leaned on a fence post and turned her face to the sky. Colours changed before her eyes, deep purple to molten gold, through soft pinks and blues. What must such a scene be like in the bush – with no sight or sound of man's presence to spoil the image? She could only imagine. But her mother had experienced the wonders of wild Africa before she died.

As she turned to answer Boney's call to breakfast, Caroline resolved to seek out those wide open spaces where nature was king.

It was all her fault. Caroline wished she'd stayed at home that weekend; then her mother wouldn't have gone on safari. She shouldn't have spent so much time with Teresa. She shouldn't have resented her mother's relationship with Boney. She didn't dare go in to him. Those familiar dresses hanging in the open wardrobe would make her cry again.

Teresa called at the weekend, suggesting they go for a ride, but Caroline didn't feel like it. She spent hours with Domino in his stable, or hanging over the gate watching him graze.

As the funeral drew near, her tears flowed at the slightest half-thought of what had happened. Boney was preoccupied with the preparations, but Caroline felt so useless. The service comforted her in a strange sort of way. She vaguely listened to the vicar talk about heaven, and cried when Guy Clayton delivered the eulogy. The whole farming community were there. Everybody cried except for Boney, who stood beside her outside the church, his arm round her shoulders while acknowledging their overwhelming sympathy.

Teresa gave her a big hug and a watery smile, but Caroline couldn't respond. People said wonderful things about her mother and kept asking if there was anything they could do… But she didn't need anything – she only wanted her mother back so she could say sorry.

"What is she going to do now?" whispered Teresa's mother.

Caroline hadn't been thinking ahead, but when she overheard the question, she had a moment of panic. Was Windmill Cottage no longer her home? Would she have to give up this life, and go back to England? She couldn't bear the thought. Yet it would be perfectly reasonable for Boney to pack her off. He was only her stepfather. She kept the thoughts to herself, but the nagging fear escalated as the week passed.

The evening before she returned to school they sat by the fire. Boney puffed at his pipe. Caroline did not want to think of him brooding alone in that bedroom with the reminders of her mother around him. The very thought of it made her want to cry again.

"Do you think we should go through Mummy's things?"

She waited while he went to the mantelpiece to top up the tobacco and tamp it down. What would he say? Boney lit up, taking several long draws before satisfying himself and then turned towards her.

"I think that's a good idea, Caroline. After all, we've got to face up to it some time, and it would be easier to do it together, wouldn't it?" He paused for another puff. "Perhaps you'd like to keep some of her bits and pieces?"

Caroline hadn't thought of that.

"I'd like to have her make-up, but the clothes would be too large for me."

"Let's give them to the *watu*, shall we?"

The following morning Caroline steeled herself to sort through the wardrobe. It was not so bad when she didn't let herself think. Then Boney summoned the servants and took the clothes outside.

"You can have these," he told them. "Take it in turns to choose what you want."

Caroline watched as the *bibis* sifted through the pile and held the clothes up against each other. They chattered among themselves as they made their choices, and were profuse in their gratitude.

It was like a purge, and she felt the beginnings of a healing.

In the car on the way to school, Boney spoke to her.

"I'm going to be lonely. You may go back to England at the end of term if you wish, where I'm sure your aunt will look after you. But would you like to stay here with me? Think about it. Perhaps we could get to know each other better. I'm afraid we've neglected you…"

If he hadn't been driving, Caroline would have flung herself into his arms.

"Oh, Boney, I don't want to leave here – I just love this country! And I'm so sorry about everything. I'll bring my horse back from Teresa's."

Boney pulled to the side of the road, and gave her a bear hug. Then he pushed her gently back into her seat.

"There's no need for that, my dear. I don't want to interfere with your friendship, and it is better for you to ride with someone else instead of going out by yourself and leaving me to worry until you get back safely. But it would be rather nice to spend the occasional weekend together, wouldn't it?"

It helped Caroline to go back to school, giving her something to do. But she was empty inside, and her heart was with Boney, all alone on the farm.

One of the nuns died. Caroline didn't know her, but the community showed no sorrow, and she sensed the excitement as everyone prepared for the Requiem Mass.

Mother Mary, her favourite nun, was trailing some vestments along the ground in the courtyard.

"Can I help you, Mother?"

"Thank you, Caroline; I have to take these for mending. You can carry this one if you like."

Caroline's knees nearly buckled under the weight of a white

41

heavily brocaded garment.

"It's beautiful."

"Yes, we keep the best for joyous occasions like this one."

Joyous? Caroline looked at the nun in astonishment.

"We celebrate the lives of our dear departed, Caroline, even though we miss them. Would you like to come to the Mass?"

The invitation appeared so impromptu and genuine, that Caroline found herself accepting it.

She borrowed a veil and crept into the back of the chapel. Dim candles lit the room and the smell of incense pervaded the air. Shadowy figures knelt in prayer on wooden pews. The priest spoke in Latin but the missal Mother Mary gave her had an English translation. The words were surprisingly similar to those of the Anglican services she attended with her mother every Christmas. She tried to say a prayer, and felt better after the Mass.

Later, she asked questions, and then began to study Catholicism, using a book borrowed from Mother Mary. Why were the two faiths so antagonistic? She took greater interest in English history lessons, and then asked Mother Mary for permission to go to chapel regularly.

"I'll have to ask Mother Superior to ask your stepfather, Caroline."

Boney gave his consent, but he wouldn't let her become a Catholic.

"You mother wouldn't have liked it, my dear," he insisted. "You must wait until you're twenty-one."

Caroline still recalled those wonderful nights at the racecourse. She would open her red notebook under cover of her bedclothes and, with a torch, read the homemade code. One night, sleep would not come. Where is Mum now, she wondered, what's happened to her?

Behind closed eyelids, she saw something. Right up close so she could have touched him, a man's face appeared. His eyes

42

were shut, his head hung to the side, gouged with dripping blood from thorns round his brow. It was so real, strangely compelling and full of misery. She could only see his head and shoulders, and the arms stretched out along a wooden beam.

It didn't last for long.

She sat bolt upright and looked around. Sleeping girls filled the dormitory. She lay back on her pillow, not knowing what to think or do.

Tears trickled down her cheeks onto the pillow, and then turned into massive sobs as she tried not to wake the others. She had been so wicked, and felt so very sorry for the pain she had caused. All that sorrow and suffering. It was her fault. What could she do about it?

In the morning everything seemed strange. Her eyes were bleary and Mother Mary noticed. Caroline sniffed and brushed at her damp face with her sleeve, trying to smile.

"What's the matter, dear?"

Caroline shook her head, and could not stop the tears falling.

The nun peered at her closely. "So, you've been converted?" she said gently. "Have you come to Christ?"

Was that what had happened? Caroline nodded. She certainly felt different and knew that life would never be the same again. But she didn't feel at all happy, and wanted to make up for all her wickedness.

There was nobody else to confide in. Teresa's final exams were looming, and Caroline didn't want to distract her. Teresa was so lucky to have that special relationship with Charles. They were living proof that people of different races could get along together.

Caroline's thoughts took flight. There shouldn't be all the hatred and terror of the Emergency. Why couldn't everyone live peacefully? Kenya was such a beautiful country with enough space for all. Perhaps one day she would be able to make a difference, and prove that white and black could live side by side. When she grew up maybe she would have a better idea of what to do.

Overcome by remorse and worried about what might have happened in the forest, she knew she would have to tell Mother Mary about their midnight escapades.

The nun quizzed her for details, and said nothing more.

Caroline tried to live a new life. One night, using her torch under the bedclothes, she flicked through the secret writing in her little red book, and then, gritting her teeth, tore it into shreds. Perhaps that would help.

After the Christmas holidays, she became class prefect, and everybody knew she would be Head Girl.

It was strange being a prefect. The other girls held her in awe and she had no friends.

She discussed the catechism with Mother Mary every evening after the nuns came out of chapel, resenting the other girls when they waylaid the nun first. They were doing it deliberately, and talked of her as 'Mother's pet' but she didn't care. Mother Mary was now her best friend.

There were whisperings round the school and some girls were called in to see the Mother Superior. They were being expelled! Everyone seemed to know what was happening except Caroline. One of the juniors came up to her.

"You'd better go and see Mother Mary, quickly!"

"Why?" But the girl wouldn't say.

Caroline sought out her favourite nun. "What's going on, Mother?"

"You don't know?"

"No!"

"You'd better go to Mother Superior, then."

The nun turned away.

Caroline crossed the quadrangle to the Head's study.

"Yes, Caroline?"

She stood in front of the imposing desk. The Superior was

new and Caroline couldn't see her eyes properly through the thick-lensed glasses.

"I've been told to come and see you, Mother Superior."

"So – what do you want to say?"

Caroline frowned.

"Do you know what's been happening?"

"No, Mother Superior."

"Are you quite sure?"

The nun studied her intently, making her feel uncomfortable, but she had nothing to hide. Caroline met her gaze.

"Yes of course I'm sure."

"Some girls have been caught breaking out of school during the night and meeting boys in town."

"Oh." Caroline now understood. Her heart gave a leap. But she and Teresa had never met boys on their escapades, and anyway, nobody knew.

"Were you one of them, Caroline?"

The denial burst from her. "No, Mother Superior!"

"Have you never broken out of school?"

Caroline could not deny it. She would be expelled with the rest of them. What would Boney think? But surely the nuns knew she was a changed person? Mother Mary would vouch for her. Had the nun broken confidence and told her Superior of their midnight escapades?

She felt the Head's eyes watching her closely.

"Did you meet boys when you broke out of school?"

"No, Mother Superior!"

She'd trusted Mother Mary. She was a new person now, and a prefect. Mother Mary understood that. Why had she been betrayed?

Mother Superior remained silent for what seemed ages.

"Well," she said finally. "I can't do anything about Teresa because she's left school, and as this happened before my time and you say you did not meet any boys, I will let you off. But I warn you we'll be watching you from now on. And I'm sure you understand that you can't be a prefect any more. Shall I take your badge now and have that stigma against you, or do you want to resign?"

Caroline scarcely gave thought to the question; she was so relieved to have escaped expulsion.

"I'll resign."

The nun nodded.

"You can do so at tomorrow's assembly."

Everybody stared as she walked up to place her prefect's badge on the podium. They believed she had been one of the 'gang' and Caroline knew they were thinking it unfair that she had escaped expulsion. But it would be no use trying to justify herself. She would go and sob quietly in chapel, and couldn't explain even to herself why she cried so often.

For her remaining school days, Caroline lived under constant suspicion. Not even when she decided to rise to Mother Mary's challenge and aim for Oxford did the nuns trust her.

CHAPTER 5

London and Oxford

Charles presented his passport at Heathrow Airport. The queue in front of him dissolved and he hurried down a flight of stairs into a large hall to claim his luggage. People were striding in all directions, the man in the brown coat in front of him broke into a run, and he was hustled towards the customs counter.

"Read this!"

He was given a bare second to focus on the plaque before his eyes, and shook his head. "I have nothing to declare."

Someone ran up and snatched his bag.

"Hey…"

But by the time he'd shouldered his camera the man had disappeared.

He stumbled over the coat trailing from his arm and lumbered into a run. He rounded a corner and saw his suitcase being hurled into the boot of an airways bus. The vehicle raced away, leaving him open-mouthed.

"It's all right, sir, you take this one. You'll get your case at the terminal."

The porter seemed to be waiting for something. Charles hesitated. He'd never tipped anyone before, let alone a white man. But he was in danger of missing the second bus. He fumbled in his pocket and produced a large silver coin, hoping he hadn't caused offence. The man touched his cap and rushed away. In the bus, Charles sat back and took his first deep breath in England.

It was afternoon. It must be afternoon. The sun was thirty degrees from the horizon and yet his watch said ten o'clock. It was going to take time to get used to this strange phenomenon. That orb, weakly glowing through the smog, seemed to remain stationary all day.

Wet glistening streets slid past. The bus came to a standstill and men on bicycles weaved in and out of the traffic, incessantly ringing their bells. Monotonous brick buildings crept by, covered with grimy filth. Did people really live there? He stared at the terraced houses lining the street. No earth, no trees; just a front door and the pavement. He thought of his home, of the patches of maize and beans, of the endless sweep of the African plains, and wondered how anybody could survive in this teeming hurrying metropolis.

At the terminal, there were more people than he had ever seen in his life. He glimpsed one black face.

"Jackson!"

Waving frantically over the crowd, Charles pushed his way through to his brother, embracing him thankfully.

"Where's your baggage?"

Noise, shouts, bangs, rushing figures, running feet, waving arms. No peace, no quiet, no rest.

A taxi took them to The Strand Palace Hotel. Charles trod gingerly over the plush carpets and wondered at the white porters, long corridors and dark rooms, comparing them to the mud huts he had left behind.

He flopped onto his bed, ready for sleep, but Jackson roused him.

"Come on, Charles! It's only morning, you know. You'd better start shopping if you want my help as I have to fly to a dig in the Middle East tomorrow."

He followed Jackson into the street, stopping once or twice to stare at the hundreds of people in overcoats that raced past. Footsteps pitter-pattered on the pavement in staccato against the steady roar of traffic, and only one or two individuals in that mass of humanity raised their heads to glance back at him.

They joined a queue at the bus stop. A double-decker loomed up and Charles was caught in the rush towards the entrance. For a second he felt at one with the surging throng and then, lodged in a seat, became a spectator again.

The way these people formed queues on any pretext astonished him. And there was a definite code among them too, for when somebody tried to push in they were severely relegated to the back. Nobody showed interest in anybody else. His eyes roamed over the pale faces half-hidden under soft caps, the pinstripe suits and shiny shoes. His hands strayed self-consciously into the pockets of his mud-coloured windcheater and he shivered. But nobody noticed.

In a department store, Charles searched doggedly through the hangers for a pair of warm slacks. A pimpled assistant spoke at his shoulder, and a torrent of unintelligible sound filled Charles's ears. He turned to Jackson in bewilderment.

"What language is that?"

"It's only cockney – London speak; he's asking what you're looking for." Jackson addressed the man politely, "We're looking for trousers with turn-ups."

The youth produced a pair on special offer. Charles walked to the cashier's desk, two people rushing past him on the way. He emerged from the queue, his pocket heavy with change.

"There's one thing you must always remember, Charles," Jackson warned as they rode the lift to the rooftop café, "the UK is not Kenya, where most people are friendly. Nobody here talks to strangers."

What a place. How can you make friends if you can't talk to strangers? In the café he studied the people reading their newspapers. One man stretched for the sugar.

"Excuse me."

"Sorry."

There was no interest. Why bother to come here at all?

Ignoring Jackson's warning, he caught the man's eye, and cleared his throat.

"Do you live in London?"

The man muttered beneath his breath, then folded his newspaper, drained his cup and left the table, tripping over in his haste. Charles, grinning, glanced at Jackson.

"What *did* you think you were doing?" Jackson was laughing at him. "If you must talk to strangers you'd better learn to discuss the weather; it's a safer topic."

Out on the pavement his steps quickened and there were fewer collisions. There was something in this hurry he supposed. But hopefully Oxford would not be quite as bad.

Jackson saw him off. He wrote down the address of a store in Carfax where he had worked as an undergraduate, and then handed Charles two hundred pounds.

"That's towards your college fees!" he shouted as the train left the station. "Keep it safe."

Buildings flashed past with increasing speed and then fields and stretches of river appeared. Neat hedgerows were shaded by trees. Charles felt cramped, somehow, in this tidy little country, but he had never seen so much wonderful green grass.

He dozed to the rhythmic chuckle of wheels over the tracks, and let his mind wander back to Kenya, and those final meetings with Teresa.

It was his lunch break, and they were on the hill again. Her deep brown eyes were troubled, but her languorous body made him catch his breath. She seemed different, somehow, so much more attractive, if that were possible. Dark clouds were rolling up the valley behind them.

"Bother – it's going to rain."

They watched the purple curtain blot out the view below, and rush up the hill. The pattering of heavy drops on dry leaves clattered closer, deafening their ears. The deluge

50

overwhelmed them. It stung their bare arms and they dived for the sparse cover of the scrub. They were wet through in seconds, and cakes of mud clung to their clothes.

Minutes later, the sun was out, and the earth steamed with wisps of vapour. Teresa's black hair was slicked in tiny coils against her profile; her flimsy blouse clung to the line of her bra. She wrinkled her nose and sniffed the air.

"I love the smell of rain on the parched earth," she said. "That earthy, humus scent makes me think of rotting leaves and wriggly brown worms working away in the undergrowth. And then little green shoots will start peeping out."

But Charles was gazing at her, conscious of a tightening in his trousers. He moved away, and tried to discuss his going, but she changed the subject.

"I don't want to think about it," she said. "Can't we just enjoy each other while we can?"

A horse developed colic, and Teresa was observing it when he persuaded her to come with him behind the stables. It was one of those rare weekends when Caroline was away, and they enjoyed the extra sense of privacy her absence gave them.

"It will be quite safe; we can hear the horse if it starts pawing the ground and tries to roll. And Daddy never comes down when I'm doing evening stables."

They settled into a depression in the grass, against the rough off-cuts of wood that formed the back of the stables, and he opened his arms.

Then Myers called.

"Teresa, where are you? Is the horse all right?"

She tore from his grasp.

"He's fine, Dad," she said, running toward the front of the stables. "I've given him a drench of warm beer, and he hasn't rolled since."

"You should be walking him out. Where've you been? What are you doing behind there?"

The voice grew louder and Charles saw a figure striding round the corner. He adjusted his clothes and hesitated, thinking of flight, but it was too late. Rather than be caught trying to escape, he had turned and walked forwards with as much confidence as he could muster.

The train drew into Oxford Station, and Charles, remembering the scene that followed, wondered how many other whites harboured vitriolic feelings towards Africans.

His first impression of the University town was one of bicycles. There were so many of them. Black gowns wobbled two or three abreast in front of his taxi. In London, the crowds had rushed to and fro with bewildering speed but with an undefined sense of purpose. Here utter pandemonium reigned. He was thankful that the sides of the taxi protected him from the chaos. But it was not hostile.

His college was a peaceful sanctuary. The imposing entrance hall gave way to rolling green lawns, which disappeared towards the river. His room at the top of a narrow winding staircase overlooked a grassy quadrangle. The grass was so beautifully green. On the other side, tall trees flanked the river. He gasped as he leaned out of the window and feasted his eyes on the vivid hues of blending colours. He had never imagined autumn to be like this.

But there was no time to stand and stare. He had to unpack, find out where to go and meet his fellow Freshers. Already two letters invited him to coffee after lunch. People were rushing up and down the stairs. Some looked as lost as he felt; others appeared to know what they were doing. He found a pigeonhole with his name on it, full of pamphlets and programs. He constantly opened his door to admit College Reps who urged him to belong to 'The Humanists' or to pay a subscription to the 'Cherwell'.

There were many questions but few answers. He went out into the cold to buy a commoner's gown, again for supplies of tea, sugar, coffee, milk, and yet again to find a desk. Then he needed notebooks and paper.

The Preliminaries of Oxford's social whirl developed into a familiar formula.

"What are you reading?"

"Which college are you at?"

"Where do you come from?"

And, if progress were really being made, "What is your name?"

He went to coffee parties and tea parties and wine-and-cheese parties, religious societies and musical societies and political societies. There were people and people and more people.

His first bitter taste of the English weather was one evening on his way to the Africa Club, setting out on his bicycle after supper, wearing a windcheater and a pair of slacks.

He met Louise the Secretary, whose enthusiasm during her presentation about a trip to Sierra Leone caused him to examine her more closely; a well-rounded blonde with large blue eyes and a friendly manner. He headed back to college and it started to rain.

It was not the strong driving rain of the tropics, but a steady monotonous soul-destroying downpour, which saturated him in seconds. It worked its way in trickles down his neck and in splashes up his legs as he wobbled through the puddles. Abandoning all caution, head down and eyes slit against the stinging drops, he raced for home. He took a wrong turn, retraced his way, glimpsed a reflector and followed it doggedly through the rivulets and cobblestones until he reached his college door.

His shoes squelched on the floor. At least he'd managed to get in before the gate closed. He'd been told that it was possible, but not easy for latecomers to climb over the spikes on the wall, and was in no hurry to put it to the test.

Oxford was a world apart. The basic worries of everyday life vanished. There were no working hours. Indeed, during those first days the subject of work hardly cropped up. Charles met his tutors and was issued with lists of lectures to attend and books to read in preparation for tutorials a week hence. A week was a very long time. Nobody asked where he was going or what he was doing. Nobody seemed to care if he worked or not. In fact, it appeared that nobody did any work. This complete freedom was bewildering.

An official envelope appeared in his pigeonhole. Charles ripped it open and glanced at the college headed paper reminding him that he owed them a term's fees. The euphoria of Oxford fell away as he realised that only half of Jackson's gift remained, and it was nowhere near the required sum.

He knocked on the door of the Bursar's office. The man smiled at him, until he counted the notes in his hand.

"What's this?"

"I know it's not enough," said Charles. "Might I have more time to pay the balance?"

The Bursar glowered at him.

"Haven't your funds come through yet?"

Charles had not even opened a bank account. The Trust had given him the first term's instalment in cash before he left Kenya.

"I have a bursary from home," he said. "But I had to pay for my flight, and there've been so many expenses since I came up."

"Well, I'll give you to the end of term – not a minute longer!"

The Bursar turned his back, reminding Charles of the summary dismissals he'd experienced from Myers back home.

The Christmas vacation was weeks away. Relieved at the respite, Charles buried his worries in the race to read enough books and write acceptable essays in time for tutorials. He joined the hordes of students cycling to lectures, gowns flying.

"You need to do at least four hours of work a day," he was

advised.

It was impossible to achieve.

He would dabble in books here and there for a few days, jotting down notes. When the tutorial loomed close, he came to know the bitter-sweet experience of an essay crisis, when pen flew across paper in a frenzied rush as ideas were bred behind a closed door bearing the telling notice: DO NOT DISTURB.

He learned to theorise and reach momentous conclusions far into the night, enjoying the stimulation of lively minds, for discussions were in earnest and ranged over every conceivable subject. In small rooms fuggy with smoke and littered with cigarette ends, they put the world to rights, defended religion, discussed politics, denounced racialism, and analysed life.

The problem of money became a nagging pain at the back of his mind.

Mzee Ondiek had said that God would provide for him, but Charles knew he needed to act for himself. The city was full of churches, bells pealed the hours over the noise of traffic. This was the country which had founded his religion.

He attended Sunday High Mass in Pusey House on St. Giles Street. The ornately robed priests, the incense, grandeur and solemnity of the occasion filled his senses to satiation. He tried to pray. He prayed more earnestly than ever before in his life. He listened to a sermon, but afterwards could not recall anything that was said. It was an awesome experience, far beyond those humble services at his Mission School in the heart of Africa.

He tried to keep busy, which wasn't difficult, but he couldn't help thinking of home, and as the days drew in and the nights grew longer the most awful depression took hold.

Charles gazed out of his window at the bleak lawn, which sloped down to dripping willows at the riverside. He couldn't focus. He felt abandoned, friendless, and increasingly out of his element. He wondered what Teresa was doing.

It was time he wrote to her, but her father must not find out. They hadn't talked about communicating before he left. She was steeped in the white settler way of living, and although he was now an academic, belonging to the exclusive environment of Oxford, the farming community in Kenya would not know how to accept him.

Perhaps Caroline would help him to get in touch with Teresa? He wasted no time.

Two long weeks passed before he heard from Caroline, and the envelope contained a note from Teresa. She was well, she missed him so, and longed to receive his first letter.

They developed a routine, writing diary notes and posting them every week. It didn't matter that the letters crossed. He enjoyed Teresa's ramblings, and the little words of love at the end that kept him going in this strange land, where nobody understood him.

She'd been monitoring his father's progress, and reported that *Mzee* was slowly gaining strength. Charles wondered how much this was due to Simaloi's potions, and how much to the fact that Mwangi was in detention. He told her about his financial worries, and she suggested he took a job to augment his income.

How could he have forgotten Jackson's advice? He found employment packing shelves, and was surprised to be in the company of other undergraduates. They never acknowledged him outside work, and he felt that it was a shameful thing having to earn a living while at Oxford.

Each visit to the shops at Carfax and down the High' was a journey into another world. The city was full of undergraduates, yet the commercial world clashed constantly with the heavy tradition of the colleges. It was this reminder that made him realise however pleasant and irresponsible university life may be, he could only enjoy it for a brief space of time. It just wasn't real.

It was real enough one Friday evening, after he'd helped an elderly lady find a pair of slippers in the store. She kept looking at him – seemed almost frightened of him – and went quickly to the check out, glancing back at him over her shoulder.

Just before closure, there she was again, this time flanked by two police constables.

"That's him!" She pointed at Charles. "He's the one in the picture you showed me."

The men approached, and before he knew what was happening, they had clapped handcuffs onto him. Anger bristled up his spine, and he dug in his heels.

"Are you going to come quietly, or are we going to have to make a fuss?"

The shorter of the two officers eyeballed him. "You're wanted for questioning at the police station, in relation to a robbery which happened on the High' two days ago. You have the right to remain silent..."

Charles waited through the spiel, and held his tongue. They pushed him roughly into an empty cell and the door clanged shut.

This was worse than anything that had happened to him in Kenya. He faced the stone-cold wall, scraping his fingers against the rough plaster as angry tears of frustration streamed down his cheeks. What robbery? He was innocent!

Later, he gave his name and address and stated that he had been at a tutorial on Wednesday at 2.30pm, the time of the alleged robbery. But they insisted on checking his alibi.

After spending an uncomfortable night in the cell, he was released at noon the following day, bristling with righteous indignation.

"How could that woman have claimed to recognise me?" he demanded.

The copper shrugged his shoulders. "A black man was

spotted at the scene of the robbery."

"And I was arrested because I happen to have black skin and a squashed up nose?"

The policeman apologised, but behind the implacable face, Charles noticed the eyes dancing with amusement. He turned away in disgust. To the English, every black man looked the same. Would he ever escape from the stigma of race?

The weather was becoming colder. Sometimes the sun shone brightly, but it made the air even more freezing. The days grew shorter. He felt cheated when dark came in the early afternoons, and he couldn't conquer an overwhelming feeling of tiredness. The icy weather, his study, his job and social life were too exhausting. No wonder the terms were only eight weeks long. How was he going to survive?

His heart wasn't in his work, and lectures were boring. Old English poets were dead and gone. Who wanted to decipher the ancient English of Chaucer, for goodness' sake? Was he reading the right subject? He'd thought he was good at language, and he wanted to be a journalist.

Louise was reading Politics, Philosophy and Economics, which sounded more exciting.

There were so many essays to write, and he didn't know what he was talking about most of the time. He tried working late into the night, but felt too tired, and never managed to get up early enough to put in the extra hours. And it was all probably in vain anyway. He couldn't imagine why they'd accepted him in the first place. What was wrong with him? He'd lost all the good sense and drive he had enjoyed in Kenya, and now he was like a jellyfish with no backbone.

He tried to find distractions, often going with Louise to the Bodleian Library. He cycled to her college, leaving his bicycle to wander with her through the park. She was immersed in revision during the final week of term.

"You need to have a clear head before your exams." He waved a map towards her. "Let's go for a ride. I've found some woods not far away."

It was muddy.

"The brambles are playing havoc with my blue stockings!" Louise showed him a ragged ladder down the side of her leg, but Charles laughed and took her hand, dragging her along the path.

The ground was thick with fallen leaves and tiny streams tumbled in rivulets down the slopes. The bare trees stood motionless. They stopped in a small clearing. There was not a movement; not even a bird or an insect disturbed the silence. Charles helped her over a stream, reaching for her hand, letting it linger in his, and they wandered deep in their separate thoughts. Louise paused to hang over a gate to watch pigs rooting in a large pen, thick with mud, and started to assess their merits.

"I used to judge pigs, when I was a Young Farmer at school."

"Did you? I was also a farmer, but we only had cattle and goats."

They cycled back to Oxford.

"I'm cold, and thirsty. Let's go for a drink."

They came to a pub off the High', and Louise pushed her bike onto the rack outside. Charles hesitated.

"Come on, they'll have a roaring fire going."

He heard some singing, and stepped aside for her, poking his nose round the door. Smoke filled the room. A sea of bright pink faces turned to him from the bar, shouting something about red roses. They stopped, and stared at Louise.

"Are you coming to join the Heritage Society?"

They weren't exactly hostile, but the unnatural silence that followed made him suddenly aware of his dark skin. Charles turned tail.

"I suppose it was rather stupid of me," he said to Louise outside. "I should've stayed to learn something about British Heritage."

Louise laughed. "I don't think you'd have learned much

from them, other than a few bawdy songs!"

They went to her room instead, had tea and crumpets, and sat on the bed together. He could smell the nearness of her, as she leafed through a book of Salvador Dali's grotesque art, but she seemed not to notice. She pointed out details in the pictures, educating him in the unusual imagery, then got up, smiling.

"I really must have an early night, Charles," she said. "It was a wonderful afternoon. I won't see you until next term, as I have to catch the train after my last exam. Have a happy Christmas!"

"Good luck in your exams," Charles remembered to say before she closed the door on him.

It was coming perilously close to the time when he would have to face the Bursar.

CHAPTER 6

Kenya Highlands

Dawn. The birds were awake and a breeze caught the tops of the gum trees. The sun moved down the stately branches, penetrating every shadow, and long fingers of light reached over the waving field of wheat towards the wooden bungalow, huddled beneath its blanket of creepers.

Caroline drew rein on a rise, her grey gelding heaving after the gallop across the stubble behind her. She patted him absent-mindedly and dismounted, hitching the reins through her arm to walk towards an overhanging pepper tree. Supporting her back against its rough bark, she let Domino graze while she watched the sun steal across the fields, touch the garden, and bathe the house in golden warmth. A lone crow flapped in the boughs above her.

Study and school routine were behind her at last; but the drudgery of a secretarial course awaited.

"Your mother wanted you to do that before anything else," Boney told her when she grimaced at his insistence. "It'll stand you in good stead, whatever happens."

Caroline gave way with grace. She'd taken the entrance exam for Oxford, and the course would occupy her mind while she waited for results. She might even be able to find a job in the interim. It was a pity she would miss Charles.

His letter lay on her dressing table. They were not so frequent now. She wondered how much Teresa knew of his relationship with Louise, and how much he knew of what went on in the Myers' household.

Last week, Dudley and Teresa had come to visit, too early for sundowners, so Caroline had called for tea.

Boney puffed at his pipe, and cocked an eyebrow at their visitors.

"What's up, Dudley?"

"Did you know that fifty bags of wheat bran were stolen from my store yesterday? I got the police, and we found them in your labour lines."

"Yes, they told me, and they've taken some of my men for questioning. It seems they've uncovered a nice little drinks factory here, making pombe from the bran. I'm sorry things are getting worse, but I'm glad you retrieved the bags."

Dudley glared at Boney. "I can't understand how you can stand by and watch. I'm fed up. This morning my best dairy cow was found with her hind legs mutilated!"

Caroline gasped. She pictured the poor cow, dripping blood, trying to pull itself along by its front legs. She hoped Dudley had put it out of its misery quickly. He thumped his fist on the arm of the chair.

"It's the Mau Mau all over again. We've got to do something, Boney. We can't go on like this."

Boney puffed at his pipe.

"You have guards?" he asked eventually.

"I have more than you. They're the worst offenders, and if you sack them, their successors aren't any better."

Ethel pushed a laden trolley into the room, her face an impassive mask. Caroline grimaced. She knew that the Headman's eldest daughter understood English, and so did most of the workers. But it was no good warning Myers. He would only snigger in disbelief.

"Tea?"

"Thanks." Myers accepted a scone. "We could close ranks, you know – operate a curfew, and lock up all strangers."

Caroline watched Boney, who appeared to be considering

the suggestion.

"What about legitimate vendors and job seekers along the roads?"

"It's our own blokes who're the biggest culprits, Boney. They hate our guts. We must work together, or we'll be back where we started."

"Have you talked to Guy Clayton?"

"You're the first person I've approached, and if we talk Guy round the rest will follow. If every farmer refuses to take on someone who has been sacked we'll get rid of the bad ones in no time."

Boney puffed into the silence and Caroline watched the smoke lose itself among the rafters.

"It's not as simple as that you know. There'll be self-government before long."

"The blacks won't be ready to govern themselves for a hundred years, Boney, any halfwit knows that! You wait, when these elections are over and the Africans find that they haven't got everything they were promised, such as houses, cars, and women, there'll be hell to pay."

"We'll see," said Boney. "Pressures are great and there's no going back. I agree they're not ready for it yet, but it will happen."

"What's that got to do with our present problems, anyway?"

"Everything," said Boney. "I'm getting on and I've had a good life. There've been ups and downs, but I wouldn't change it for anything. I want to stay here and I want to live in peace."

"But…"

"Yes, the thefts… We can't go on like this. It's time we treated them like human beings instead of brainless idiots. They are intelligent you know, although sometimes it's hard to fathom their mentality."

Caroline saw his eyes mist over, and she shifted in her chair. She knew what was coming.

"I still can't make my Headman understand my rage when I find my cows grazing in the wheat fields. His attitude is, it's the *bwana's* wheat field and the *bwana's* cows, so what's he grumbling about? Can you beat it? And yet it is logical, in a way…"

"That proves my point. Don't you see?" Dudley interrupted. "Let me tell you a story…"

Caroline exchanged glances with Teresa, and inclined her head toward the door.

"It was after that bamboo fiasco," Dudley was saying. "Remember, before the men were sent for screening? I forced that Mau Mau driver I had, Mwangi, to come with me to the races – didn't trust him on the farm without me there. The *watu* asked him to buy goods for them, and he was cheated of the whole bloody lot! I found him in the morning, scared stiff but I made him face the music," Dudley sniggered. "It's just typical. Why give them wages when they don't understand the value of money? And you talk about them having brains? I bet if you built them modern houses they'd board up the windows."

Teresa gripped Caroline's arm as they stepped onto the veranda.

"No wonder Mwangi hates us so much, Caroline. I'm terrified of that man."

"Don't worry," Caroline tried to soothe her. "He's still locked up and you'll probably never see him again."

But Teresa wasn't listening.

"Do you remember when that old bibi started to shake, with tears down her cheeks? And the young girl next to her giggled, and then everyone surrounded him, falling over themselves with laughter."

"It *was* amazing," said Caroline. "They have an incredible sense of humour and generosity of spirit." She paused, thinking. "And as he was a Mau Mau leader they wouldn't have dared to demand repayment."

"Maybe not," said Teresa, "but he'll probably hate us all the more when he comes out, because we were witnesses to his shame."

Caroline felt in her pocket, "I have another letter for you from Charles."

She stood by as Teresa read it.

"He's having a good time over there, and you're going off next year."

Caroline shook her head.

"Now, don't you deny it – I'm positive you'll get in! I know I'm not brainy enough, and I'm happy now that Daddy has given me charge of the racing stables." Teresa brushed back her hair. "Would you like to come with me on Sunday? Who knows, I might even saddle a winner."

"I'd love to," said Caroline, "but I must check with Boney first. He's still lonely, and I don't think he's looking forward to me going to Oxford."

Teresa stuffed the letter into her pocket.

"I wonder how this will all end."

"You mean you and Charles?"

Teresa nodded.

"Well, I hope you two get together one day – it's about time the people in this country learned to live with one another, and what better way is there than intermarriage? You still love him, don't you?"

"I think so, but it's hard when you haven't seen each other for so long."

"He's mentioned Louise again?"

Teresa nodded.

"Something like that was bound to happen. But so long as he still writes to you... Has Dudley had any more suspicions?"

"None at all, thanks to you. I don't know what we'd have done without you, Caroline. But sometimes I think there is no future for us. How could Daddy ever accept our relationship, and how would we manage, coming from two such different worlds?"

Caroline could find no answer to that.

"We'd better get back to the house," she said. "They'll have had a couple of drinks by now and your father will be in a better mood."

Dudley was speaking. "You'll not support me then?"

"I'm afraid not," Boney answered. "I want to stay here. My Headman makes the others work better than I can. He gets his rake-off. They're not that disorganised. But as long as I've enough to pay my way I can turn a blind eye. Life's too short. If I were younger I might have listened to you, but now I want to live in peace."

Caroline had a sleepless night.

She envied Teresa's opportunity to become part of Kenya's history. She loved this country, with its freedom, and wide open spaces. This was her country; she felt it in her very being. She loved its people, and ached to become part of their progress. Teresa's mother, a Catholic, would have reservations about Charles, but he could take instruction. There wasn't that much difference between the two faiths as far as she could see. It was Dudley who would rant and rave. His reaction to Boney's story was typical of the man.

Caroline remembered the poor cow being hamstrung in the paddock. That sort of thing should have ended when the Kikuyus were sent away. There was still an official Emergency in force. She glanced out of her window. She always slept with the curtains open to let in the moonlight, and every morning awoke with the dawn. The diamond shaped security bars were etched against the starry wash of the night sky and the curtains swished softly against them.

A sharp crack sounded from the direction of Boney's bedroom and Caroline jumped. Another crack, and then another, as if the wind were raining gum pellets onto the roof, except there were no gum trees near the house. She turned towards the wall and stilled beneath her blankets, ears

66

straining for any other sound. Silence for a while, and then a sudden series of deafening cracks, as if the roof were being sliced in two.

Caroline's heart stopped thudding. She remembered Boney telling her that the contraction of the corrugated iron roof made those frightening noises in the night, especially after a hot day, and turned to face the window. Another reason for having her curtains open was to make sure that no one lurked in the garden. So long as she kept awake she felt that nobody would break in. She stayed watching for what seemed like hours. Her eyelids drooped and she shook herself several times. It was only when the first streaks of dawn lightened the sky that she let herself sleep far into the morning.

She had missed her dawn ride.

Boney was at the table, a mound of bacon, eggs, sausages, tomatoes and mushrooms on his plate. A rack of toast was at his side, with a silver dish of farm butter curled into grooved spirals. A cut glass bowl of homemade orange marmalade stood in the middle of the table, a spoon glistening at its edge.

"One thing your mother did was to teach Ethel how to serve an excellent breakfast." Boney bit into a sausage.

"I'm glad you didn't send me back to the UK after Mummy died," Caroline said, helping herself to some porridge from the side table. "I wouldn't be happy anywhere else in the world." She never let her sleepless nights spoil her love of the country, nor did she admit her fears to Boney.

"You must see the world before making up your mind, my girl."

"I'll come back when I graduate, I've got that feeling."

She looked out of the window at the rolling wheat fields beyond the garden hedge. Soft cumulus clouds, still rose-tinted, were drifting gently against an awakening sky. It was changing into a deep blue as she watched. She thought of a future when she would play a part in the emergence of this lovely country, and turned to Boney.

"You'll still be here, won't you?"

"Don't worry, I'll stay until I'm thrown out, which I trust will be never. But it will be different for you. So many people are leaving Kenya and there won't be many eligible young men around. Would you want to marry a black man?"

Caroline made herself think. Would she? How could she know? It was all very well having lofty ideals... She didn't answer. It would be too risky. She might find herself talking about Teresa and Charles.

She put her arms round Boney's neck.

"Daddy..."

"What are you going to wheedle out of me now, young lady?" Boney disentangled himself gently.

"Nothing much – only, Teresa has invited me to the races next weekend..."

The Parade Ring was a soft spongy green bordered with bright red and yellow salvia flowers. The centre bed, a mass of crimson and orange, was surrounded by a circle of outward-facing white chairs. Caroline studied the gleaming racehorses being led round by their uniformed *syces*.

Eleven horses were running in the major race of the afternoon. Joint favourite was Guy Clayton's filly, Black Bombshell, with a white star on her chest. This was Teresa's first time as official trainer for Clayton. But Caroline's attention was caught by a rangy bay gelding being led up behind the favourite. She glanced at the race card. His name was Atlas, and this was his first outing.

A band of jockeys entered the ring, their colours adding to the festive air. They separated to go to their trainers for last minute instructions. The bell rang and Caroline watched Teresa check the filly's girth and give the jockey a leg up. He was one of the world's top riders who had flown from Ireland especially for this race. The horse cavorted off the path before circling the ring and emerging onto the course.

The owners and trainers dispersed, and Caroline saw Teresa and Guy Clayton leaning on the rail to watch the warm-up gallop to the start. A young man was with them, short, with wiry hair receding from his forehead. He had Guy's distinctive Roman nose. She joined them.

"Have you met Brian?"

She smiled up into a warm pair of brown eyes. Although she'd often been to parties with his younger brother Ian, Caroline had never met Brian.

They approached the bookies' stalls and Guy placed a bet. Caroline noticed that Atlas's price was drifting and fumbled in her handbag.

"I think I might put five shillings on Atlas," she said to Teresa with a laugh, "just for fun. But I'm going to do it on the Tote."

"Why do you fancy that one?" Brian asked her. "I know nothing about horses, except that they bite at one end, kick at the other and are damned uncomfortable in the middle."

Caroline laughed. "You don't ride?"

"Never! I've only come to support Dad this once."

"Well then, let me show you."

The others disappeared in the direction of the owners' boxes, while Caroline led Brian along the row of bookies and chose one with the most favourable odds for Black Bombshell.

"You must support your father," Caroline insisted. "But I'm going to have a Tote flutter on Atlas. Look – his price is drifting even further."

"Why don't you use the bookies?"

"I've discovered the Tote gives better odds most of the time, and anyway it's safer having an each-way bet. If Atlas doesn't win, I'll still get something back so long as he is placed second or third."

"There's another one with a short price," said Brian. "So, having done my duty by my father I'm going to put a saver on Turning Point."

"Have you seen it in the paddock?"

"No."

"I never back a horse without studying it first," she said, looking at her race card and noting that Turning Point had only won one of his last four races.

"I wouldn't know what to look for anyway," replied Brian drawing out his wallet.

They went to the Tote where Caroline placed an each-way bet on Atlas and then wandered together towards the grandstand. She glanced at Brian's lapel. He was wearing an Owner's Badge.

"I'll see you after the race," she said. "They won't let me up into the boxes."

"I'll come with you. Dad won't miss me."

They barely had time to find seats in the public stand before the rising murmur from the crowd was echoed by the commentator.

"They're off!"

Caroline focussed her binoculars. Bombshell was streaming along easily at the back, half a length ahead of Atlas. Turning Point was in the middle of the field. As they passed the halfway mark, the three horses paced stride for stride, closing slightly on the leaders. Approaching the final bend, Bombshell was on the inside.

"...with Atlas lying fourth as they come towards the straight and the gap is closing... as they come into the straight, Bombshell goes a little wide, closely followed by Turning Point..."

People were beginning to shout, drowning out the commentator's voice. Caroline's hands were shaking and all she could see was a moving blur. Tossing aside her binoculars, she stood up.

"...and with only three hundred yards to go, I can see Turning Point making a strong bid for the lead."

Caroline started to shout as the leaders approached the stands. The crowd was going wild with excitement as Turning

Point rapidly gained ground and the horses flashed past the winning post.

"Did she do it? She did, didn't she?"

The loudspeaker crackled back into life. *"There will be a photograph for the winner."*

"Did who do it?" asked Brian.

"Bombshell, of course!"

They jostled the crowd emptying from the grandstand and threaded between chattering groups on the lawn below. Caroline hung over the railings of the winners' enclosure. Bombshell was the last to come off the track. Teresa and Guy were waiting together with the owners and trainers of Turning Point. The horses, sides heaving and sweat flecking from their necks, were being walked in circles by their *syces*.

"Who won?" She heard the jockey ask Teresa.

"I don't know. What do you think?" Caroline sensed the excitement in Teresa's voice.

"It's hard to say, my dear," the jockey replied with the calm born of experience. "It was very close."

As Caroline watched, he placed a hand on Teresa's shoulder.

The crowd pushed her against Brian.

"What are you so excited about?" he asked. "You didn't back Bombshell or Turning Point, did you?"

"No. But I put an each way bet on Atlas on the Tote, and he came in third. Wouldn't it be wonderful if Teresa won for your father! And whatever happens, you will have won some money too."

The loudspeaker crackled. *"The winner of the fourth race is…"*

Caroline could hardly listen. The crowd roared, and she hadn't heard. Then she watched Bombshell being led into the winner's enclosure. As Guy Clayton was handed the trophy, and the jockey and Teresa received their mementoes, she was aware that she had a silly grin on her face which became wider as she turned, remembering Brian beside her.

"I'm so pleased for Teresa. You know this is her very first win!"

But Brian had withdrawn the bookie's ticket from his pocket.

"I must go and collect my money."

Caroline pushed her way through the crowd and, lost for words, hugged Teresa.

"I knew I'd start winning races as soon as Jack came back to ride!"

She was hanging on the jockey's arm, and Caroline saw him giving her an intimate smile as she pecked his cheek. It was good for Teresa to think of other things, instead of moping over Charles all the time, Caroline told herself.

She found Brian again in time for the sixth race and they watched his choice enter the winner's enclosure. She stood beside him at the ringside for the last two races.

"You can see if a horse is ready to win by the fitness line along the belly," she explained. "Look," she pointed at the flank of a passing horse. But Brian was an unwilling listener.

"I'm having enough luck without all your theory," he laughed. "Would you like to celebrate with me at the Corner Bar this evening?"

"I'd love to – another time," answered Caroline. "Today, I'll be going back in the lorry with Teresa."

"That's a date, then. I'll keep you to it!"

CHAPTER 7

Oxford

Charles walked into Magdalen College, tiptoeing along the wide stone passages while the eyes of greatness bored into him from the portraits and statues along the walls. He marvelled at his audacity in stepping up the stairs, worn down by the feet of famous men, and wondered how he had come to be in such a venerable institution. The lecture was taking place in the dining room, and here, too, the atmosphere was heavy with tradition.

But he no longer stopped wondering if he was really here.

He belonged now, and it had happened so unexpectedly.

At the end of the first term, the Bursar had again quizzed him about his finances, and then allowed him more time to pay. Charles had wondered if the change in attitude was something to do with his arrest, as the Principal had called him in to offer apologies on behalf of the College. He managed to scrape his way by working through the vacations, and borrowing whatever he could from friends and family. During the summer, he'd earned enough to cover his debt. He changed subjects, and looked forward to his new course in Politics, Philosophy and Economics, even though it meant an extra year in Oxford.

Midway through the term, he was summoned to the Bursar's office, and his previous suspicions were vindicated.

A Canadian scholar had won funding from his country, but couldn't claim it without forfeiting the College scholarship.

The College had decided to offer Charles half of it. It would not entitle him to wear a scholar's gown, but as he was starting a new degree, the money would hold until graduation. Was he interested?

Charles basked in euphoria for several days. He celebrated wildly along The Broad, and treated friends to meals in expensive restaurants. The term's allowance disappeared in no time, but then he took control of himself.

He was now in his final year. It was some time since he'd gone through his finances. He did the calculations again, and then again. He had money to spare!

A travel agent told him the fare to Nairobi. He had enough for a flight home over the Christmas holidays. How wonderful it would be to go home, touch base for a short while, see Teresa, and enjoy the sunshine, before coming back to brave the worst months of winter and his final exams.

He made the decision. After all, it was his money. Not for one moment did he think there would be objections from his family. How could they? They would be so proud and pleased to see him, and so would Teresa. Charles booked his passage, and couldn't wait to tell them. Teresa's reply was encouraging, if not ecstatic.

But Jackson's letter from Cardiff University where he was lecturing was brutal in its outright refusal to let him go home for Christmas.

It's too soon, and you still have study to do. If you go, you might not want to come back. We both know what it is like in the British winter, but you must endure for the sake of your career and your country. I did. And as for Teresa Myers, leave that woman alone! She will rain evil spirits on your head.

Charles pulled a face as he read Jackson's reference to Teresa. How did he know about her? But his brother was wise, and had endured three unbroken years in this country. Charles steeled himself for the duration. Disconsolate, he sent off a letter to Teresa, with a note for Caroline explaining his change of plans. The long dark weeks stretched before him.

He caught a coach to Cardiff, where Jackson met him. His brother lived in a tiny terraced house on the high end of a steep street lined with identical buildings. The only distinguishable features were the varying colours of the front doors. As Charles stooped low to enter a bright orange door, he was greeted as an old friend. Jackson's landlady Ella, a plump woman in her fifties, never stopped talking, and he could have listened to her lilting Welsh accent for hours.

He accepted a cup of tea, and let her chatter drift over his head, as he thought of Teresa. He'd received a letter with disquieting views on Kenya politics in the run up to the primary elections for the reserved seats, confined to European voters only. He wasn't sure whether they were hers, or an echo of her father's opinions.

All the parties seem to be contradicting each other and are very vague. The Africans make wild statements and then twist them when challenged. Generally speaking, we favour the Coalition, which aims to protect minorities. But, even though he betrayed us by supporting African aspirations, Michael Blundell and his New Kenya Group will probably take most of the European seats.

What dismays me is this 'Kenyatta cult', and the wearing of Kenyatta badges. Also that man Macleod, as Daddy describes him, is in favour of releasing Kenyatta from detention. In one way it is better to release him. We would then be dealing with a man and not a myth. But to us the reason against his release is much stronger. It would be a complete betrayal by the British Government of the loyalists who suffered so much during the Emergency, and of all decent people in this country.

My views on politics sometimes get a little mixed. I am not quite sure what's going to happen, but I do know that this is home for me, and I hope there'll be a place for us in a new Kenya.

People like you, Charles, will help bring it about.

The teacups were empty, and Charles realised he had devoured three slices of yeast cake. Jackson suggested going for a walk. Ella stood on tiptoes to give him a peck on the cheek.

"Charles, our house is always open to a handsome man like you."

The village pond was iced over.

"It might be firm enough for skating soon," Jackson said.

It started to snow. The pavement was silver, and Charles picked up a piece of snow. It felt soft and crunchy.

"What's happening back home?" he asked his brother, mentioning the passage from Teresa's letter. Jackson still disapproved of their relationship, but Charles was happier now that he could talk freely about it.

"Kenya politics is a mess isn't it?" said Jackson. "I don't think Teresa is right in opposing Kenyatta's release. The whites are trying to sacrifice what is best for present day Kenya, in the interests of an obsolete minority. The Mau Mau have lost their bite now, and the loyalists have played their part. Kenya is faced with different problems, and it isn't fair to keep the mud of the past stirred up. Some people will be hurt, that is inevitable. Whatever the outcome, Jomo Kenyatta is going to be released. The whites must face it, and let him out of detention before the elections, so the confusion can blow over."

"Those are my ideas, too," agreed Charles. Then he remembered Mwangi. If the Emergency were lifted, his enemy would be released. Jackson had told him their father's health had stabilised. Would Mwangi renew his vendetta, causing further deterioration? He kept the thought to himself.

"I believe that a clearer view is given to those like ourselves, Charles, away from day-to-day issues, and yet closely connected with the country. Certainly the ideas would be less impassioned – don't you agree?"

But in her next letter Teresa did not agree.

It is difficult to forget the past and very wrong to ignore those heroic people who fought for the right during the Emergency. I think it is shameful but, unfortunately, Macleod thinks they can be forgotten. He encouraged the settlers to come in the first place, and is now deserting them, and handing everything over to the Africans. The British Government will never be respected in this country again – by any race. You should see the apathy here. We know one person who five years ago was offered five thousand pounds for a small farm. He sold it recently for five hundred.

I hope that things are not going to be as bad as a lot of people believe, but my parents are going almost crazy with worry. Money is flowing out at a fantastic rate. In Daddy's opinion, Kenya will be bankrupt in three months unless something is done to restore confidence. But hopefully there won't be much violence.

Maybe Kenyatta is going to be released, but it really goes against the grain. Don't think I am a diehard racist. How could I be? But we are sick and tired of seeing how expendable the Kenya settlers are in the eyes of men who have spent a mere fortnight out of their lives here. I suppose politics is a dirty game and will always be.

Charles hoped that politics would not ruin their relationship, but there was no time to worry about that now; he had studying to do before going up for his final two terms at Oxford.

He heard Fenner Brockway speaking on Africa but was disappointed, as the politician merely summarised the situation in each country. The questions afterwards were more interesting. Brockway expressed sympathy with the view of the white settler as an annoying stumbling block on the way to independence. Charles was gratified that a prominent Englishman should take the African side. He mentioned the discussion to Teresa, but she was worried about the rising nationalism in Kenya.

There's frightening talk of a common roll. Of course it's the right thing to have, but what will happen to the white farmers, and the Indian businessmen? We're such a minority, we'll be disenfranchised, and we've been encouraged to put so much into the country.

He went to stay with a friend on a farm in Kent for the Easter vacation. They drove past miniature fields tidily bound by hedges, through sunken lanes arched with trees. The sun pricked through the latticed fronds, and newly budding leaves were outlined in soft green shades against the blue of the sky. There was no room for two cars to pass, and they had to reverse into small indentations in the bank to give way.

A farmhand in his mid-thirties, who tended the battery chickens and sixty sheep, pulled funny faces at Charles.

"What do you do with all those hens?" Charles asked him.

"We sell the eggs in the local market and when they're past laying, we wring their necks for the pot."

The man looked at him strangely, as if the answer were obvious. Charles knew he was reinforcing the stereotype of an ignorant black man in the labourer's eyes, but the concept was unfamiliar, and he wanted to know more.

"And the sheep?"

"I shear them, Charles. We sell the wool in town every year."

He gazed at the white blobs of the sheep burying their black faces in the lush green pasture.

"At my home we have about six hens scratching in the dirt around our huts, and a dozen goats for family use," he said thoughtfully, wondering how long it would take his people to move away from subsistence farming to commercial enterprise.

The parents were a friendly couple who, when they had recovered from their first sight of a black man, asked him questions about his home and his family's former pastoral life. But he saw that they could not visualise the endless dry plains of Africa.

Louise called to see Charles in the first week of summer term.

"I've just won two places in the ballot for a college canoe on May Morning," she said. "Would you like to come?"

It was 4.00am. He waited downriver of the boathouse, clutching a flask of hot soup. Louise and her two friends rounded a clump of weeping willows. They were crouched in the bottom of the boat, muffled in windproof jackets, their paddles waving erratically.

"Thank goodness we've got one man, at least," Louise said as the canoe grounded beside him.

He removed his shoes and waded into the freezing water, then stepped into the flimsy craft. It wobbled violently, and the girls shrieked with mock fear. He wondered how deep the river was. He didn't know how to swim.

There were no seats. The three girls knelt in the bottom of the boat, a pool of water swishing round their knees. Charles took an oar and settled in the stern. They drifted out, paused for last minute adjustments, and paddled downstream. Now and again one of them would hum a tune or put on an unexpected spurt, making them bump into the bank, or a branch, or a boat ahead.

Before long the river was full of punts holding people huddled under blankets. Paddling less erratically now, they passed remnants of all-night parties on the banks, the sleepy figures sitting bleary-eyed in front of a few glowing coals.

Near Magdalen Bridge, the river was congested with every type of craft imaginable. They came to a full stop about a hundred yards from the tower. Charles jumped into the shallows and tied the canoe to some branches. The girls disembarked carefully onto the slippery bank and a path, hung low with damp foliage, led them forward.

They found a vantage point facing the tower, and settled to watch and wait.

The bells began to peel the hour. There was dead silence over the river, invisible under its carpet of punts. A huddled crowd hung over the bridge. The thundering traffic stopped. Even the birds were quiet in the clear morning air, as pure and heavenly singing rang from Magdalen Tower. The whole world paused.

The spell broke when the choir dispersed, and the punting parties tried to extricate themselves from their muddle.

"Let's wait for the river traffic to disperse before we go back," suggested Louise, taking his hand.

They jostled up the High Street and into the Square beside the Radcliffe Camera, following the pipes of the Morris Dancers. But it was hopeless trying to see anything. People were climbing up scaffolding, scrambling onto trees, and scaling walls in their efforts to get a view. Charles found a couple of small oil drums and they took it in turns to balance on them and watch the colourful handkerchiefs and hats of the bobbing dancers.

A terrific crash drowned the music, as a tree collapsed under the weight of the people on its branches. After a brief pause to make sure nobody had been injured, the dancers announced they would proceed to The Broad.

Charles and the girls made their way back to the river, which was now empty except for a lone punt fastened to the opposite bank. Charles watched them bale out the canoe, and bought some hot soup before embarking for their return.

Louise caught her toe on a protruding root, and slipped down the bank, feet first into the icy water. Charles caught hold of her shoulders and drew her out, he turned her round and enveloped her in his arms, taking off her sodden jacket and substituting it with his sheepskin-lined coat. They stood there until she stopped shivering. She gave him a little smile, and he made her sit on the privileged stern seat as they paddled upstream.

They rested often, observing the awakening students who had camped on the riverside. He heard fires crackling, and saw huddled figures warming themselves. An appetizing whiff of frying sausages reached him from the banks. Somebody was playing a mouth organ as they rounded one bend, and the high-pitched clangour of bagpipes greeted them at another. They paused to watch a group of kilted dancers perform a reel in the long grass.

Charles left the girls to drift through 'Dame's Delight', and they in their turn got out of the canoe before 'Parson's Pleasure' where 'Ladies are not allowed'. While the others walked along a path screened from the river by bulrushes, Charles hauled the canoe up the rollers and paddled it alone for twenty yards through the forbidden area, avoiding the nude men who frolicked in the water. He noted that it only reached to their chests.

When they arrived at the boathouse, it seemed as if he had lived through a whole day, instead of just a few hours. He had two essays to write in three days, and had done no research. He recovered his coat from Louise. He hadn't had a chance to talk to her alone all day.

"We're having a staircase party later in the term," he said. "Would you like to come?"

"I'd love to." She smiled. "I haven't been to one yet."

"Neither have I."

Charles waited for Louise at the entrance to his college. She was late. He hadn't seen her since May morning, and wondered if she'd forgotten. He walked up the cobbled street and back again. As he was about to give up, she appeared on her bicycle, her scarf unravelling behind her.

She was red in the face.

"I've come from a disastrous hockey match. My shins are bruised, I went over on my ankle, and we lost. I've only just had time for a quick shower."

81

He helped to chain her bike, and led the way to his corner of the quadrangle. The staircase was overflowing with people. He'd been told these parties were classed as the typical summer entertainment in Oxford. They wandered from one room to the other, clutching their glasses, drawing on their cigarettes, and shouting over the music.

They danced, gyrating from one leg to the other on the same spot. The dim rays of a street lamp shone through the window. Charles wondered idly if someone would smash it before the night was over. Bottles accumulated on the windowsills, cigarette butts were crushed on the floor. The tempo increased, and steamy couples strayed past, hand in hand, looking for somewhere comfortable. Louise detached herself.

"I'm going," she said. "I've got a squash match tomorrow, and need a good night's sleep. I must bathe my ankle too. Don't bother to see me out."

But he walked with her to the gate, and helped unlock her bicycle. Charles had no enthusiasm for sport, which Louise had become more involved in as the terms went by. He didn't sleep that night, and in the morning he and his friends faced a stiff bill for replacement of the street lamp which had, in the end, been smashed.

He found an invitation in his pigeonhole from the East Africa Society. He could not remember joining them, but they were holding a social evening at the imposing Rhodes House, so he went along.

The room overflowed with people and buzzed with talk. For once, whites were in the minority. In one corner, an intense discussion was taking place between the son of a European settler and a Kikuyu from the Mount Kenya region on the question of federation of the East African states. In a small space in the centre of the room, couples were swaying to the strains of jazz. Charles spotted a white girl peering through the door, and then she ducked back. He went after her and asked her to dance. She was blonde, with heavily made-up eyes, which she demurely lowered as he took her hand.

She told him about her political leanings, and he admitted there was something about communism which appealed to him. Perhaps Africa was more in line with the concept of communal ownership, than western capitalism? After all, his tribe never had any trouble with land before the white man came to carve it up. They wandered wherever the rains made the grass grow, and the land renewed itself behind them. It was there for everyone. They would raid the Masai, or the Kikuyu for cattle and women, but the warfare was natural and healthy.

The news of the murders of a family in the highlands made him think of Teresa once more. Their correspondence had dwindled, but when he wrote to her through Caroline, she declared it was the Mau Mau again. The authorities were playing it down and her father had gone off on one of his tirades. She was confused and unhappy, and he did not know how to console her. They didn't exchange any more letters.

His exams loomed nearer and he had time for nothing else but study. His final weeks were dedicated to intensive hours in the library while the rest of Oxford cavorted in the sunshine.

Finally, no longer self-conscious in his gown, Charles entered the high-roofed examination halls at 'Schools'. The life-size portraits on the walls exaggerated his insignificance. Under the ornate architecture he scratched at his desk while the city's muted clatter continued outside the massive doors.

As the University gathered itself for another wave of May Balls, his thoughts turned to the future. There was an opening for him as a junior reporter in Fleet Street, London.

PART II

1961 – 1963

The Mau Mau rebellion precipitated the granting of Independence to Kenya in 1963. There was a major exodus of settler farmers in the run up to Independence, as they took advantage of the British Government's compensation program for improvements to the land which had been allocated to them in the early 1900s.

CHAPTER 8

Ngorongoro crater, Tanganyika

Caroline opened Charles's letter. With her departure only a few months away, she had written hoping to make contact with him when she arrived in Oxford.

I'm delighted you've been accepted into Oxford, and I'm sorry I won't be able to show you round. After my finals, I'm going to work in Fleet Street for a few months before coming home. How is Teresa? Please tell her I asked.

Caroline wondered about passing on Charles's message.

Teresa was earning a good reputation as a trainer, and despite the uncertain political climate, their stables were full. She had imported a stallion from South Africa and begun a breeding program. Caroline reflected on her friend's tenuous relationship with Jack, the jockey who came from Ireland during the UK off season. The man was married. She would have to pick the right moment to talk about Charles.

After the landslide victory of the Kenya Africa National Union in the elections at the beginning of the year, the Emergency was lifted. The Kikuyu workers were released from detention and most of them returned to their previous jobs. It was as if they had never been away.

Boney had taken on the Myers' driver, Mwangi.

"I will not have him back here again, Caroline," Teresa told her. "I've got used to the new one now, and although he's not as good as Mwangi, I feel much safer."

"I've heard from Charles. I wrote telling him I'll be in Oxford later this year. He asked after you."

They were riding together on one of the rare Saturday afternoons when Teresa wasn't at the races. Teresa dug her heels into her horse's flanks, and galloped him up a grassy hill. Caroline followed, eyes alert for hidden ant bear holes, which would be fatal for her horse. They drew rein at the top. Teresa's inky black hair fanned across her face. Her eyes looked troubled.

"Jack will be here in August," she said. "I guess I'll just have to wait and see."

Time was running out. Caroline felt she hardly knew Africa, although she'd lived here for most of her life. She'd never been to the northern desert, nor had she stayed in a game park. Most of her free time was spent curled on the sofa, reading and dreaming. The Ngorongoro crater in Tanganyika sounded such a romantic place, and it had a large concentration of animals.

The rains had been good, the harvest was coming in, and Boney expected a bumper crop. Then it would be time for their annual holiday. Caroline chose her moment one weekend after supper. The eucalyptus logs in the fireplace cracked loudly, creating sparks as the flames shot up the blackened chimney. Flakes of soot drifted onto the carpet. Then the fire settled, and Boney's face reflected the warm glow. Caroline handed him a cup of coffee.

"Might we do something different for our holiday this year, Boney?"

"Why on earth?" He took the cup, splashing the hot liquid onto the saucer in his surprise.

She laughed, "I know you like to do the same thing every year, and I really don't mind. But, just this once, before I go away, I'd love to try somewhere else. Like the northern district or even Ngorongoro..." She rolled the name round her tongue. "I've never been on safari…" She sat at his feet, gazing into the fire, dreaming of men in khaki shorts, sitting round a campfire while somebody strummed on a guitar.

Boney took a sip of coffee.

"You deserve to do something special before leaving, my dear. If we have a good harvest, I could leave the Headman to look after the farm. I might ask Guy Clayton to drop us in Arusha on one of his monthly flights. He's offered to take me often enough."

"Oh thank you, Boney – I never dared think…" Caroline flung her arms round him.

He disentangled himself, laughing. "Remember, I can't promise anything; and now, my girl, it's long past my bedtime."

They met Guy at the airstrip on his farm. Boney had invited him to join them on safari, but there was another figure standing by the tiny aircraft.

"D'you remember my son Brian?"

Boney offered his hand. "I last saw you as a teenager," he said.

Caroline was behind him.

"We've met before, at the races," Brian said to her. "I'm sorry I haven't contacted you since, but it's good to see you again."

Guy handed them into the rear of the plane.

"I've never flown before." Caroline fastened her seatbelt, trying to ignore the nervous flutters in her stomach.

"There's a paper bag in the pocket in front of you," Brian said, his eyes twinkling.

They rattled along the grass runway. It seemed such a flimsy machine, and Caroline gripped the handle in front of her as they turned into the wind. Guy roared the engine, and they rose steeply over the farm. He banked before clouds enfolded them, and Caroline's stomach gave a lurch. When they

89

emerged into the sunlight, she peered through the window at the country below, trying to distract herself by identifying landmarks. But they were soon enveloped in cloud again. They hit several pockets of air. She felt nausea welling up, and stared resolutely at the greyness outside. She glanced at Brian who winked at her and then stared at the seat in front, his face turning pasty. She held the bag before her mouth, but that made it worse, so she put it back. She closed her eyes… would the journey never end? When she was about to reach again for the pocket, Guy called out.

"Hold on, folks, we're there!"

They touched down on the dusty strip outside Arusha township, and trundled to a stop. Brian handed Caroline out of the plane. Her legs felt shaky, and she wobbled against him, before taking a deep breath, her arms stretched to the sun.

Boney had booked a self-drive Land Rover through a local tour company, and he went to collect Mwangi, who had arrived on the bus the day before. After a reviving cup of coffee, they prepared for the long drive via Lake Manyara to the Ngorongoro crater.

The road was deeply corrugated and the best path was always on the wrong side. They passed the oncoming vehicles without mishap, dust enveloping them in a thick blanket. Caroline sat in the rear seat, sandwiched between Brian and Guy. Brian's leg, thick with soft curls, brushed against hers. A tingle raced through her. They shifted position often. If she turned, ostensibly to look out of the window, she could study his profile and marvel at his long eyelashes, and her knees would again touch his.

Two hours swept by.

They came to a sleepy village nestling under a canopy of umbrella thorns. The yellow branches glowed in the hot sun. Brian bought them ice-cold sodas at a wayside *duka*. A herd of enormous elephants encroached on the road, blocking the way up a tortuous escarpment, before they emerged on a plateau above Lake Manyara. They stopped for tea at the lodge overlooking the lake, which was lined with a thin border of flamingos.

"Not nearly as many here, as in our Lake Nakuru," mumbled Caroline, dropping some cake crumbs onto the paved floor of the patio. She watched as a flock of superb starlings swooped in a mass of glossy blue, orange and white from a nearby thorn tree. They squabbled over the crumbs, and then stood by waiting for more.

"But those elephants we saw at the foot of the escarpment were much larger than any you can find in Kenya," Brian reminded her, smiling warmly, his eyes brim-full with humour.

As they were about to leave, a woman emerged from the lodge, dressed in traditional African garb. Voluminous folds of cotton in bold patterns of red, black, and green, adorned the ample figure. A red and yellow headdress rose in striking splendour over the chubby face, which was flushed with sunburn. She swept forwards, her garment brushing the floor. She produced a camera cluttered with lenses, adjusted the focus, and in a loud American drawl tried to direct the African tour guide into position at the door of their minibus. He was a slight man uniformed in spotless khaki, and regarded her with despair, but posed obligingly.

Caroline could not resist the spectacle. She caught Brian's eye and reached for her camera.

"This will be one for the album," she whispered as she included the tourist and the tour guide in the frame, and clicked the shutter.

She noticed Mwangi watching, and smiled to include him in the joke, wondering what he thought of it all. His implacable eyes, reduced to pinpricks of black stone, bore into her. They flicked towards Brian, and then he turned away. Caroline stood, transfixed, as the bus rumbled into life and disappeared from sight. She wished Boney hadn't brought him along as driver. But she didn't blame Mwangi for resenting the foreign tourists who were so out of place in their beloved Africa.

"Come on, Caroline – we're waiting for you!"

Boney tapped on the bonnet of the car, and Mwangi started the engine. She joined Brian on the back seat.

They stopped for the night at a farm hotel, hidden behind a screen of bushes. Small flares lit up the pathway to the dark reception area. Brian handed Caroline her coffee after dinner, and they sat beside the fire together, leafing through wildlife magazines.

His hair curled away from an already receding forehead. His prominent nose dominated a generous mouth. When he smiled, or drew on his cigarette, she glimpsed stained teeth, crowding against each other. But he had such friendly brown eyes, and exuded a feeling of warmth, and security.

The road snaked up the volcano towards the crater rim. Dense bush revealed an occasional glimpse of the farmland below. The air chilled, and they passed patches of bracken and groundsel.

They turned a corner, groaned up a steep rise, and the crater opened out before them. Mwangi parked the car at a lookout, and they walked to the edge, glad to stretch their legs. A thunderstorm was progressing along the opposite wall, its deep purple clouds contrasting with the faint browns and greys of the sunlit plain far below. On the left glimmered a lake, behind a tiny patch of forest. Caroline let her eyes wander round the vast rim of the crater. The great canopy of sky overwhelmed her, she breathed in deeply, savouring the immensity of the scene. The breath of Africa filled her being. This was her country, her home.

Grey clouds rolled in from the slopes, tumbling over each other in silent frenzy as the wind picked up, and stinging drops of rain sent them running for the car.

They continued to the lodge, slipping and sliding in the mud, and passed a herd of buffalo, their glistening backs showing above the long grass. Wooden buildings were perched haphazardly overlooking the crater rim, with more buffalo grazing the lush pasture between them, like domesticated cattle.

They found their rooms. The three men shared a large cabin. Caroline enjoyed a double room to herself. She saw Mwangi walk towards the labour lines after he had unpacked the vehicle.

"Don't forget, I'm taking you into the crater tomorrow morning," he called to her.

Was there a sinister tone in his voice? He was a strange man, his beady eyes unfathomable in a wizened face. He never said much, and seldom smiled. She supposed she couldn't blame him. After all, he'd only come out of detention a few months before. It would be enough to change any man. He always wore a faded red fez, but she had seen him once in a rare moment without that protection, and was surprised at the long coils of black hair that sprang from his scalp. She could see why Teresa felt uneasy in his presence.

Caroline treated herself to a hot shower, fuelled by a wood fire outside her bathroom. A bitterly cold wind penetrated her thick pullover as she sidled past a buffalo and ran to the main building to join the men for dinner.

They awoke to a swirling mist. Visibility was so low, that the ranger doubted they would leave the lodge, let alone venture into the crater. They waited for forty minutes, but the cloud still hung over them. A park vehicle, its headlights gleaming weakly through the murk, crept towards the gate.

"It is very thick out there," the warden said. "But it's possible the cloud is only settled on the rim. You will only know for sure if you try."

Mwangi waited in the driver's seat, but the warden stopped them.

"You're not allowed to go in your own car," he told them. "You have to use a park vehicle, and the ranger will drive you."

Mwangi engaged the warden in a heated exchange.

"What's he saying, Brian? They're talking too fast for me."

"I don't know, Caroline. He seems to be overly anxious to come with us."

Boney and Guy were transferring their picnic and spare clothes into the park vehicle. The warden won the argument, and Mwangi, his eyes glittering with rage, stomped past them to disappear into the mist.

"I'm glad he's not taking us," Caroline said. "He gives me the creeps."

Brian laughed. "He's only a driver, Caroline, a mere human being. He can't harm you – especially when I'm here!"

He engulfed her with his arm, in mock protection.

"There are just two roads; one into, and one out of the crater," warned the ranger, "and there's no room to turn round. If we go down, and you can't see anything, we'll still have to drive all the way round and come up the other side, and you'll have to pay for the whole day."

"Let's take the risk," decided Boney.

The precarious track wound downwards in a series of hairpin bends. Travelling at walking pace, they emerged beneath the cloud. A sheer precipice appeared on Caroline's left. There was nothing between her and a two thousand foot drop except for the shaking side of the sliding Land Rover. She eased nearer to Brian on the back seat.

What had appeared as a brown plain from the lookout on the previous day became acres and acres of undulating grassland covered with black specks. As they approached, the specks were transformed into massed herds of wildebeest and kongoni. Hyenas slunk away from chewed bones, their ugly heads turned backwards, watching; wild dogs quarrelled over bloody carcasses; vultures crowded over the pungent remains of a Thomson's gazelle; and a pair of silver backed jackals scurried out of sight.

Caroline stood on the back seat beside Brian, looking

through the roof hatch. She pointed to the west. Two young rhino were dozing in the early morning sun.

They approached the beasts. She marvelled at the enormity of their grey bulk. The folds of their mud-baked hides betrayed dark cracks of moisture. The driver parked the vehicle on a hillock, the sun behind them, and switched off the engine. Caroline's ears became tuned to the muted sounds of the animals around them. One of the rhino lumbered to his feet, looked at them briefly, and began to rub his prehistoric head over the back of his companion. Their hides grated harshly as they made contact, backwards and forwards, the loud rasps strange amid the twittering of birds and the gentle calls of the antelope.

They approached a patch of scrub on the far side of the crater. Yellow grass interspersed with thorn scraped under the chassis.

They stopped, and all was silent. The ranger indicated to their left, a cautionary finger over his mouth. Caroline could see only bush. Then she discerned two watching eyes. She looked closer, and saw a pair of cocked ears, and an inquisitive nose poking through a thorn bush only three yards away. A cub lay there, perfectly still. She scanned the scrub. Lion surrounded them; several females and three cubs.

She made room for Brian, and Boney and Guy squeezed together to stand on the front seat.

Brian moved, his camera ready, while Guy scanned the bushes with his binoculars.

"There's the male," he mouthed.

He had come up behind them. Every inch of his proud, black-maned head and lithe body lived up to the title of King of Beasts. He stood erect, taking his time to scent the air, and then walked majestically past them.

"He's drawing our attention from the pride," whispered Guy.

The lion stopped a couple of feet away, disdaining to look at them, and then he insolently marked his territory, tail high, in front of them. A strong smell of urine tainted the air.

They lingered, savouring the scene, until the pride melted back into the dappled shade.

They followed a track across the plain towards the forest. A cheetah surprised them, coming out into the open, its black rosettes in smart contrast against the tan hide. It jumped the ditch beside the road, and then walked in front of them for a hundred yards before bounding lightly into the long grass, muscles rippling with latent strength. They caught glimpses of elephant far away across a swamp, and then drew up in a glade surrounded by umbrella thorns for a late lunch.

It was a relief being able to talk normally again. Birds competed with their chatter and cheeky cordon bleu finches hopped towards the fallen crumbs. The men disappeared behind some bushes, and Caroline wandered towards an opening in the forest. It was so peaceful. A lone impala raised its delicate head to watch her, and then bounded away. What a different world it was down here. She didn't want it to end.

The exit road was long and steep. Every twist threatened to break the vehicle in two, while wooded chasms yawned up at them with frightening frequency. At the summit they paused to look back at the vista of unspoilt Africa spread out below.

"I shall never forget this day as long as I live," said Caroline. She and Brian were standing on the lawn overlooking the crater after dinner. Stars carpeted the skies. She shivered, and Brian included her under his overcoat.

"Neither will I…" he said, squeezing her gently, "for more than one reason."

She found herself responding. She felt secure and comfortable nestling against him. Then, embarrassed, she broke away. They went back into the lodge, but before they parted for the night he stopped her.

"Would you like to come dancing with me when we get back?" he asked. "The Nakuru Athletic Club is having a Ball next month."

Caroline paused, not yet ready to think outside her day's experience, but she felt honoured that he should want to take her out.

"I'll give you a call in the next week or two, shall I?" he said.

Relieved that he understood her hesitation, she nodded. In the weeks that followed, whenever she was about to drop off to sleep she would recall that private moment on the crater rim.

CHAPTER 9

The Kenya Highlands and Mt. Kenya

The band played a catchy piece, and Caroline's feet tapped in time with the beat. Brian had gone to buy her a drink. She could tell after the first dance that he didn't have a natural rhythm, but at least she could let herself go for the rock n' roll numbers. She glanced around. She didn't know the rugby crowd, and everybody else on their table was dancing.

Brian returned.

He took several long swallows from his beer, wiping the froth from his lips. It was too noisy for conversation. They sat watching the dancers, and he pointed out the members of his team, leaning close to her ear, but she only caught half his words. Her feet were still tapping. He offered his hand. Her strapless navy blue and white spotted dress swirled in full circle as she turned gracefully to the music of a fox-trot. He stepped on her toes a few times, apologising awkwardly. They couldn't say much in the din that surrounded them. At the next pause, he held her at arm's length.

"We're not getting along very well, are we? I am no dancer... like to come outside for a moment?"

He led her onto the rugby pitch. Behind them, the clubhouse was alive with lights, laughter, and the clinking of glasses. They moved beyond the arc of light, away from the loud music in the background. She liked being alone with him.

"It's peaceful out here – and cool."

She admired the canopy of stars, and they stood in silence, savouring the night air. She felt him watching her. He was so quiet and serious. She knew she could depend on him... for what – for not making advances towards her? She almost wished he would.

"I suppose we'd better go back," she said.

He faced her, placing his hands on her shoulders, then hesitated, and turned her away from him so that she looked towards the lighted clubhouse. He kissed her lightly on her bare shoulder, and then, with a gentle nudge, guided her before him. The kiss burned her skin, making a permanent impression on her senses. He led her back to the dance floor and held her tight against him until the music stopped.

Every other weekend he drove the hundred miles from Nairobi, and they explored the countryside together. Their favourite place was the rim of Mt. Menengai, the volcano overlooking Nakuru town; smaller than Ngorongoro, it had its own dramatic character. They stood on the jutting promontory and looked over the dense scrub in the crater depths, interspersed with black mounds of glistening lava, a dark, forbidding country.

"It's the third largest crater in the world," Brian told her. "I read that somewhere."

Caroline gazed beyond, at the vastness of Africa, which rolled through patterned farmlands, across hills and plains into the hazy distance. As evening fell, grey clouds crept along the crater depths and swirled up the cliffs, snatching at them with wispy fingers, as the wind caught and tossed the vapours into nothingness among the trees.

They walked towards the car, but a sudden movement in the long grass near the forest distracted them. Brian turned off the track, parting the stalks in front of him.

"Careful of snakes!" Caroline warned.

She followed, treading in his footsteps. As they approached

the thrashing, it increased, and she saw the soft brown hide of a female impala, its eyes wide with fright. One leg was caught in a loop of wire.

"It's a trap, but the wire hasn't tightened too much. I'll see if I can free her."

Brian caught hold of the leg and the animal stilled. She seemed to know they were trying to help. He struggled with the wire, and eased it over the hoof. He let go. The doe stood there for a second, then moved her leg and took a small step. She bounded away and the grass closed behind her. It was as if it had never happened.

Brian coasted the car down the mountain, his arm round Caroline's shoulders. She snuggled against his tweed jacket, eyes closed, smelling the smoky maleness of him.

He had a friend who drove a racing car, and they supported him regularly at the Sunday track meetings in town. Caroline did not enjoy the noise of the cars screaming endlessly round and round the steaming track, the taint of burnt rubber, and the loud-mouthed crowd slurping ice creams and dropping their rubbish beneath the makeshift stands. But she went, because it meant she could be with Brian.

She preferred the horse races, which were sometimes held on a Saturday afternoon. She enjoyed the soft green track, the animals, their coats rippling with vitality, and the excitement of betting on Teresa's runners. But Brian liked to watch rugby then, and she was often torn between the two.

She waited for him in the car while he bought a take-away supper after a match. A crooked street lamp glowed weakly through the windscreen. She reached over to open the door as he approached arms full. He eased himself into the driver's seat and turned towards her to put the package into the back.

His arm brushed her shoulder. He kept it there, and then moved her gently to face him. His eyes were deep brown, flecked with amber lights. His lips found hers, then lingered. A deep welling of giving flowed from her, and she melded her spirit into his. She drew away, to gaze into his eyes in the light of the street lamp, then responded again, losing herself.

He talked as if it were the most natural thing in the world that they should spend their future together. She liked to savour the purity of her sensations, and was in no hurry to make plans. Besides, their embryonic love was no match for the heady triumph of her being accepted into Oxford.

"I've never climbed Mt. Kenya before," said Caroline. "I know you have – would there be time for us to do it, before I go?"

The romantic sight of the snowy peaks rising above the northern horizon on a clear day always made her catch her breath.

"If you wish, my dear, I'll organise a party of rugby players and their girlfriends. But you'll have to train first – it's a tough trek."

"I'll be okay; I play enough hockey and tennis to keep fit."

They booked into a self-service cottage at the Naro Moru River Lodge. Manicured lawns sloped towards the river, its opposite bank overgrown with foliage. Caroline explored a path leading away from the lodge. Sunbirds danced among the flowerbeds and a giant kingfisher perched on a dead twig, motionless above a pool. A turaco flashed its red wings and settled on a tree, then flowed upwards into the canopy with long smooth hops.

The following morning cloud enveloped the mountain. Brian and Caroline filled the boot of his car with heavy packs, and drove the porter-guide up the mountain behind the others. Mud huts nestled among maize patches lining the route through the lower slopes. After the park entrance, the car groaned at the gradient and the altitude, battling over the corrugations through dense tropical forest before reaching the road head. The others were waiting impatiently.

Two porters opened the boot of their car, grabbed a full rucksack each, and disappeared up the track. Wally, the club hooker, determined to shoulder his own, hung on grimly as another porter tried to relieve him of it. Caroline opened hers, separating immediate essentials into a small emergency pack between her and Brian while the remaining porters hung round impatiently.

"Why didn't they warn us about this last night?" complained David, the fly-half. "My pack has disappeared up the mountain, and I haven't even got a sweater or a bar of chocolate on me."

"They will be waiting for you at the lunch stop on the vertical bog," Symon, the guide, explained. "The porters always go on ahead. Don't worry; I am here to look after you."

When everyone was ready, David disappeared up the track.

"You must keep together!" Symon shouted after him. But he was too late.

Before they had walked five hundred yards up the steep forest path, Caroline was puffing heavily.

"It's the altitude," Brian said. "You must take frequent rests."

At least it wasn't too hot. By the time they reached the misty moorland, she had gained her second wind.

She dreaded the vertical bog. Brian had warned her that its two-steps-forwards, one-step-back ordeal was the worst part of the ascent. They emerged from the trees. Great tufts of swamp grass alternated with white clumps of groundsel, their flower stems rotted into sentinels. Some of the stalks were bent over, half-broken and dry; but the occasional late yellow blossoms revealed what it would have been like in season. The mist played hide-and-seek with them, allowing tantalising glimpses of the surrounding countryside under the cloud.

In the end, provided she took it slowly, it proved no great hardship.

"That's because the ground is dry," Brian told her as they stopped to look back. "We're lucky."

The main road to Nairobi wound into the distance, and the Park Gates nestled in the forest thousands of feet below. Had she really climbed that far?

Wally laboured under his forty-pound pack, which contained a luxurious camp bed, the reason for his reluctance to let it out of his sight.

"I can hear my heart thumping all the way," he admitted.

At least she could experience the bliss of taking off hers, and walking on air every half hour as she and Brian passed their joint pack between them. David dropped back to persuade Wally to off-shoulder his burden, and Caroline noticed his relief when they stopped for lunch ten minutes later.

They stood against some high rocks to eat their sandwiches. The clouds opened windows onto the plains below, but offered no view of what it was like on either side, or above. They plodded on. Another rest, and Teleki Valley stretched below, with a blessed downward path to the valley floor. The sun did not exactly shine, but the mist lifted enough to allow them a view up to the hut.

"How much further to Makinder's Camp?" Caroline's legs were folding. "Have we gone more than half-way yet?"

"It's only just half-way," Brian consoled her. "But it's an easier walk, and it won't take so long."

They fairly whooped down the valley side, the groundsel towering over them on stilted stems. While crossing a stream Caroline slipped, wetting her feet and Brian made her change into dry socks. Her back was feeling the strain, and they had hardly started after the others when the hail came. It stung her face and hands, and clattered against her anorak. After a very long ten minutes they arrived at Teleki Hut, crowded with sheltering climbers.

Porters lined the floor, sleeping soundly. A bespectacled climber fairly smothered his small son with a warm blanket on a high bench. David's girlfriend Jenny, snug and cheerful, had arrived before the hailstorm.

Caroline felt a headache developing; it increased with a vengeance, and David produced some painkillers while Brian looked for drinking water. When the weather eased, Symon pronounced it safe to start, and they completed the final stage to Makinder's Camp in no more than a steady drizzle.

Caroline, lagging behind, looked at her watch.

"Is it really only three o'clock?"

They were allocated tents numbered 1 – 5 but each tent had four different numbers painted on. She claimed the nearest empty one and dumped her burden, then, armed with a gas stove, tea, cocoa and soup, invaded the grimy dining tent.

Brian drew water from the fast-flowing stream above the camp. There were no latrines. Caroline cleaned the table by pouring hot water over and wiping it off with newspaper, which came away black with filth.

Before dark, the clouds swirled lazily round the mountain, partially unfolding the dramatic scenery. With Brian, she sought privacy in a hidden hill fold a short distance away from camp, huddling together to savour the spectacle. He pointed upwards.

"Can you see Diamond Glacier?"

She raised her binoculars and picked it out nestling between the twin peaks of Batian and Nelian, a hard glistening mass cut short by a wall of ice halfway up the cavity.

Two runners clad in nothing but brief shorts and trainers, passed below them, every sinew of their muscular legs working visibly.

Symon approached. "They are Norwegians, training for the Olympics," he said in reply to Caroline's query. She noticed his mouth turn down in disapproval, and then he gave Brian a severe warning.

"You mustn't go out of sight of camp; I need to know where you all are."

Two hours later, one of the runners was rushed down by the Mountain Rescue team.

"He's suffering from mountain sickness," Symon said. "He'll be taken to Nanyuki Hospital. It can kill you, if you don't get down immediately."

Caroline's headache cleared, and only faint nausea reminded her of the altitude. Then Brian succumbed, but a timely dose of pills restored his appetite and strength. They retired early onto damp mattresses.

Caroline's fingers brushed against Brian's ear, and he leaned over to kiss her lingeringly. She turned in her sleeping bag, curving her back into the warm arc of his body, her nerves tingling every time he moved.

Snow dropped in soft plops on the tents during the night, melting where it fell. By morning, clouds roofed the valley walls, which were now glistening white to almost halfway down. Diamond Glacier, topped with snow, had doubled in size.

"Today we acclimatise," Symon told them.

Another party had left early for the summit, but one member returned to camp, having given up on the scree.

Caroline felt surprisingly energetic, and Brian asked Symon to lead them on a walk up the ridge behind camp to Tarn Hut. They hadn't gone far when Caroline's will failed her.

"I can't make it."

Brian put his arm round her shoulders. "Don't worry, my darling, we've got all day. Just take slow, steady steps, and stop whenever you feel like it. I'll stay behind you."

Her body gradually became accustomed to the exertion.

The steepest gradient was towards the top of the ridge. Little pockets of snow nestled among the alpine flowers. With the end in sight, her legs took her more surely on. Not even a headache marred the moment as she stood with Brian enjoying a brief view between the clouds, of the camp far below.

"We must be about level with the snowline on that valley wall opposite."

They topped an incline and enjoyed a stretch of level ground. A miniature plain studded with boulders and loose rocks opened out before them, but she couldn't see more than fifty yards ahead.

"It's like a moonscape," Caroline said.

Over another ridge, she gave a cry of pleasure. The Tarn lay below, still and cold under the clouds, with a hut standing aloof and forlorn against the rocks on the far side. Caroline remembered a photograph she had seen, of the peaks towering over the Tarn, their reflection mirrored in the water. She looked longingly up where she sensed the mountain mass to be, but there was only impenetrable mist. They scrambled down to join the guide, who was brewing coffee at the waters' edge.

Caroline's headache and nausea returned. It felt better when she was moving. "Isn't the water clear."

"Are there any fish?" asked Brian, peering down. But the guide didn't know.

It began to snow miniature flakes. Then the clouds parted to reveal Diamond Glacier beneath the peaks. Deep crevasses traced ski-lines across the fresh fallen snow. The sun warmed the scene momentarily. The scree on the opposite wall stretched before their eyes, with its winding tracks between the rocks.

"Is that what we've got to climb tomorrow?" Caroline cried. "It's so long and steep."

They crossed another shoulder of hill, and the lower portion of the scree, much steeper, came into view. Caroline gasped. David's red anorak moved along the lower slopes. Brian called, and the mountains echoed his voice, returning it, muffled, to their ears. They both shouted, and David spotted them, waving. They returned to camp by a circular route, and on the way, Caroline picked up some stones mottled in pastel shades. However, a few hours later, the orange, blue and brown colours faded, so she threw them away.

After a hearty lunch, it poured with rain and more snow came. Parties of climbers trickled into camp, soaked through and shivering, telling of five hours' continuous rain all the way from the road head. Caroline kept the kettle hot, and handed out cups of coffee and chocolate as people arrived. Some were totally unequipped for the conditions. Then she persuaded Brian to walk along the valley floor with her towards the peaks.

Meandering along the stream's trickle, pausing to admire the alpine flowers in pockets of rubble, and coming together for the occasional kiss and cuddle, they arrived at the bottom of the scree. She looked upwards, craning her neck at the steepness of it. A faint path zigzagged up the loose pebbles.

"Shall we try it for a little way?" she asked.

"Let's leave it until tomorrow; I don't want you to be defeated before we start."

Brian turned resolutely back. She gazed wistfully at the mountain walls, the lower reaches of Midget Peak, and up at Point John towering above, and then followed him.

That evening, for a brief few minutes, the sun shone warmly through the raindrops. People emerged from their tents, to marvel at the vision of a brilliant rainbow, etched in a perfect arc against the dark face of Point John. Hurried exposures were taken and cameras clicked before it faded, leaving them with a cloud-interrupted view of the peaks in the swift fall of dusk.

Caroline set the alarm for two o'clock in the morning. The mountain was stark above them, against the moon-washed sky. She packed their heavy sweaters in a rucksack for Symon to carry. Brian lit the way, while she plodded along with the rest behind her thin circle of torchlight. The higher they climbed, the weaker became the beams, until Brian's battery gave up the struggle against the cold.

They rested a while at the foot of the scree.

"Remember, everyone, the recommended programme is ten

steps and then stop!"

To Caroline's delight, she found she could manage twenty steps. But she stayed with Brian who had retreated to the back of the line. They lost sight of the others. Brian shouted, and a torch beamed out the path for them. A welcome pause, and a sip of water when they joined the others, perched precariously on some boulders, but nobody felt like eating. The night was clear. A light winked in the camp far below. A brighter mass beamed further away, and Caroline concluded it must be the little town of Nanyuki.

If she turned her head too suddenly, it hurt, and when she looked towards the mountain she was disappointed at the dark mass, concealing its mysteries.

"I wish we'd started later so that we could enjoy the view in daylight," she moaned.

The longer second half of the scree had an easier gradient, but the gap between Caroline and the rest of the party grew longer. She could no longer hear Brian's steps behind her. Their stops became more frequent. Caroline suspected he was trying to give her a psychological boost. The others pushed on, uncomplainingly enduring long cold rests while they stopped to wait.

It clouded over, and Symon called them together. "Keep to the right of the path," he said. "There's a sheer drop on the left."

Caroline could see nothing. They reached the snowline, and she trudged deeply into the footsteps of those before, noticing how the snow retained the patterns of their boots. Only ten steps at a time now, and after each stop it was harder to summon the will to get going.

"Let me go in front of you. It might encourage you to go faster," suggested Brian.

"It's no good," she called after a few minutes. "Wait for me!"

They swapped places again.

It started snowing in earnest, and the wind buffeted against her. They sheltered near a large rock, and a party of climbers passed them.

"Keep one behind the other!" they were cautioned. "Don't forget the eight hundred foot drop on your left."

It was difficult to imagine anything in that thick, wet blanket of cloud.

Caroline heard a shout, and raised her head. Top Hut beckoned, its windows dimly aglow above a drift of snow. Knee-high boulders encrusted with white impeded her progress toward the haven. She sank onto a bench, and a wave of nausea hit her. People were slumped against the wall, their faces inward masks of misery. Wally lay under a bench. Only Brian remembered to apologise for their intrusion to some thickly blanketed figures draped on the top bunk.

"That's okay!" a cheerful voice replied. "You're the second party through today; we're used to this sort of thing."

It was half past six in the morning.

The hut was divided into three rooms lined with benches and bunked sleeping areas. Fur-caped heads and muffled hands protruded from dark blankets. People began to stir. It was cosy.

"Ready now?" Brian consulted with Symon.

The night sky had lightened, and Caroline stepped into a swirling blizzard. She was thankful to be on the move again. Her head cleared, and she felt fit, but she had to stop frequently. The others were out of sight. David came bustling back.

"Come on now, we must go faster or we'll freeze, we can't stop and wait for you two any longer."

He took Caroline's arm.

"I can't go any faster."

"Can't *you* go slower?" Brian asked. "Then you would stay warm without having to stop."

They approached the edge of the Lewis Glacier at a snail's pace.

Symon paused to probe the deep snow with his ice axe, before leading them onto the glacier. As she stepped down from the wind-whipped rocks onto the sheltered smoothness of the snow-encrusted ice, Caroline experienced a feeling of absolute exhilaration. An expanse of unmarked snow stretched into the limited distance of her visibility. Each step she took gave her added buoyancy.

She could scarcely see the guide, a bare ten feet ahead of their line of plodders. Muffled figures carefully stepped into the footprints of the one before. Then, to her right she saw the reason for their caution, a fold of snow revealing the corner of a treacherous crevasse. They stopped, while Symon veered left in a wide arc, but his ice axe sank to the hilt in the snow before him. He returned to the cleft and prodded.

Another party caught up with them, clumping heedlessly over the virgin snow, making a mockery of their caution. But when they saw the dim outline of the crevasse the newcomers backed off in alarm.

Caroline wanted to carry on. The cloud around them lifted briefly, and the summit of Point Lenana was now visible. Only twenty yards of glacier separated them from the target. But Symon shook his head.

"I don't know how big the crevasse is, and there could be another one immediately beyond."

"What about those rocks? Can't we try them?" Caroline indicated an outcrop to their right.

The guide shrugged. "They are loose and dangerous…"

After some hesitation, they decided to trust his judgement, and reluctantly turned back. Caroline knew she could have made the top, and she saw that Symon was upset.

"I have let you down," he said, "but it's too dangerous."

"It's not your fault."

The other party attempted the rocks, but didn't get far before giving up.

A biting wind, lashed with stinging snow, accompanied

them back to Top Hut, where they stopped to change into dry gloves and balaclavas.

Half an hour later, the sun emerged, and their world transformed. Behind them stormed the blizzard; in front stretched Teleki Valley, with the tents of Makinder's Camp tiny in the distance. At their feet, yellow clusters of alpine flowers awakened beneath their crust of snow. Caroline turned her head – no longer sore – and gazed in eager anticipation at the mountain.

The foot of the Lewis Glacier appeared beneath the mist, the sun gleaming whitely on its slopes, with the tiny Curling Pond below, iced over. Point John, a gigantic column of time-eroded wood, towered above them, the light catching its varied hues. Grey clouds swept among the higher peaks, allowing glimpses of Nelian with Diamond Glacier at its base. But Batian remained shy.

On the other side of the valley, Caroline saw the still waters of the Tarn, and marvelled that she and Brian had climbed there the day before. Then she looked down... and back up...

"How could we possibly have climbed so far?"

Brian laughed. "Now you can appreciate the wisdom of starting off in the dark. If you'd seen how far it was, you'd never have made it; be honest!"

The others hurried on, but Caroline lingered, taking photographs, savouring the scenery, and enjoying the crisp mountain air. This was God's world – her world!

Behind them on Point Lenana, the blizzard still raged. She slid laughing down the scree, and walked briskly hand in hand with Brian along the valley floor to camp. It was half past nine in the morning.

"Come on, you two! We want to get down in time for lunch," said David.

"What's the hurry?" asked Caroline. "We're not due back in Nairobi until evening."

The gentle gradient up the wall of Teleki Valley was a

pleasant change from the flat valley floor, as Caroline's legs were now accustomed to climbing. They watched a white curl of cloud billowing lightly before them through the gap. It rolled onward down the slope in relentless envelopment. They plunged into it, and suffered its damp ministrations. The bog ran rivulets of water through the slushy mud. The tufts of swamp grass were too big to step over. They stumbled and slipped downwards, thankful that conditions had been easier on the way up. Climbers approached them, slithering their way up the slime, some of them wearing light cotton shirts, shorts and trainers, their faces eager with anticipation.

"How long is it to the snowline?" they asked.

Caroline sheltered with Brian beneath towering rocks to eat her lunch.

She emerged beneath the rain, and gazed upon the rolling slopes of moor on either side. White clumps of groundsel dotted the landscape. It all looked so fresh in the sunlight.

The forest at last! But this felt the longest part of the descent. Caroline moved, a slow automaton, and Brian had to frog-march her down.

"Did you enjoy that?" he asked.

They were sitting on a bench overlooking the Naro Moru river in the grounds of the lodge. Brian nursed a large glass of beer; Caroline was enjoying her first taste of shandy. The others had left for Nairobi.

"Of course I did! Do you need to ask?"

"Would you do it again?"

"With you? Yes!"

"I love you."

CHAPTER 10

Nakuru

They settled into a routine. Brian travelled the hundred miles from Nairobi to see Caroline every weekend, and the enormity of the decision before her became apparent. They talked about the future in a general way, skirting round the subject of her University career. She told him that she meant to become a Catholic.

"I met my Uncle Ed's girl friend the other day," Brian told her while they were parked under the spreading pepper tree outside her house, after an evening at the cinema. "He's my father's elder brother, and lives in Mombasa. They came up because his horse was running last weekend. Did I tell you that Teresa trains for him?"

"I didn't even know you had an uncle in Mombasa."

"Well – Meg is awfully nice. She and Uncle Ed are very much in love but she won't marry him because she's a Catholic and he is a divorcee. Although he was the innocent party, she considers him still married. She doesn't seem to think that it is just as bad to be his mistress. It is in cases like these that I get upset about Catholicism."

"But if Uncle Ed's girl friend were a real Christian she wouldn't be his mistress," said Caroline. "I don't think you should judge the religion by the people who outwardly belong to it."

She hesitated, wondering how he was going to take what she was about to say, and then decided to say it anyway.

"I don't mean this personally, but anyone who goes against the Church like that really has no right to say that she belongs." She put her hand on Brian's arm. "Very strong words. I hope you won't take umbrage?"

Brian covered her hand with his and gave her a smile.

"Religion is not just one religion," he said. "It is a number, interpreted differently by different people like Christians, Muslims, and Buddhists. But most of them have a God, and a Christ of sorts."

Caroline didn't know anything about Muslims and Buddhists, so she kept quiet.

"I don't think I've expressed myself very well," he continued, stretching his arm round the back of her seat. "I'm very conscious of the fact that we talk about religion, and I like it. But we sometimes get out of our depth, don't we?"

Caroline laughed. "Shall we talk about politics, then?"

"That's even worse!"

"Okay." She looked at her watch. "It's getting late anyway, I'd better go in."

She raised her face for a protracted goodnight kiss.

Caroline knew that Brian's politics were similar to those of his father, though he was not as extreme as Dudley Myers. She felt differently; she couldn't help seeing the African point of view. Perhaps it was because she had not, like Brian, been born in the country.

"When I was in London," Brian told her, "I saw an old film called 'Come Back Africa' about the life of a poor black in South Africa. I felt like getting up and walking out because of how they represented the European as hard-hearted and bigoted. But if you disregard the exaggerations, you get an idea of the lot of the African who has had civilization thrust upon him, and you realise that what is happening now was inevitable from the first time the white man set foot in Africa."

"You also realise, I hope, that the white man is not the only one who counts," Caroline said, shifting her position to face him more fully. They were side by side on the sofa in his parents' house. Guy and Angela were in the packing shed preparing strawberries for export with the *bibis* who sorted the fruit and packed it into punnets ready to catch the early morning flight to Europe. Caroline and Brian would take turns with them to supervise the women.

"I think that Verwoerd's ideas of the superiority and importance of the white man in his role as 'the leader and the creator' are totally wrong. We're all humans and although we may differ in many areas, I refuse to believe that the white man is any more special than the black. Verwoerd isn't realistic. He is talking about something which, if he only looked around him, he would realise just isn't true."

Brian glanced sideways at her. "Of course not, but you can't deny that the Africans are still some way behind the whites in their development."

"What development, Brian? What makes you think we're any more developed than they are? By which standards are you measuring?"

Brian raised his voice a pitch. "You can't say that they are advanced enough to govern themselves in our present international environment. They just don't know enough, they need more experience, more education."

"You're just as bad as Verwoerd!"

Caroline flopped back into her seat and let out a huff of frustration. She felt so helpless, arguing against him. He seemed to know much more than she did. Why couldn't the Africans govern themselves however they wished? How could the whites dare to say they knew better? She'd heard the farmers talking about Jomo Kenyatta's recent release, and how he had asked them to stay on in Kenya, declaring the need to forgive and forget and build a prosperous nation together. She found it astonishing, and humbling that he should show such a Christ-like capacity for forgiveness. The whites could certainly learn a thing or two from the Africans.

But she didn't want to upset Brian further. Thank goodness she'd never told him about Teresa and Charles. He wouldn't understand.

Brian tried to put his arm round her shoulder, but she didn't feel like responding.

"Let's talk about world politics, then. I've devised a plan for future world peace. Would you like to hear it?"

"Hang on," said Brian, getting up to open another bottle of beer. He brought her a soda and settled back beside her on the sofa.

He stretched his arm along the back of the sofa and took a lock of her hair, twisting it round his finger.

"I'm ready for the fray, now," he teased. "Tell me your great idea."

"The answer to the whole problem, of course," she said, "is for UNO to dissolve itself and let someone impartial, who is above the petty politics of any particular country, take over and act as an all-powerful judge in world affairs."

"And who might that be?"

"I don't know... He must have power, and the complete confidence of the heads of the various governments. In that way, the world could in fact be one government headed by one man – but of course, he would have advisors. If everything were brought openly to this court, there'd be a far better chance of world peace and co-ordination between the different races and nationalities.

"There's my nice castle in the air," she grinned. "How to achieve this, I haven't worked out. The person had better start quickly gaining the confidence of the Khrushchevs, Kennedys, de Gaulles, Mboyas, and Mbutus of this world. Of course, he must be impervious to the intoxication of power, and have the respect of mankind."

Caroline paused.

"The only person I can think of who fills the bill is Christ.

What a conclusion! But I suppose it's the natural one, as when he comes again he will bring an endless period of peace. That is what we want, isn't it? It seems as if every problem has its solution in Christ. Though I must confess, he didn't come to my mind when I was thinking up my dream-person."

Brian laughed. "Your solution for the world is quite impossible – but a good try. Don't you know that there is in fact a World Court at Le Hague?"

"Oh, is there? You see how ignorant I am!"

"But it's not very effective." Brian tapped his cigarette into the ashtray at his side. "I wondered when you'd think of Christ… but perhaps you're putting religion on a pedestal, which may not have any connection with us as we are. Maybe I'm wrong. I think we can try and lead good lives; some, like me, fail but when everything is subject to strict rules then I'm not sure that we're fulfilling our purpose."

"I know my solution for the world is impossible," said Caroline. "But it's fun to ramble on. Religion is a personal thing, but no one can live up to his ideals if he strives entirely alone. I think of the Church as a kind of society that you join with others to help achieve your aims. That's why I believe that people should belong to one, whatever it is. It's up to the individual to find the right one.

"I'm sure, whatever you say, that religion should play a large part in life, and if everyone were Christian, the world wouldn't be in such a mess. But we're imperfect beings, and it is up to each one of us to do what we can in accordance with our beliefs."

She stopped.

"Have you finished?"

"I suppose so – for now!"

"Well." Brian looked at his watch. "It's time we went to do our stint at the packing shed."

As the time for Caroline's departure drew nearer, she noticed that Brian was drinking more often. She didn't object when he headed for the bar with his mates after rugby matches, for she'd made friends with the other wives and girlfriends. But she noticed when he slurred his words, and came to recognise the signs of too much alcohol whenever a particular sheepish look crept over his face.

One evening she joined him at the bar and drank more than her usual glass of wine. She felt extraordinarily relaxed, and couldn't think straight. Silly jokes made her laugh so much she couldn't stop. It was embarrassing, although nobody else seemed to notice. She hated the feeling of not being in control of herself.

Brian's team were due to play at the coast one weekend, but Caroline did not go with him. She had no desire to sit at the bar with the rugby crowd, and perhaps it was time they gave each other a break. The past few months had been wonderful, but she needed space to think. In a way, she felt too happy; she didn't deserve to be so happy. She was lucky having Brian to love and be loved by, but how could it last?

"I feel that my life so far has been too smooth," she said. "I should be doing something I don't like."

She stopped, wondering how to say what was on her mind, and afraid that he might not understand. But it was too important not to say. She waited until he had pulled up under the pepper tree and turned off the ignition. They had come from a Sunday at the races, and Brian would be driving back to Nairobi that night.

"I will say it: sometimes I feel that I should give up seeing you, because I'm not meant to enjoy such wonderful happiness. It's not good for my character."

She thought she was explaining how much she loved him, but Brian was silent.

"Wouldn't the world be a wonderful place if everybody lived for the enjoyment of each other?" she went on. "But even then, by bringing happiness to others, we are also making ourselves happy, and this is another example of selfishness!"

Brian turned on her.

"No, I don't understand your attitude," he said. "Why should you feel that you should be doing something you don't enjoy, and how on earth do you know that your character suffers because you do what you like? It most certainly is not a form of selfishness to give happiness to others. You seem to think that to be happy is a sin. It is not a sin at all. The only sin is in doing something which is not right but which makes you happy. If it is any consolation to you I wouldn't have thought that your life so far had been easy. You've lost both your parents, although you've been lucky in having a stepfather who, in my opinion, is one of the world's best. Why should a man have to suffer? I don't understand you. Why are you not meant to be happy?"

Caroline was shocked into silence. She had hurt Brian, the person she loved best in the whole world. She did not know what to say.

It was late, and he had to get back to Nairobi. Boney would have left the front door unbolted for her. She clicked the car door open.

"I'm sorry I've hurt you."

But Brian leaned over to draw her back in.

"I am not hurt about this. I am just bloody annoyed. You cannot combine fatalism with religion. Make up your mind which it is going to be. I know that sometimes I am a fatalist but I don't think that I try and precipitate it."

Brian glared at her. Caroline took out a handkerchief; she had been feeling a cold coming on all afternoon. Then he smiled.

"However, my darling, I do appreciate your telling me, and I do love you all the more for it, because it must have taken a lot of guts."

He pulled her to him.

"I've a good mind to spank you! Turn over."

119

Caroline found herself lying face down in his lap, while he gently padded her bottom with his bare hands. She pulled herself away, mortified by the indignity, even though she knew he was half in jest.

"How dare you!"

She flung herself out of the car, slammed the door, and ran into the house.

CHAPTER 11

Charles pushed aside his typewriter and stretched his back, folding his arms behind his head, and looked up from a paper-strewn desk. It was good to be home again, but what a contrast it was.

The traffic on the street below his first floor offices was snarled again, and a cacophony of honking drifted through the window. A wild clangour overrode the noise, and he went to the windows to watch a fire engine trying to leave its station opposite. People crowded along the pavement, gawking.

A barefoot youth, his clothes in tatters, jumped into the road. With exaggerated gestures, he blocked the path of a car moving slowly up the left hand lane. He forced it to the centre of the road. The opposite lane was at a standstill. The youth, frizzed hair standing out from his head, approached another vehicle, waving it to the centre. Others followed the cue, leaving a narrow passage by the pavement. The crowd overflowed round the traffic from the opposite side. Then the youth strutted and gesticulated at the marooned fire engine, which had quietened in defeat.

The red monster stirred, and edged out to creep up the wrong side of the road. It bumped across the centre dustbowl of an enormous roundabout below the newspaper offices, and re-started its siren, which faded up the hill beyond.

Charles clicked his fingers at a reporter, gesturing him to follow the fire engine.

"And see if you can find that youth who directed the traffic, we might have a use for him."

He turned his attention to his editor, who placed a hand on his shoulder.

"It's good to see you have a sharp mind for the job, Charles. But have you visited your father since coming back from London?"

Charles shook his head.

"A man must confer with his family before starting a new career. I feel guilty for demanding your services as soon as you arrived. Take some days off at the end of the week. Give my greetings to your father, and see if you can come back with a story for me."

First, he had to think about getting there. His VW Beetle saloon was fine in the city, but would it make the journey upcountry? His cousin James had sold it to him. Charles negotiated his way down Grogan Road through the chaos of pedestrians, cyclists, crabwise lorries and battered cars.

He turned into a *jua kali* yard, littered with vehicles in various stages of disrepair. A quagmire of puddles filled the barren patch of ground.

Charles stepped gingerly between the stagnant pools of the 'open air showroom', which he planned to feature in a future edition of the newspaper. He guessed that the secret of James's success was insistence on cash for every transaction.

He paused beside a pair of bare soles protruding from beneath the chassis of a station wagon, and addressed his cousin, keeping his distance until James had discarded his overall. Underneath, he wore a checked shirt and a faded pair of trousers, torn off below the knees.

Charles pondered on why Africans had adopted the white man's trousers, but not his habit of wearing shorts unless forced into them, like policemen. There could be several reasons. There were so many stories to be told. One day he would publish his own magazine, and not have to write in the style and content dictated by an editor.

"What's the news of many days?"

"Not bad news. Are you well?"

"Yes. I am well."

"And everyone else?"

"All well. What of work?"

"Well. It goes on."

They ordered mugs of tea at a nearby canteen. Charles accepted the mixture of milk boiled up with tea leaves in water, scooped from a wide brimmed *sufuria* bubbling over a coal brazier. He told James of his proposed visit, and his doubts about the car. James wanted to sell him one more suited to rough roads, but Charles refused to trade in his Beetle.

"It's only for one *safari*, James. Can't you have a look at it, and fix what needs to be done? I know there's a hole in the exhaust."

James waved towards the half-dozen cars awaiting his attention and shrugged his shoulders.

"I have too much to do already," he said.

"I'll make it worth your while." Charles knew the paper would give him a generous allowance for the journey. "And one day perhaps I'll find you a better location for your garage."

The mechanic finally agreed to have his car ready for the weekend.

"You're lucky it's a VW and there's no problem with spares," James said.

Charles escaped the Friday evening rush hour by leaving work early. He followed the cracked tarmac through the Kikuyu Reserve towards the Rift Valley escarpment, and could not help feeling uneasy as he drove past the densely cultivated smallholdings, marked out with sticks, bamboo poles or cactus hedges. Everyone was preoccupied with politics, but you never knew with the Kikuyu. There was always the risk of falling victim to thugs.

He left the reserve and descended the hairpin bends to the

valley floor. There was no room for two vehicles on the narrow strip of tarmac. Charles had to move his left wheels off the road whenever he met a car from the opposite direction. The lip was jagged, and sometimes six inches high, causing the Beetle to jolt alarmingly. A fast-moving sedan hogged the road, bearing down on him. He veered off the tarmac and wobbled along the corrugations before finding a place to bounce back up again.

On his left, the escarpment fell steeply into a wooded drop, a graveyard for many vehicles. Flimsy barriers gave protection for only the most dangerous of the hairpin bends. On his right, above the perpendicular bank were dense slopes of forest, and he swung the wheel to avoid fallen rocks.

He passed the chapel at the foot of the escarpment, which had been built by Italian prisoners during the Second World War. As he swung through the tight left hand bend, he remembered *Mzee* Ondiek taking him there as a boy, to give thanks for a safe journey down the escarpment. He'd noticed the cracks in the paint of the Mary and Joseph statues, and thought how old they must be. It was the first time he had seen a stained glass window.

The road widened, cutting a newly graded swathe through the grasslands on the valley floor. Dust swallowed him at frequent intervals as cars whizzed by. When he topped the rise to Mt. Longonot, a blissful section of tarred road took him down to the sleepy township of Naivasha.

He was not even half way there.

After buying a freshly baked roll at the inn, and relieved that he didn't have to make this journey regularly, Charles tackled the final leg in the dark. Approaching lorries never dipped their lights, and cars crowded him from behind.

His plucky Beetle groaned up the opposite wall of the Rift Valley and he turned off the highway down winding tree-lined tracks through fields of maize towards his family home. The sump scraped over the raised grass centre and then the car

124

grounded. Its wheels spun uselessly over the sunken tracks. He got out. Soft rain was falling. But before he could kneel to see the extent of the damage, shadowy figures came out of the darkness.

There were muttered greetings and, after a quick study of the situation, four strangers lifted the VW bodily sideways.

"Keep your right wheels on the middle grass, and don't fall into the ruts again!" they advised him.

Several times he slipped and skidded back into the deep tracks, and by the time he reached home, the exhaust had broken off.

Mzee Ondiek greeted him. White fluffs of hair protruded from his scalp. His face had an unhealthy greyish tinge, and his body was more stooped than Charles remembered. They squatted on rough-hewn stones outside the hut for a smoke, and Charles was filled with a timeless sense of peace.

This was what mattered, one's family and home, the earth, the country. His father could only vaguely have registered the 'wind of change' in Kenya, with no idea which way it was blowing. The old man expected him to explain unfolding events. Where should he start?

"The UK papers said nothing about Kenya while I was at Oxford," Charles began. "Africa hardly exists for them. Those I spoke to didn't know whether they wanted Kenyatta to be released or not. Perhaps the UK was trying to ignore us in the hope that the problems will go away. But their government will guarantee the whites something for their farms, and maybe we will have our land back."

"But if all the *wazungu* leave, where will our people get jobs?"

"I agree they mustn't all go. It's complicated, but there are some who should leave."

'Like Bwana Myers?'

Charles nodded. "There's no place here for people like him."

Mzee choked on his cigarette, coughing up the phlegm.

"That cough is bad."

"When you left, I had to fight the *thahu*. The charms Simaloi gave me worked, but the curse left me weak. Sometimes there is a fierce fire in my chest, but I've got used to it now."

"Mwangi's curse?"

The old man nodded. "I haven't seen him, but when the fire comes, I know he isn't far away."

Charles stirred uncomfortably.

Now that Jomo Kenyatta had been released from detention, and the Emergency lifted, Mwangi was a free man. Charles wondered where he was.

***

Nakuru

Caroline was in despair. Had she spoiled everything?

Perhaps it would be for the best; otherwise, could she ever have the courage to make the break when she went to Oxford?

She thought about marriage, although they had never discussed it. She didn't feel ready for it. There must have been a purpose behind their falling in love, and she hoped with all her heart that they would eventually spend their lives together. But there was her career to think of.

A letter waited for her on Wednesday morning. Unfamiliar writing was scrawled over the envelope. She turned it over to see Brian's name on the back. Had he written to break everything off? The boss summoned her for dictation, and she put the letter in her handbag.

It was a particularly busy day at the office, and Caroline worked through the lunch hour. She was afraid to read the letter in public, and when she left in the afternoon, it lay unopened in her bag. Instead of joining Boney by the fire after supper, she excused herself.

There were two sheets of flimsy blue paper in the envelope, and she turned to the second one. He still loved her!

She treasured the thought, before reading from the beginning.

My Darling Caroline,

I am sorry I got angry with you. I'm afraid I was a bit harsh. I cannot stop loving you but I do think that you make problems for yourself, and darling it doesn't make it easier for me. If you have good fortune, accept it with grace.

I hope your cold is better and do look after yourself. Don't you dare even try and break with me. I love you too much. Brian.

She thanked God for the reprieve, and wrote back, finding it easier to compose her thoughts on paper without the distraction of his presence.

I admit I've been wondering if God wants us to break off. I am afraid that I've hurt you. You see now what kind of a girl I am; as well as try and inflict sorrow on myself, I do it to you.

She received his reply by return.

If that is the way you feel, then I will make the break, because I would hate to think you were not doing so because of lack of courage. Why should it be God's will that you break with me? If it is going to be a matter of principle with you that it is I or God, then I give in. Why you cannot combine both, I don't know.

She didn't know what to say when he arrived to pick her up the following weekend. They drove to the rugby club, and Caroline chattered inconsequentially in the car. Brian played in the curtain raiser, and she joined their celebrations at the bar after his team won. A sheepish look crept over Brian's face, and she pulled at his sleeve. His driving never seemed to be affected by the amount he drank, but there must be a limit somewhere, she felt.

"I've agreed to play up in Kitale next weekend," he told her.

He didn't ask her to go with him.

On the way back the sun filled the sky with a lustrous pink glow.

"Isn't it beautiful!"

He put his hand over hers, laughing. "You're always looking at the sky, aren't you, my dear!"

She hesitated. At least he wasn't cross with her.

"I got your letter."

"Oh."

He parked under the pepper tree, turned off the ignition, and faced her; she could not see his expression in the faint moonlight. He slid his arm along the back of her seat.

"Well?"

"I'm sorry if I hurt you," her voice came out in an unfinished squeak.

Brian looked straight ahead.

"It's not only between me and God, is it," he said. "There's also Oxford, and your career."

She was grateful that he'd said it for her. But it didn't make it any easier. She had got into Oxford, didn't he realise what an honour that was? How could she not go?

"I love you, Caroline. You know that?"

She nodded. "And I love you too – so much!"

He took her hands in his.

"Would you marry me?"

"Yes."

She said it immediately. This was what she wanted – what she'd been waiting for, and when he kissed her, gently and lovingly, she snuggled into him, smelling the familiar whiff of tobacco, safe in his arms. What a wonderful man; with him, she could be herself entirely, and fear nothing. Then she stiffened.

"But?"

"Yes, but," she admitted. "Would you mind if it wasn't yet?"

Brian took a deep breath. "I knew that was coming," he said. "It's all right, I can wait – I think."

Caroline paused as another thought crossed her mind; she wondered if this was the right time, but when would it ever be the right time?

"Even if I became a Catholic?"

"Yes, darling, even that; I know if you become a Catholic it'll be because you really think it is *the* religion. You know I don't like it but I love you, and would still marry you."

"Would you mind if I prayed for you?"

"I wouldn't object at all if you said prayers for me. You are the only one who is entitled to, and I know it would be genuine. You are quite incapable of being anything but genuine, my darling."

But he was pensive, and Caroline knew that he wanted to say something else.

"What is it?" she asked.

"The next three years will be hard, and we'll both change," he said. "We must do – but one thing never changes, and that is a person's basic qualities and faults. That's why I feel someday we'll have a full and happy life together; because we have a common upbringing and share so many interests."

Caroline agreed.

"But I want to say one thing," he continued.

She waited.

"We mustn't promise each other anything."

"But I've just said…"

"I know, my dear, but it won't be fair on either of us to make a long-term promise. You're going away to another country. You must feel completely free."

What trust! What a wonderful person he was. Caroline knew she would love him forever, and there was no need for promises.

Boney telephoned her at work ten days later.

"Angela Clayton has just rung," he said. "Brian has had a car accident."

Caroline's heart stood still.

"He's all right, but a bit shaken. The child in the other car is in hospital."

"What happened?"

"We're not sure. It was on his way back from a rugby match in Kitale last night. He sends you his love."

"It was on Sunday evening, after we'd had a few beers," Brian told her over the telephone. "I was giving two players a lift home. A car passed in the opposite direction. Another came immediately behind him but I didn't see it because of the fog and the dust until it was a few feet from us. I had no chance to do anything. It looked to me as if he was trying to overtake the first car but the police say that I will have a job to prove it."

"I'm so glad you weren't hurt."

"Fortunately not, apart from minor cuts and bruises. But one of the kids in the other car had cuts on his face which didn't look too good. The police said if the crash had happened three inches further to the middle of the road we would probably all have been killed."

"You must have been going quite fast?" The words came out before Caroline could stop herself. They sounded accusatory. But he appeared not to notice.

"Probably. Unfortunately my car is a write-off, so I don't know what I am going to do. I won't be coming upcountry until the insurance is sorted, I'm afraid."

"I've written you a letter, I posted it last night."

"You got mine?"

"Yes. I was so pleased to get it. Oh, Brian. I love you so much! Please be more careful in future?"

Caroline wrote every week, her letters sometimes crossing Brian's. Once the insurance money came through, he bought a new car, and when he came upcountry again, she noticed that he had changed.

He was moody and short-tempered, and the carefree happiness had gone from their lives.

Caroline's day of departure drew nearer. Their Sunday night leave-takings under the pepper tree became more protracted, and they could barely contain their passion before she forced herself to open the car door, and creep back into the house.

Something was burning inside Brian.

"I don't know how I'm going to manage without you. I just can't bear the thought of you going," he said one evening.

Caroline had been putting off even thinking about it. The college had recommended some books for her to read before going up, but she could not summon any enthusiasm.

"When I get there, I think I'll try and change to a more recent subject than British history at the time of the venerable Bede..."

"Not *if* you go there?" Brian emphasised the second word, which forced Caroline to react.

"I didn't say *if*!"

"Caroline, I can't stop thinking about you and me. Things have changed. Perhaps it's the accident, I don't know. But life is so short – I don't think I can take it. You're bound to meet someone else, lots of people..." Brian faced her. "If you go to Oxford, we must break everything off. Completely. It's the only way..."

This was unexpected. She couldn't answer him.

He took her hand, and raised it to his cheek.

"Or else...marry me now."

She still couldn't speak. Then a strange relief filled her being. But she would need time to think it over. Brian would understand.

She loved him. She could have lost him. If she loved Brian, why was she even contemplating going to Oxford? What did she want from Oxford anyway? Did she really want a career now? She couldn't pursue a career and still have Brian. That was not possible any more.

CHAPTER 12

"There's a white settlers' wedding up-country next Saturday. With your Oxford background, you'll blend in better than these ruffians here."

Charles raised his eyebrows. He'd returned from a political meeting at the coast, and had a report to prepare. There was so much going on, now that Kenya approached internal self-government, who would be interested in a white man's wedding at this time in history?

"Who is it?"

"The son of Guy Clayton. You must know the farmer, he wants to call in a favour. But I also need you to look out for a man called Dudley Myers. His daughter, the racehorse trainer, will be bridesmaid. This Myers man is a big pain for us. He is a loudmouth, and hates the Africans. He's written several unprintable letters. See what you can get about him."

Charles gave his editor a knowing look, but his mind was racing. He would see Teresa again, but did he want to? What would happen when she saw him? She had never replied to his last letter from Oxford.

Would she even recognise him? He knew that, to many whites, one African was indistinguishable from another. He had started a paunch, the mark of prosperity, and he patted it proudly. Five years had passed since he'd seen her.

"You can take a long weekend."

Charles thought about home. It had been a good year for rains, and the maize harvest would be in. Drinks would be flowing freely in the beer halls, and he'd be able to pick up material for a few stories. Independence was in the air, and the whole country poised with expectancy that Jomo Kenyatta would be Kenya's first President.

He stopped at a roadside hotel to change into formal clothes, and arrived at the wedding reception in the garden of Guy Clayton's farmhouse in time to join the end of a line of guests.

What was he doing here? As the reporter, he didn't have to greet the bride and groom, but he stayed in line. A group of farmers huddled nearby, glanced in his direction. Apart from the waiters, he was the only black man. Teresa faced him, a frangipani flower over one ear. He caught a glimmer of astonishment in her dancing brown eyes, and then he was greeting her, offering his hand, drinking in her beauty. She pressed his palm, but looked nervously over her shoulder at the farmers. Her father watched them.

"Where the hell did he come from?"

The remark, though muttered into the man's beard, reached Charles and stabbed at his heart. He moved on to greet the bride.

"Charles! How wonderful that you've come to report on our wedding. Have you seen Teresa? But of course you have! Isn't she lovely?"

With Caroline, he turned to watch Teresa as she talked to the vicar, her noble profile olive against the afternoon sky. She wore a lemon yellow gown, falling in silky folds round her limbs, which Charles glimpsed in soft outline as she moved. She didn't look like either of her parents, nor, he knew, did she have their temperament. Remembering his mission, he forced his eyes away from her.

"Not as lovely as you, Caroline," he said gallantly.

Her blue eyes sparkled; her auburn hair was a mass of curls under a fluffy veil. A few freckles on her nose had defied the make-up artist. She wore a traditional white wedding dress, spread out stiffly round her slim figure. Placing a hand on her new husband's arm, she introduced them and Brian shook his hand warmly. The man was scarcely taller than Caroline, his hair had already receded from the temples, and his coat tails failed to disguise a stocky figure. Charles marvelled that she should have given up Oxford for this man, but they obviously adored each other. He positioned the bridal party against a backdrop of trees for their formal photographs, making a beautiful picture. His palm still tingled from that warm handshake. Perhaps Brian was one of those rare *wazungu* with a genuine feel for the African as a fellow human being, in which case Caroline was a lucky lady, and she deserved him, for she, too, empathised with Africa.

Charles withdrew into the background to observe the guests. A waiter in full-length white *kanzu* with a red cummerbund and fez blocked his line of vision. He was bending over a group of ladies seated under a garden umbrella, offering them a salver of toasties. Charles moved his camera to capture the scene.

The waiter glanced up, and Charles interrupted a look of pure malevolence as the man limped away with an empty tray. There was a familiarity about that face…

He remembered his brief to find out what Dudley Myers might be planning. The farmer stood with a group on the fringe of the lawn, beer bottle in hand; a giant of a man, his wild black hair framing a pock-marked face, eyebrows meeting fiercely over the bridge of his nose. He was the only one wearing shorts, and although the Emergency had ended, he had a revolver strapped in full view round his waist.

Charles drifted over to stand against the hedge behind the men, and raised his camera to take shots of the guests against the backdrop of Lake Nakuru, which shimmered in the distance. He knelt in the shade of a bougainvillea to change films. He could hear what the men were saying, and as the afternoon wore on and the empty bottles accumulated, the voices became louder. They had no regard for who might be listening, least of all an insignificant black photographer, and Charles knew how to make himself dissolve into the background.

"No, Myers, you can't just send everybody away, there'd be hell to pay."

Guy Clayton stood with his back to the hedge. He had lost weight since Charles had last seen him.

"Don't I know it," replied Myers. "Perhaps we should massacre the bastards…"

An uneasy silence followed, and someone coughed.

"And then what would you do for labour?"

Myers waved his bottle in Clayton's direction. "It's not only the thefts," he said. "Prices are falling and costs rising, you know that. Machinery keeps on breaking down, and you can't get anything fixed. I don't even enjoy going to the races any more. Everyone is leaving, and some of the fields are down to only two or three horses. It's just ridiculous!"

As the whingeing continued, a couple of farmers turned away from the group, but others joined in. Charles remained in the background. He heard Myers boasting about leading Kenya Regiment patrols in the Aberdare forest. Some of the wazungu were as bad as the Mau Mau they were hunting. He had heard horrific stories about both sides, and he despised Myers for leaving his women alone on the farm.

Myers ran his fingers through his hair. "You can't win in this goddam country. There's no future, and the situation is getting me down. Sorry, Guy, I understand your point, but I'm afraid I can't take it. I hope the happy couple are going to leave. I'd have thought a boy with Brian's intelligence would go a long way in the UK."

"They've decided to stay on," replied Clayton. "Brian missed Kenya. He turned down an offer from a law firm in London, and after all, Jomo Kenyatta has asked us not to go. You must give it to the young, they've got guts."

"Or else they don't understand what's happening," scoffed Myers.

"Do any of us really understand? It's so hard to tell the future."

"If there is any future…"

"I suppose it depends on one's attitude."

Myers glanced at Clayton testily. "All right, all right! My wife is always on at me too, about the way I treat my labour. But I could never kow-tow to them like Boney."

Clayton downed his drink and turned away to mingle with the guests.

"Why don't you say something at the Settlers' Meeting next week, Dudley," he called over his shoulder. "But don't raise your hopes. Most of us want to stay. Those who don't are on their way out anyway, meaning no offence, of course."

Dudley smiled wryly. "There's probably something in what you say, Guy. Don't think we haven't considered leaving before now, it could be the answer."

Charles felt he had enough material to satisfy his editor. Would Teresa leave the country with her parents? Charles caught sight of her on the other side of the garden and moved in that direction, taking a piece of wedding cake from a waiter on his way. The man held Charles's eye in a brief moment of hostility before disappearing in the direction of the kitchen.

Then Charles knew – it was Mwangi, the man who had cursed his father.

Caroline and Brian went inside to change, and he moved to the veranda steps to take position for a photograph of the happy couple as they left for their honeymoon.

The bride emerged, gaily clad in a floral cotton dress, and tossed her bouquet into the crowd. And there was Teresa, arms lifted, laughing as she caught the flowers. She was beautiful. Charles met her eyes over the heads of the guests. Everybody followed the bride and groom to the field where their get-away car had been prepared, and Teresa and Charles found each other among the remnants of paper napkins and champagne corks littering the lawn.

Raucous laughter drifted from the field, and he heard the loud bang of a firecracker. Finally, a clattering of empty cans faded down the driveway. The guests began to dribble back, and Teresa turned away from him, pretending to tidy up the tables. He watched her scrape half-eaten pieces of wedding-cake and abandoned wedges of marzipan from the china plates. But there were waiters to do that. He grasped her wrist, forcing her to face him.

"I must see you again," he said.

"How?" Her eyes darted towards the returning guests.

"I'll try and arrange to cover the racing news for the paper. Then we can meet up. Please, Teresa?"

She hesitated. A waiter came towards them and started to clear away the debris. Teresa moved out of his way, and then Charles recoiled as the man spoke to him in Swahili.

"What are you doing with that stupid white girl? If I tell your boss, you will lose your job!"

Charles raised his arm, but Teresa came between them.

"Are you out of your mind?" she hissed.

He stepped back, but Mwangi hadn't finished.

"I know who you are, Charles Omari Ondiek, the man who took my job when your father wounded me. His days are numbered, and when he dies, the *thahu* will go to that bitch who should have died years ago, and become part of the Mau Mau oath to kill her father."

Mwangi insolently jutted his chin towards Teresa, and then he picked up a tray and turned towards the house.

"Watch out, for the curse will end up with you!"

Teresa's eyes widened. "What was he talking about?"

"Nothing."

"It's not nothing; I know enough Swahili to understand something about a curse and a Mau Mau oath! What's happening, Charles? Mwangi was released from detention a

138

while ago. I refused to let him back to work for us, but Boney took him on, and lent him to us to help with the wedding. I've never liked him."

"We can't talk about it here," Charles replied nervously.

"Well, I want to know!"

Charles saw his opportunity.

"I'll meet you after the races next Sunday, and we can go somewhere for a quiet drink."

The editor accepted the wedding story, and Charles told him that Dudley Myers was thinking of leaving the country.

"I know people who'll be glad to hear that news. The man has been a problem for many. Can you keep in touch, and tell me when his departure is planned?"

Charles could hardly believe his luck.

"If I attend the Nairobi races, I'll be able to keep up to date," he said. "The daughter is a trainer, as you know."

"That's a good idea. You can take over the reporting of the races. I have better things in mind for you, but this must take priority until the man leaves."

Charles waited for Teresa outside the trainers' enclosure. She wore a smart navy checked outfit, and a hat designed to ward off the sun with an attractive ridged effect inside the brim. He admired her openly as she approached.

"I've been told to report regularly on the races," he said. "So we can be quite legitimate. Hard luck in the last race – I thought you were going to win it."

"So did I. The owner was disappointed; the jockey seemed to stop riding him in the last few strides. Sometimes you wonder about these jockeys, but I wasn't allowed to put up Kiprotich."

"Oh?"

"Some owners still think only white jockeys can win races."

He led her to an empty chair in the members' area under the

grandstand, and bought her a glass of wine. People were packing up, but a few die-hards were propped against the bar at the other end.

"I can't stay for long; I have to see the horses safely into the lorry."

"You're not driving them back, are you?"

"Not this time. I'm staying at Muthaiga Club for the night. I still want you to tell me about what Mwangi said."

"Shall we go to the Corner Bar for a curry? I'll book a table, and you can come when you're ready."

The Corner Bar was the only decent curry house in the city where people of all races could feel comfortable.

"That's a good idea. I'll see you there," Teresa finished her drink. "I'll be about an hour behind you."

There were several tables available, and Charles chose a secluded corner. This was one of his favourite haunts, although he had not come here with a white girl before. They were shown to a table secluded behind a trellis by an expressionless waiter.

"Have you been on a date with a black man before?" asked Charles.

He saw her surprise. She glanced round. A white couple were at a table on the far side of the room, and an African in suit and tie was at the bar, a glass of beer beside him. "No I haven't. There's nobody I know here, not that it matters."

"Don't worry. It's a good place for us to be."

"I know. The jockeys talk about it, I've been here before, and the curries are excellent."

Relieved that she felt comfortable, he watched as she gracefully took a folded napkin onto her lap, then raised her head to meet his eyes. What an extraordinary women – a girl with her white settler background dining with him, quite naturally, in public. In Oxford, this would not be remarkable, but Kenya was not even independent. The tables filled. Some contained people of all three races, but most were not mixed.

140

Teresa looked smart, and composed. Charles noticed the other diners glance at them, and felt a flutter of pride.

She ordered a mild chicken masala, and he ate a hot Madras curry, allowing the red peppers to scorch his mouth. He dipped into the *raita* yoghurt mixture to cool it, before taking more mouthfuls of the spicy dish.

"Now, what's all this about Mwangi and a curse?" Teresa asked, as she tore at her *nan* bread, using it to scoop up the sauce. "And why does he hate us so much?"

"Do you mind if I ask you a question first?" said Charles. "When you were still at school, did you have any adventures?"

"What do you mean?"

Charles searched her face, seeing nothing but bewilderment. He reached forward, and placed his hand over hers, fondling the back of it with his fingers. He watched her expression altering as she tried to remember.

"Caroline and I used to break out of school," she said slowly, and he nodded in encouragement. "We went on long walks to the racecourse a couple of miles away in the middle of the night. We did it six or seven times I think, over a couple of terms, and then stopped when I had to do my exams. Nobody knew."

Charles leaned back in his chair. "Did anything happen?"

"Nobody found out. We were just kids. How did you know?"

"I'm asking you if anything happened on one of your walks."

Teresa was clearly confounded. He could see she had difficulty remembering.

"It was so long ago, and I haven't thought about it for years. What's all this about?"

"Trust me, Teresa. Just try and remember."

She took another mouthful of chicken. He watched her, and saw her face change. But then she put down her fork.

"My mind's a blank," she said. "Is it important? And what

has it got to do with Mwangi?"

Charles could have enlightened her, but he wanted to hear Teresa's version of the story. In a way, he was being a coward for putting off the evil moment, but he told himself it would be easier for them both if the news were broken in stages. He didn't want to frighten her, and he needed an excuse to see her again.

"Maybe you should ask Caroline if she remembers anything?"

They finished their meal, and stood outside in the car park. He drew her to him, and kissed her lightly.

"Shall we meet again next race day?" he asked.

"Yes. And I'll ask Caroline in the meantime."

The Indian owner greeted them like old friends. They took the same table and ordered the same dishes. The dim décor created an intimate environment, as the waiters padded barefoot between the tables.

Teresa wiped her mouth with the damask napkin.

"Caroline did remember something," she said. "On our last escapade we had a fright. A large animal or something suddenly crashed in the forest near us. We ran away as fast as we could, but that was all. I'd completely forgotten about it."

"That was Mwangi," said Charles.

"Mwangi?"

She sounded utterly bewildered.

"Were there guards at the school, Teresa?"

"Yes. We would hide behind the dining room curtains and time them on the beat."

"One of those guards was my father, *Mzee* Ondiek. He used to follow you."

"Did he? But we were never found out!"

"I know. He was trying to protect you from the Mau Mau, and he speared one in the forest."

"Mwangi?"

"Yes."

"While we were there, walking along the racecourse…"

Charles could see that she realised the danger they had been in.

"That's not the full story," added Charles. "My father pulled his spear from Mwangi's thigh, and hurried back to the school to be there when you returned."

"So?"

"Mwangi put a curse on my father. It's a very strong curse, and he hasn't been able to work since. Our tribal sorceress tried to counter it, but he is slowly dying. I've been to see him again since Caroline's wedding. He stays on his bed all the time."

"But that's just superstition…"

"I know you don't believe in curses, Teresa. You and I are Christians. But there is still the supernatural, and even though my family have been going to church for many years, there are things which cannot be explained."

"Mwangi said that your father's days were numbered."

"Yes."

"What else did he say? Something about me."

But Charles did not want to tell Teresa that Mwangi had been stalking her that night in the forest. He didn't know how much Teresa knew about Mau Mau oathing ceremonies. But she had to be warned.

"Your father is an unpopular man," he said. "Mwangi was trying to get at him through you."

Teresa shivered, and Charles could see the fear in her eyes.

"I'm glad I didn't let Daddy take him back onto the farm. But I have to warn Caroline – he mustn't stay with Boney a moment longer," she said.

"That would be wise. Mwangi said one other thing; he claims the curse will fall onto you when my father dies."

"Nonsense. I don't believe in such things. We'll get rid of the man, and that'll be the end of it."

Teresa took up her fork, and finished her meal. But their conversation had destroyed the pleasure of the evening.

"Shall we meet again next time?" Charles asked as they said goodbye.

"I don't see why not."

He resolved not to mention Mwangi again. Their dinner dates were becoming a pleasant habit.

CHAPTER 13

Caroline slowed the car and turned into the first bend of the escarpment. She stopped at the lookout to check on baby Paul. He was asleep. Allowing a chink of air through his window, she locked the car and walked along the wooden platform that jutted precariously over the Great Rift Valley. Souvenir vendors lined its sides, their cheerful chatter blending with the rumble of traffic behind her. She leaned on the barrier to savour the vastness of Africa. It was her habit to pause here on the way up country.

She glanced round. A man in a fez was sidling along the walkway towards her car, so she hurried back.

Jewel-like Lake Elmenteita appeared behind the shoulder of a cutting, a touch of pink showing round its edge. Then Lake Nakuru twinkled at her. The last time she came, the soda bed was a swirl of dust, but water filled it now, and a thick band of pink lined the shore. The flamingos were back. Menengai loomed behind the town, its sides rising into a dark crown of forest on the rim of the crater. A fire burned on the lower slopes, the smoke rising in white wafts over the town.

Her thoughts turned to Brian. We must go up there again, she said to herself. He'd gone to London on business. This was their first separation since the wedding, and she looked forward to having a weekend alone with Boney.

Caroline gave him a bear hug.

"It's so good to see you, Boney. I feel I haven't been here for years," she said, manoeuvring Paul's basket from the car.

145

"You haven't stayed since your wedding. I've been feeling quite neglected," said Boney, taking up a pile of terry nappies.

"I know. You make me feel guilty."

Caroline thought of Angela Clayton, who insisted on them staying in the guest wing she had fitted out for them. Angela was going to miss her only grandson when they left for South Africa.

"But the Claytons aren't going to be here much longer, are they?"

"No," admitted Boney. "The transfer of their farm to the land bank is almost complete, so they'll be off within six months, I reckon."

Caroline fed Paul and put him down for the night, and then joined Boney by the fire, sitting at his feet like old times. She felt his hand caress her hair.

"How are you, really?"

"It's different without you, Caroline, but we struggle along. My Headman is aging fast. His time in detention didn't help. I suppose I'll have to try and find a replacement."

"I hope you got rid of Mwangi?"

"I did, with some regret, as he is an excellent mechanic. Since he left, my tractors always seem to be breaking down. But he wasn't a pleasant character, I agree. I suspect he was one of the hard-core Mau Mau, the reason for his stay in prison until the end of the Emergency. Why did you insist I sack him?"

"He threatened Teresa – something to do with vengeance against Dudley, and I promised her I would talk to you. I told you that. Don't you remember?"

"I'm getting forgetful in my old age, my dear."

Boney picked up his pipe and stood to knock it against the mantelpiece. He looked frail, more like a grandfather than a father. He must be lonely here, thought Caroline.

The door to the lounge opened, and a pleasant-faced woman came in, bare foot, wearing a cotton frock with a blue jersey stretched across her ample bosom. Caroline had to look twice before she recognised the uniformed maid who had served them at table.

"Do you need anything else, Bwana?"

Boney patted his pocket. "Where did I put my tobacco?"

"It's in the bowl here, Bwana, where you always keep it."

Ethel went to the table beside the radio, and handed it to him with a smile.

"Thank you, my dear. That's all for tonight."

"*Kwaheri*, Bwana."

"Goodnight, Ethel."

The door closed quietly behind her.

"Ethel looks after me very well," said Boney. "You probably don't remember the Headman's daughter? I discovered her after your mother died. She wanted to go on a cookery course, and now my dinner parties are the talk of the district. She'll probably leave me one day, to work in a hotel."

Boney tamped the tobacco into his pipe, and felt in his pocket for a lighter.

"By the way, I've invited Guy and Angela round tomorrow night, with Sheila and Dudley Myers, and of course, Teresa. It'll give Ethel a chance to show off her prowess. Hope you don't mind?"

Caroline knew that Angela would want to see Paul.

"May we ask the Claytons round earlier, so they can be with Paul before he goes to sleep?" she asked. "Then I needn't visit them on Sunday."

"Of course."

"And would you mind if Teresa stayed the night? She can share my room. It's ages since we had a long chat."

"Good idea."

Caroline came from the bedroom after checking on Paul, and helped Boney hand out the liqueurs.

Dudley Myers paced the floor, while his wife played with

the fringe of a cushion on the sofa in uneasy silence, her nervous fingers weaving it into a plait. She was such a quiet mouse of a woman.

"It's not only the thefts and the politics," Dudley said. "We can't go out of doors without fear, and life will never be the same again. Kenya is going to end up as another Congo, I'm sure of it. Everybody is talking of leaving before Independence. I know the payment from the British Government to settler farmers is a pittance, but at least we'll get something back."

He ran his fingers through his hair, and turned to Caroline.

"What's that husband of yours doing in London? He'd be a fool not to look for a job over there. If you've any sense, you'll take your baby and make a new life away from all this."

"Oh, Daddy, why don't you stop ranting and just enjoy it while we're still here?" Teresa's voice rose to a whine.

Caroline widened her eyes.

"What do you mean?"

They all stared at Dudley.

"I suppose I'd better tell you; everybody will know sooner or later. We're off to Australia on a ten pound ticket." He clenched his fist. "But I don't like being defeated by a bunch of blacks. Wouldn't Africa be a wonderful place without them!"

"What am I going to do without you, Teresa? I'll miss you so much!"

They were in the bedroom. Caroline sat at the dressing table, shaking out her hair. It had lost most of its curl since she'd had Paul.

"We've hardly seen each other since you moved to Nairobi."

"Yes, but you know what I mean…"

The baby was asleep under the window, in the wicker basket she had lined in blue quilt. He looked so snug and peaceful, lying there, thumb against his cheek. She tweaked his blanket, and then turned back to sit on the bed beside Teresa. The fire had gone out of her friend's eyes.

Caroline wondered whether she still saw Charles after the Sunday race meetings in Nairobi. Teresa was right; they had drifted apart since her marriage.

"Do you have to go with them?" she asked. Teresa was well over twenty-one. "When was the decision made?"

"The news came through last week," said Teresa. "I have to go. I've got no money of my own, and our owners are already transferring their horses to other racing stables. My stallion has been sold. The boat leaves Mombasa in three months' time. It is better this way, as Daddy has done enough damage. I have to go too, before anything worse happens."

"What do you mean?"

Teresa got up and sat at the mirror, releasing her gleaming black locks from the tight coil she used during the day.

"You remember when I asked you if Boney could get rid of Mwangi?"

"Yes. You said Charles had found out he was a dangerous man. But what's Mwangi got to do with anything?"

"Well, it all started that last time we broke out of school…"

"You mean when we heard the crashing in the forest?"

"Yes. It seems such a long time ago. That noise was made by *Mzee* Ondiek, the night guard at school who saw us break out. I know this must be hard for you to believe, Caroline, but *Mzee* was trying to protect us from him. Then Mwangi put a curse on *Mzee* for wounding him, and preventing fulfilment of his oath."

"How on earth do you know all this?"

"Charles told me. He's *Mzee's* son, remember."

Caroline raised her eyebrows. "It's amazing that so much happened that night, with such consequences – have you told Charles you're leaving Kenya?"

"I haven't seen him. His father died. *Mzee* claimed the curse was killing him, and there was no point trying to fight it any longer. Charles took some leave to arrange the funeral and help sort out family matters. Oh Caroline, I'm so afraid…"

Caroline put her arm round her friend. "Why, Teresa? Surely that's the end of it?"

"*Mzee's* death has changed the curse; it's me he's after now. When Mwangi lay in wait for us that night in the forest, he planned to use me to destroy my father."

This amazed Caroline. With Teresa's upbringing, she shouldn't be affected by such a primitive matter.

"I've found out more about Mau Mau oaths," Teresa continued. "They're horrible. He was going to take my…my entrails, and make Mau Mau recruits eat them in a ceremony which would bind them in an oath to murder my parents. If they didn't do it, then the oath would kill them." Teresa's voice faltered. "Mwangi's oaths work. He's told Charles that if we carry on seeing each other, he'll be in danger, too. I mustn't see Charles anymore. I can't let him suffer because of me, and I have to leave the country so the whole horrid thing will go away."

"But if Dudley and Sheila leave, surely Mwangi can't touch them," said Caroline, feeling herself becoming caught up in this bizarre situation. "And there'd be no point in targeting you?"

But Teresa said she had to leave.

Her friend, who was so strong and resilient, and who knew what to do in any circumstances, collapsed onto the bed and covered her head. Caroline heard her sobs through the blankets. She left her alone. It would be best for her to cry it out, and they would face the problem again in the morning.

Paul woke Caroline for his early feed. She changed him and put him down, and then joined Boney in the breakfast room.

"We had a great party last night, Boney, and Ethel is a gem, isn't she?"

"I know, my dear. And may I compliment you on being an

excellent hostess?"

Boney put his arm round her shoulders, squeezing her close. She smiled up at him. She didn't feel quite so worried about him, now that she knew about Ethel. Maybe they were more than just employer and cook, but it wasn't for her to judge.

"Where's Teresa?"

"She's still asleep. We had a long talk last night. I'm worried about her, Boney. She's upset at having to leave, and I'm going to miss her!"

She went to check on Paul. Teresa stirred, then sat up and threw her blankets aside. Caroline heard the sound of retching in the bathroom.

"I must have eaten something bad last night."

Her face was pale, and she staggered weakly through the door. This wasn't like Teresa – she was never ill.

"Are you sure?" asked Caroline.

"I know what you're thinking…" Teresa hung her head.

Caroline stared at her.

"Well?"

"I don't know," said Teresa. "How can I know for sure? My period is late, but I've never been that regular anyway. Oh my God! If I'm pregnant on top of everything else, what am I going to do?"

It was a genuine prayer, Caroline knew. Her mind started racing. What would she do in the same circumstances? But it might not be true.

"You don't know for sure."

Teresa faced her. "It is true," she said, "I am pregnant. This isn't the first time I've been sick, and it's over eight weeks since my last period."

"So – you've got to face it," said Caroline. She was surprised that Teresa should be in this predicament. She'd always seemed so much in charge of herself.

Then she remembered her own dilemma over Brian, and her decision to give up Oxford to marry him. Her family and

151

many of her friends thought she'd made a mistake, saying she had thrown away the chance of a lifetime. But the power of love was too great. She remembered her words to Brian on their wedding night.

"I have given up my career for you, I need to keep myself occupied – I want five children!"

And now here was Teresa, facing a similar turning point in her life.

"I don't know what to do."

"You need to tell your mother."

But Teresa shook her head, and Caroline understood. Sheila had always been dominated by Dudley. Caroline could not imagine her being any source of strength for Teresa, and Dudley would explode with wrath at the news. She marvelled again at how they could have produced a daughter so different from them both. But they would have to know eventually. Caroline thought of Australia. She'd heard that the Aboriginals were virtually extinct, and anyway, they were a primitive tribe. What future would Teresa's child have in a white dominated country? Caroline did not have to ask her if it was Charles's.

"You'll have to tell Charles."

But Teresa shook her head vehemently. Caroline felt so inadequate.

"Well, you know I'll help you all I can. We've got a bit of time to think things out…"

The train coiled down the wooded track. Through the tops of the waving pines Caroline glimpsed the plain below. The engine disappeared from sight round a bend, and then emerged on the edge of a precipice. The whole breath-taking vista was visible. A steep slope of tangled undergrowth swept downward to the valley floor, dotted with thorn bushes and yellow with drought. The volcanic outline of Mt. Longonot rose, blue in the distance. Beyond, the land disappeared into a haze, and golden bars of sunlight interrupted the darkening sky to illuminate patches of the enormous expanse of the Great Rift Valley.

She was going to collect Paul from the Claytons after saying goodbye to the Myers family in Nairobi. She stared blankly at the trackside stations slipping past the window, wondering at the turn events had taken.

On their arrival in the city, they had checked into the New Stanley Hotel in the middle of town. Dudley and Sheila had final arrangements to make, so Caroline and Teresa went window-shopping. Teresa was disconsolate and grumpy, despite Caroline's best efforts to make the most of their final time together. Then she had an idea, and without thinking it through, Caroline made the fateful suggestion. What would have happened if she hadn't spoken?

"Shall we phone Charles? I'll make the call, and if he's not in the office, we'll take it as a sign…"

She could see that Teresa was tempted. She spoke to Charles, and they arranged to meet him at the Thorn Tree café for lunch.

"I want you to promise me you'll never tell him I'm having his baby."

Caroline made the promise.

She saw Teresa'a eyes light up when he appeared, but, before their order arrived, her friend lost control of herself. Charles put an arm round her shoulder, and Caroline got up.

"Can you ask the waiter to bring my meal to our room? I'll see you later."

"Thanks, Caroline."

She met Dudley coming out of the hotel foyer.

"I'm on my way to sell our car," he said, dangling some keys from his hand. "I've hired another one for the day. But I can't find Sheila or Teresa to follow me in our old jalopy to the garage."

Caroline had to distract his attention.

"Would you like me to drive it for you? It's in the back street

153

outside the rear door, isn't it?"

She brushed past him, turning his shoulder and made sure Dudley followed her back down the corridor, to the rear entrance. They drove in convoy down the dual carriageway to a garage in the industrial area. It had been raining, and the yard was awash with stagnant potholes. A man emerged from the office.

"Are you Mr Meghji?" Dudley asked.

"Sorry, sir, Mr Meghji is on safari. Can I help?"

"He agreed to pay me two hundred pounds for my car," Dudley led him towards Caroline, who was gingerly trying to avoid the puddles. "I told him I'd bring it in today."

The dealer cast an eye over the battered Ford station wagon and probed inside the bonnet. Then he scanned the paintwork and examined the tyres.

"When did Mr Meghji see it?"

"He hasn't. I told him the mileage and he quoted the figure."

"We can't give you two hundred pounds for this car without Mr Meghji's instructions. Please come back tomorrow."

"I'm not here tomorrow. What can you offer?"

"A hundred pounds."

"Make it a hundred and sixty, and it's a deal."

"A hundred and ten – and no more."

With vehement spluttering and enraged objections, Dudley had to capitulate.

Teresa was not there for dinner. Dudley quizzed Caroline, who did not dare to confess that Teresa had lunched with Charles. But he challenged her.

"She's been seeing that nigger again, hasn't she?"

Caroline said nothing.

"Hasn't she?" Dudley brought his face close to hers, and the people on the next table looked up. Sheila laid a hand on his elbow, but he shrugged her off. "I knew something was up, when I saw him at your wedding. I'm not stupid, you know."

It was after office hours, and Caroline didn't know where Charles lived. They could do nothing, and she felt so guilty. She couldn't sleep that night.

The following morning she telephoned the newspaper and spoke to Charles, but he confirmed that he'd said goodbye to Teresa at the Thorn Tree. Dudley grabbed the phone and questioned him rigorously.

"Damn the girl!" he shouted, turning to Sheila. "I knew no good would come of this!"

He rounded on Caroline. "You knew all about it!"

Caroline denied it, and Sheila tried to quiet him.

"You know she didn't want to come with us, when we told her about her past, dear," she said. "Teresa is over age and we can't force her. But perhaps she'll have second thoughts..."

Caroline did not understand. "What past...?"

But Dudley interrupted her. "There's no time," he said. "We're flying to Mombasa this morning, and have to be at the airport within two hours. We can't miss our boat."

Caroline drove them to the airport.

"I won't give up trying to find her," she said. "I'll let you know."

There was a long queue at the check-in counter, and they sat in awkward silence, drinking coffee before the flight was called. She watched them through the passenger gate, and Sheila turned to give one last wave, before disappearing.

Caroline climbed the steps up to the waving base. There were only one or two people waiting in the blazing sun. Exit farmer Myers, she thought with some relief, casting a swift look up at the overcast sky. Half an hour later she watched the jet rise like a screaming bird and disappear into the clouds.

The train pulled into Nakuru Station. Caroline still didn't know what to think. Why had Teresa disappeared at the last minute? Was Charles telling the truth? She could understand why Teresa didn't want to leave Africa, but to make such a drastic decision took courage.

Boney met her, and she told him the news.

"I'm hardly surprised," he said.

"Why?"

"Well, she's adopted, you know. They couldn't have children, Teresa was abandoned at birth, and they took her in. We were all astonished that Dudley agreed to it, but I think her mother might have been Italian, like Sheila."

"Teresa never told me…"

"I'm not even sure that she knew. But if she did, she would hardly tell."

"Why? I'm her friend after all!"

"People said that Teresa's real father was a worker on the railway," explained Boney. "Perhaps her mother was raped – who knows? Her mixed blood has become more evident as she's grown older; it's made her into a most attractive woman. If Sheila told her, I suspect she's gone to look for her roots."

This new dimension made Caroline feel a little happier about her friend. If Teresa were indeed looking for her roots, perhaps she would instinctively know how to go about it. But it was a dangerous time for any girl to be alone in Nairobi.

She could do nothing for the moment, however. Brian was due back from London, and they were going on holiday to the coast with friends before he returned to work.

CHAPTER 14

The minister stood at the graveside, his black robe billowing in the wind. His voice, intoning the prayers of the dead, reached her in gusts above the noise of traffic along the main road. She didn't hear the actual prayers. She didn't register much about the funeral, except that Boney and Brian's parents had flown down for it; and, above all else, she had to keep a grip on herself. If she broke down, everybody else in the small crowd of friends grouped in the graveyard would also burst into tears.

Nobody came near the mound of earth waiting to be heaped onto the coffin. Caroline stopped ten yards away; the others straggled out behind. The prayers ended and she could scarce gulp out a broken Amen. The minister bent down and took up some earth, throwing it onto the coffin, then in silent strides he retired towards the waiting wreaths.

Caroline approached Brian's grave. She picked up a handful of clodded earth and let it slip, thud after thud, onto the coffin lid. Each dull thud went through her like a dagger, but she went on, as if bent on self-persecution, until there was no trickle of earth left in her grimy hand.

Brian. She pictured him, lying there under the lid in his little blue bathing pants. Gone now; stiff and cold. So sudden.

She tore her eyes away from the gaping hole before her and raised them towards the palm tree on her left. Its swaying trunk bent gently towards the grave. She looked up its ringed bark; up and up until the few green fronds swished against the blue sky. Her eyes squinted and watered at the merciless glare of the heavens, then found rest with a small white cloud.

Brian. Where are you? You know the Answer to Life, now. Can you see me here, my darling? Brian! Her heart cried out and tears welled. Brian – I love you.

Alone now.

The others were at the row of wreaths, reading the labels and standing in hushed groups. Nobody joined her at the graveside. She approached the flowers, and people started to pick them up and turn towards the mound of earth. She found a small wreath. Somebody had written on the label.

To my darling Brian, with love from Caroline and Paul.

Not alone. How silly of me. Thank God for little Paul.

She turned. She could feel their eyes watching her, sympathy welling up at the tragedy of it all. She knew what they were thinking. What will she do now, a young widow with a six-month-old baby? Why do things like this have to happen? Such waste; such a fine, promising life cut short.

A lump stuck in her throat. Sympathy was the hardest thing of all to bear. She managed a smile at friends who had travelled for miles to be there. She found it easier, thinking of them, and thanked them for coming.

They said nothing – just responded. Silent tears were rolling unashamedly down Jenny's face. It's all right, Caroline's eyes pleaded with her. Don't cry. Don't cry for Brian; don't cry for me. It's done now. Look ahead. Don't look back – look ahead.

She found it easier, those first weeks, to concentrate on the present. She didn't know what she was going to do in the future. Her brain was too numb to think that far ahead. She fed Paul, bathed him, and played with him, and thanked God and Brian for him. Many times she thanked God for him. Paul kept her sane, kept her from withdrawing into herself. He was such a cheerful, winning little soul with an impish grin and a mischievous way that it was easy to laugh when he was around.

The lease on their Nairobi house was up, and she returned

to the city to pack up their wedding presents, and her clothes. Friends had put Brian's holiday clothes into a suitcase for her. She didn't want to touch it, but remembered Boney's principle when her mother had died. It would be best, she knew, to face up to it now. She opened the case, and trying to suppress her feelings, drew out Brian's crumpled shorts and shirts. She put them with his suits and shirts from the wardrobe, and divided them into piles for the people on the farm.

She took Paul to stay with Boney, and stood by while the *watu* riffled through the clothes and gratefully made their choices. She knew Brian would have approved. Afterwards, it was as if a shadow had lifted. She visited the Claytons, but they were about to leave the country. She went back to the coast, and lived with Brian's Uncle Ed and his Catholic girlfriend. She liked Meg. They went to church together a few times. Caroline remembered how she had pontificated to Brian about Meg not being a true Christian if she continued to live with his uncle. She felt ashamed. Life was more complicated than it seemed.

Her mind was bruised, but she didn't blame God. She wanted to understand, to get over what had happened to her, to survive the next few years.

She knew what people were saying.

"Why don't you go to Oxford, and get your degree?"

How could she go to Oxford and leave her baby? And she didn't want to leave Kenya. But would it be best to do so? Teresa had faced a similar dilemma. If only she were here.

Caroline made herself think back to the time when she and Brian had last been together. A suspicion was forming in her mind, and she needed to remember...

On the first day of their coast holiday, Brian had shouldered the cine camera, which he had bought in the London duty free. They'd wandered hand in hand down the path to the beach, leaving Paul in Jenny's care. Their bare feet sank into the sand. The beach was tiny, bordered by two rocky points. Rough ridges of coral showed beneath the water.

"We'll have to find a better place for Paul," said Caroline, rounding the point to their right. "Look over here – the sand goes on for miles!" She ran along its firm surface, and then bent to pick up a butterfly shell. She put on her goggles and floated face down among the rocks to gaze at the silent world below. Electric blue streaks flashed in and out of the seaweed. Bright red and yellow apparitions came and went in swift succession, black and white zebra fish flicked past in dazzling shoals and, lurking beneath a dark overhang, a large orange monster cautiously eyed the waving green world before him.

But Brian hadn't followed her. She strolled back. The incoming tide lapped in wavelets against the coral. He was standing on the path, his stomach protruding slightly over his light blue bathing pants, cine camera at his face. She watched him experimenting with the zoom, following the continuous motion of the waves, and then panning out to include the foliage on the headland and beside the path. He turned to include her as she approached him, laughing.

The following afternoon they went surfing in the spring tide, leaving Paul asleep on the veranda beside Jenny who was immersed in a paperback. She didn't even look up when Brian called goodbye.

There were no surfboards in the house, but he had picked up a yellow inflatable mattress. He waded out into the high tide, floating the mattress through the water, before turning to surf a breaker. Caroline, content to paddle in the shallows, watched him catch some thrilling runs onto the sand.

"It's your turn now." He pushed the float over to her.

"No, you carry on. I hate getting my head wet."

"Come on! I'll show you," he insisted.

He went with her as she tried to dive through the mounting waves. He held her tight as the breakers pulled and pushed at her. Eventually, she managed one exhilarating run, and started back to catch another wave. But she felt a strong tug at her legs, and stumbled. Brian was there to support her, but she floated the mattress over to him.

"The current is too strong for me, I'm going in."

She battled the sucking waters of the receding tide, until she reached the beach, and then turned to watch Brian.

But she couldn't see him. She noticed the yellow mattress drifting near the shore further down the beach, and ran back towards the headland to get a better view.

Then she saw him peacefully floating on his back further out to sea than expected. Clambering wildly over the coral rocks towards the house, she shouted for help.

She paused for breath, and watched him turn over and strike out for a canoe, which was anchored nearby. It was a native dugout, with wide stabilisers smashing violently into the heaving waters. Just as he reached it, a wave slapped up and dashed him away. His arms flew up, and he heaved half out of the water before submerging backwards. Had she seen a figure in the boat, etched in silhouette against the waves? It was too far away to be sure.

She renewed her efforts to race up the stony path, shouting for David.

Minutes later, she stood on the cliff with a pair of binoculars, waiting to direct David towards Brian. David was a good swimmer but he seemed to take forever to put on his flippers. Then she couldn't see Brian. She searched the chopping waters for him, lowering the binoculars to the shore, then up again towards the distant reef. There was something to the left, near the point, and she waved to David. He struck out strongly, then pushed aside some driftwood, and stopped for further direction. But she saw nothing but deceiving pieces of floating wood. Nothing.

Later, a motorboat set off from the shore, and before dusk, an aeroplane swooped low over the waters, zigzagging in its search.

Caroline ran down to the beach and turned northward, clambering over rocks and through deep pools to round several points in the scraggy coastline. She approached each promontory with fresh hope, but on rounding it, her heart gave a sickening lurch as nothing but the foaming breakers greeted her empty gaze. It was getting late and she had to feed Paul. She turned and wandered back along the waters' edge.

The tide had receded, the sky was darkening, and a few stars twinkled through the clouds. Her mind was full of horror and anxiety.

This can't be happening to me; of course we'll find Brian... Oh God! Her heart cried out, Thy will be done, Lord. But please God find Brian for me – find him and help me!

They found his body an hour later, washed up by the rock pools below the path. It was exactly the same spot that he had photographed the evening before.

The policeman asked her if she wanted a post mortem.

"We tried to resuscitate him," he said. "But there was no water in his lungs. Your friend has formally identified him. I don't think you should see him. There's a bruise over one side of his face."

"That must have been when he was hit by that boat," she said, allowing herself to be led away.

The thought of cutting up her dear Brian was too much to bear. What was the point? It wouldn't bring him back to her.

She looked out his cine camera and sent the film to be developed, witnessing Paul's early attempts to lift himself up on his arms. His little head jerked in awkward wobbles before he collapsed into swimming motions on his belly.

She remembered how Brian had lifted him from the cot on that final morning, and brought him into bed while she prepared a bottle. They had lain together, father and son, looking up at her from the bedclothes, and she'd wondered if this would be the start of a family tradition.

The end of the film dwelled on the restless motion of the waves. It zoomed in and out, before panning towards the point. And then there was the final moment when she approached, her laughing face filling the frame.

"Had any more thoughts about adoption?"

Boney made his weekly telephone call. He had told her before that friends of friends had made the tentative offer. But Caroline recoiled in horror at the thought. Paul was her lifeline. Thank God she had changed her mind about Oxford. Thank God they had battled with family and friends, and got married. Now at least she had some wonderful memories, and little Paul to keep her company.

But she couldn't go on like this, putting off the day when she would have to think for herself. Teresa was somewhere in Nairobi. Perhaps she could go and live there, take in paying guests? Then she would only have to find a part-time job. She blessed Boney for insisting on her doing that secretarial course.

PART III

1965 – 1976

Jomo Kenyatta, a member of the Kikuyu tribe was Kenya's first President. He went to mission school, and after furthering his education in England and Russia, he returned to Kenya, and played an active part in politics. He was arrested in 1952 for implication in the Mau Mau movement, and finally released in 1961. During his term of office, Kenya was a two-party Republic.

CHAPTER 15

Kenya's Independence celebrations passed Caroline by, causing hardly a ripple in her life. Absorbed with her own problems, she had little time to keep up with news and politics.

Afterwards, she sensed a pause as the country settled. Visions of the Congo atrocities were kept fresh in her mind by daily newspaper coverage, and with her friends, she watched and waited for their worst fears to materialise. But nothing happened, and business started moving again.

She rented a large house in the Nairobi suburbs and acquired two paying guests. The Government initiated a Tripartite Agreement, requiring the unions to accept a wage freeze and employers to expand their labour force by a third. Caroline did her bit by employing Onyango, the Clayton's ex-house servant who was embarrassingly grateful.

She trained Njeri, one of Ethel's daughters, to look after Paul. It was not long before Caroline felt able to leave him safely at home with her. The contributions from the paying guests merely covered her living expenses and she felt the need for outside stimulation and challenges.

An agency found her some temporary secretarial work and a middle-aged man with beady eyes and a portly figure called her regularly. He sold pharmaceuticals. They faced each other over his executive desk as she took shorthand notes on her knee.

"Have you read the latest Reader's Digest?" he asked.

"No, why?"

"There was rather a good joke in it, the best contraceptive nowadays is still the old-fashioned 'No'."

Caroline laughed politely.

"I have received lots of different samples lately."

She felt a sly brush against her knee under the desk and stopped smiling.

As realisation dawned, she felt a slow creeping blush spread over her face. How could he? What right had this bloated, middle-aged, pompous specimen of humanity who called himself a businessman, to make such a suggestion and in such crude terms? All right, she was a young widow and perhaps he thought she was fair game, but he had grossly mistaken his temporary secretary. Even if she'd wanted such consolation, did he really believe that she would require it of him, when there were so many far more attractive men around?

A long minute passed as she flicked over the pages of the *Manufacturing Chemist*. She could feel him watching her. Then he started dictating erratically and senselessly. Silence again. The fool, she wasn't going to help him.

"What are you thinking?"

Caroline shrugged. "Nothing."

She took down a couple more letters and then rose to type them out.

"I'm afraid I can't come to you again for a fortnight," she said.

That was perfectly true as she'd arranged to go to another office. But if he needed any further convincing, this was her opportunity. Caroline left.

Then she could laugh. What a situation, and what a pathetic old geezer he was.

There was so much more to offer the country than wearisome temping; it would be exciting to become an integral part of the growth, to get away from superficial white society and make a difference to the people who really needed her.

A new business magazine was advertising for an editorial assistant. There would be no harm in trying for it. She squeezed herself into her only suit, which had been a perfect fit before she'd had Paul, and drove to the station end of Government Road. It took her a while to find a parking spot.

A thin carpet covered the floor of the reception area. Two brown leather armchairs rested at careful angles across the far corner, facing a table bearing an ashtray and a copy of a magazine called 'Growth'. A low bookcase near the door bulged with sheaves of news releases.

Caroline composed herself on one of the chairs.

The door to the next room squeaked as it opened.

"Please come in."

The man in a pinstripe suit didn't look at her directly as he motioned her through the door, and then turned to ruffle the papers on his desk.

She stared at him.

"Charles?"

He had changed, grown round the midriff, and a thin moustache bristled above his lips. She supposed she must have changed too. Her figure was not what it used to be. Hadn't he recognised her?

He returned her gaze, then tweaked his tie and adjusted the red carnation in his buttonhole, his mouth widening into a smile.

"Have I altered that much, Caroline?"

"I didn't know it was you…"

He motioned her to sit opposite him, and she opened her bag to withdraw the letter inviting her to interview and scrutinise the name at the bottom.

"I dropped the Ondiek from my professional name," he explained. "Omari rolls off the tongue better." He paused. "Caroline, I was very sorry to hear about Brian."

She smiled, nodding away his awkwardness, but wondered why he hadn't disclosed his identity when inviting her for interview.

"There is so much we have to say to each other, Caroline.

I'm glad you applied for the job. We must talk. But now…"
He looked at his watch and took up his notes. "I only have
half an hour. Are you still interested in working here?"

Caroline nodded.

"Have you any experience in journalism?"

"No," she said. "But I'm keen to learn and as I said in my
application, I've always been an avid reader, and my English is
good."

"I'm looking for an assistant who might eventually become
editor of the magazine."

Charles showed her the last edition, pointing out a few
errors in spelling and grammar. "Plenty of room for
improvement, don't you think?"

Caroline flicked over the pages and smiled back at him.

"You can see it deals with small businesses. We'll be doing a
feature on a different one every month. I want to encourage
those who are making progress, and in the new Kenya there's
plenty of scope." He sat back in his chair. "What have you
been doing since we last saw each other?"

Caroline made a dismissive face. "Not much," she said.
"Some temporary secretarial work through an agency. But now
that Paul, my son, is at playgroup, I have time for something
more challenging. I've always wanted to be a journalist."

"You won't be doing much journalism in this job," replied
Charles. "But you will learn how a magazine is put together."

In her mind, journalism and editing were much the same. It
sounded exactly what she was looking for.

"Would you like the job?"

It was almost too good to be true. "I'm certainly very
interested."

"Naturally, I'm looking for someone who isn't always
watching the clock," Charles said.

"Of course not."

"And you'll appreciate I'm not in a position to offer a huge
salary. In fact, to begin with I can't afford more than a

commission on space."

This meant nothing to Caroline.

"Magazines depend on advertisements for income," explained Charles. "Selling space is easy really once you have the contacts. And I'm sure you must know many people in Nairobi."

"A few... I'm not sure they'd be the right ones, though."

"I'll give you forty per cent commission to start off with, which is very generous. But I expect you to assist me editorially as well. Do you agree?"

Caroline wondered if anyone else had applied for the job.

"Could you give me an idea of how much I would earn in a month?"

"That depends on how successful you are," Charles said. "You could earn as much as sixty pounds – could be more..."

He rose to show her to the door.

"Can you start at the beginning of next month? I'll send you a letter confirming your appointment. Then we can catch up with each other's news."

During the first weeks Caroline spent long hours at the office learning the job and perfecting the magazine. Once she settled into a routine, perhaps she would be able to keep more civilised hours. After the first month, she accompanied Charles to meetings and press conferences, and wrote her first feature article.

Charles sent her to interview his cousin James, who had a garage in one of Nairobi's back streets. She described the open-air showroom, applauded the enterprise, and took a photograph of James leaning against his van.

"I'm sure James's business would grow if he found better premises nearer the centre of town," she told Charles when he invited her to lunch.

"Probably, Caroline, but it's always a struggle to find the right place at the right price." He lifted his glass. "We're here to celebrate our bumper edition and it's time to catch up with each other."

She studied the menu.

"I expect you've been wondering if I had a part in Teresa's disappearance," he said. "Well, I was as shocked as you were. Have you heard anything?"

Caroline shook her head.

"She told me about Mwangi and a curse, and she seemed to link it with herself and your father. You know more about that than I do. It's strange, in this day and age. I can't believe that Teresa would take something like that seriously. But it wasn't the only thing that was troubling her."

"I assure you, Caroline, that Mwangi's curse was real, and connected with a Mau Mau oath. My father was seriously affected by it and his death hastened because of it."

Caroline was surprised by Charles's response as she knew he was a Christian.

"You said there was something else bothering Teresa?"

"That's not for me to tell, Charles. But she may have gone to search for her roots."

"What do you mean?"

"I only learned after she disappeared that Teresa is adopted. Apparently, her real father was descended from a worker on the railway, when it was built from Mombasa to Lake Victoria at the turn of the century. She was abandoned at birth."

Charles did not hide his surprise. She watched him chew on a piece of goat meat and discard the gristle onto his plate.

"I've always felt that Teresa was unlike her parents, and now I know why. I'm relieved that she is no blood relation of Dudley Myers. But it is dangerous for her to be on her own in Nairobi."

"Do you know how we could trace her?"

Charles beckoned a waiter and ordered coffee.

"My relative, Jackson, works at the National Museum on the fringe of the Indian suburbs. He might have some ideas."

Charles took Caroline to see his printers. The offices of Messrs. Kundi Singh and Brothers were off a dirty side street in Nairobi's industrial area. The girl at reception, swathed in a black sari, raised her eyebrows in sullen enquiry and then opened a door to look for Mr Singh. The insistent clack of printing machinery filled the room.

"He's busy. Can you come back in two hours?"

"I'm busy, too," answered Charles. "And we can't come back. Please tell him I have my assistant with me and I won't keep him long."

There were no chairs in the room. Caroline wandered to the window and absent-mindedly traced a finger through the dust on the sill.

Mr Kundi Singh emerged from the workshop. He wiped inky smears down his overall.

"Good morning, Mr Omari."

He unbuttoned the coat and flung it over a chair, then ushered them into an office cluttered with files.

"I want you to meet my new assistant, Caroline. You'll be seeing a lot of her as she'll be looking after this side of the business for me."

Mr Singh flicked at a straight-backed chair with his handkerchief and invited Caroline to sit. It wobbled on the uneven floor as she adjusted her dress. He turned to Charles.

"So…we're carrying on, then?"

"We're late starting this month I'm afraid, as Caroline had to learn the job. She'll bring you copy first thing next week."

Mr Singh turned and bowed to Caroline. "I'll be very pleased to work with you, ma'am." He pressed his palms together and bowed his head. "It will be an honour."

Then he looked pointedly at Charles. "You'll come and see me privately?"

"Yes, Mr Singh, as soon as I can. And now, if you'll excuse us…"

Caroline found herself conducting all future dealings with

Mr Singh, and whenever it was necessary for Charles to be there, he insisted that she came with him.

She realised that he was taking full advantage of this period of golden opportunity. In these uncertain times so close to Independence, Indians and Europeans dared not refuse to do business with emergent African entrepreneurs, and having herself as an employee added another dimension to Charles's prestige. But Caroline didn't mind when he paraded her in public. She enjoyed being a part of emerging Africa; she had always dreamed of doing this.

She made an appointment to see the Managing Director of a motor company. Mobey's was an industry leader, and Charles wanted her to plan a supplement on cars. A couple of the salesmen had been members of Brian's rugby club and she had seen the MD once at the Nairobi Cathedral, while singing in the choir for a Cabinet Minister's funeral. The MD had courteously showed some African VIPs to the front pew, his face a picture of grovelling reverence.

Surely he would be sympathetic towards a fledgling African business? And perhaps she could persuade him to take a full page advertisement.

The office was on the top floor above a showroom. She knocked on the door. The room was surprisingly modest. At his invitation, she perched on an upright chair, and offered him a copy of the magazine.

"What are you doing working for an outfit like that?"

His aggressive tone startled her.

"People like you don't help matters. Don't you realise that African upstarts like this man are out to make their fortunes?"

Caroline forced herself to relax back into the chair and listen. Clearly, she wasn't going to make a sale.

"These people don't have any capital, and they use naïve white girls like you to further their ends. You think you're helping but all you're doing is making a fool of yourself. You should take my advice and go back home."

The man slapped the magazine onto his desk, leaned forward and glared at her.

Caroline refused to let herself be intimidated.

What insufferable bad manners! She wasn't even going to bother to tell him that Kenya was her home. She rose from her chair and, picking up the magazine, left the room. She steadied herself as she negotiated the steep stairs.

What hypocrisy! How could someone in that position be allowed to carry on in business holding such views in a newly independent country?

Luckily, they were not all like that. She discovered the Asians were the easiest to win over. They seemed afraid not to buy space and she learned to take advantage of this by booking them up for several months.

The paying guests did not cover all her costs and her finances were suffering. She caught Charles in his office before he left work one afternoon.

"I have prospected for advertisements, written articles, interviewed people and supervised the printing of your magazine," she told him. "I have learned a great deal thanks to you, but at a cost. I've been staying on into the night to meet deadlines and I hardly ever see Paul. I've worked three months for you now, and I'm still waiting for my cheque."

She folded her hands in her lap, watching as Charles struggled for words.

"But, Caroline, you're paid on a commission basis. You agreed to that in the beginning."

"I know, and I've calculated that I've earned nearly two hundred pounds."

Charles could not hide his surprise. "I don't disagree, Caroline. I'll have to work it out. But you can't expect to be paid until the advertisers have paid me."

She hadn't thought of that. "You don't expect me to chase people for money as well?"

"You won't have to chase them all, but they do take time to

pay."

"You're telling me I'll have to wait even longer?" Caroline rose from her chair. "I've rent to pay and food to buy as well as you. I understood I'd be getting a monthly pay cheque, and I think I've been very patient."

"Look – I've been having some cash flow problems." Charles delved into the inner pocket of his jacket. "I can give you forty pounds for the time being. Will you take it?"

Caroline caught her breath and almost felt sorry for him. He didn't have to pay her from his own pocket. But she needed the money, and accepted his offer. He reminded her of the generosity of her commission.

"I admit that under the circumstances, the commission is worth waiting for," she told him.

He held up his hand before she left the room. "Caroline, would you dine with me this evening?"

She tried to conceal her surprise, then composed herself. "I'm grateful to you, Charles, for giving me the opportunity to learn about the magazine world, and I'm proud to be part of it. I'm trying to repay you by working my best but I have my own social life to lead."

"You've had social lunches with me before. What's the difference between lunch and dinner?" Charles's voice was steady.

Caroline clenched her jaw. "I've always considered our lunches as strictly business. If I'd thought they were anything else, I'd never have accepted."

"I admit that I made the luncheon invitations under cover of business, Caroline, but I also hoped they would lead to a more personal relationship between us. Surely you could not have been unaware of this?"

He rose from his desk and came to stand before her.

"Let's not talk about the lunches. I'm now asking you as a man if you'll have dinner with me tonight."

"Thank you very much, Charles, but I'm already doing

something this evening."

"Tomorrow then, or any evening of your choosing?"

"I have a friend who's jealous about my time."

"A special friend?"

Caroline hesitated, but she replied truthfully. "Not particularly."

Charles seemed to be propelled by an inner compulsion. "Are you refusing me because you don't like me, or because of my colour?"

The words hung between them, as he walked to the window.

"Would you like me to resign?"

"Of course not, Caroline."

"In that case, you'll forgive me if I don't answer your question."

She moved towards the door and he stepped round to open it for her. She did not look at him. What did he think he was doing? First, he'd refused to pay her and now he was becoming personal.

Of course it wasn't because he was black that she didn't want to go out with him. He should know that by now – hadn't she lunched with him on countless occasions? Anyway, she'd always thought of him as Teresa's.

Perhaps she should look elsewhere for a more reliable job. Unfortunately, she really enjoyed the publishing world even though the space-selling side of it was tedious.

There were no further luncheon dates, but the magazine rapidly increased its circulation and stature under the influence of her enthusiasm.

But financial matters were again distracting Charles. The printers were more open about their repeated requests for payment, and Caroline knew that he was being threatened with eviction.

"Will you help me face the landlord?" he asked. "I need more time."

She went with him in his car to the Company Head Office. They parked in the private courtyard.

But the landlord was unyielding. "You've only to sell that car of yours to raise the money. I'll give you a week," he said.

Caroline felt humiliated and resentful, and Charles said nothing on their return journey.

He dropped her at the office, saying that he had an idea. The following day he greeted her with a proposition.

"My relative, Jackson Ondiek, is working on a dig in the Rift Valley. Remember, he studied palaeontology at Oxford? Would you like to do a story on him?"

Caroline's eyes lit up, allowing him to tempt her further with a story about a cave in the vicinity, connected to a tribal legend.

"Simaloi, my grandmother, is our tribal sorceress and custodian of the cave of our ancestors," he told her. "I don't know where it is, but I suspect that Jackson does, and his profession may have something to do with what it contains.

"See what you can find out from him. It would make a great scoop for the magazine. I'm afraid I can't pay for your petrol but I think you will enjoy the experience. Jackson is a fascinating fellow."

CHAPTER 16

Caroline contacted Jackson to arrange a day for their meeting at Olorgesailie. She would take Paul and Njeri with her.

"I want you to go on the last weekend of the month," Charles told her, disregarding her dismay. He knew how stressful it was to put the magazine to bed in time. Why the hurry?

But she was excited at the chance to get away from Nairobi, and grateful for the opportunity to uncover a piece of Kenya's history. These were intensely interesting times. She was helping African industry and furthering African ambitions, and it made her proud.

While Paul slept on a mattress in the back of her station wagon, Caroline cruised along the tarmac, which wound down the escarpment behind the Ngong Hills.

She allowed her mind to wander, marvelling that someone with her background should be privileged to have a place in this new world. But to succeed in identifying herself with the African cause she knew there would be sacrifices to make. She would have to forego her security and her way of life, and be prepared to see herself swallowed up in the national effort.

Caroline felt tempted. She had tasted the exhilarating uncertainty of an enterprising African endeavour and knew the rewards of witnessing and being part of a new birth would prove worthwhile.

She swung off the tarmac to avoid a pothole, and Paul whimpered in the back. Would realising her ideals be fair on him? She would have to think about that.

Her blouse was sticking to the back of the driver's seat. The tarmac ended and her car rumbled along the corrugations, dust billowing in great clouds behind her. Paul was bouncing on the mattress at the back, and Njeri had to climb over and comfort him when he bumped his head. Caroline nearly missed the track to the prehistoric site, as its crooked wooden signpost was camouflaged against the dry scrub. She drew into the compound, and a crested barbet flashed its red and yellow feathers from an acacia tree.

Jackson was taller than Charles, and of slighter build. She guessed he was much older. He greeted her in impeccable English, and showed her into a refreshingly cool thatched hut. Paul began to bounce on the bed, and Caroline handed him a drink.

"I don't think you should take your boy where we're going," said Jackson. "It'll be much too hot for him."

She left Njeri to look after Paul and, taking her notebook, followed Jackson. Some American tourists clambered up the rocky steps towards them, mopping their brows.

"It sure is hot down there…" they drawled as they passed.

The landscape stretched into the distance, miles and miles of parched African plains dotted with thorn scrub. They reached the first level and Caroline took shelter under a tin roof, wiping away the sweat, which was running in rivulets down her brow. A wooden rail separated the walkway from an earthen pit. The sand had been scraped back to reveal a large skeleton.

"It's a fossilised hippo."

She stared. She had never seen a fossil before. This one was enormous. Jackson pointed out the bones of its rib cage and directed her to the explanatory notes on the wall behind.

"Not many outsiders have heard of our hippo, all the focus has been on the hand axes. We've got an elephant too, but he's too far away for visitors."

They lingered in the shade. It was stifling hot out there, but

Jackson motioned her on down the rough path to the valley bottom. Her shirt stuck to her back and its sleeve stained brown as she used it to mop the perspiration from her face. Jackson seemed unaffected by the heat. A crude wooden walkway lay suspended over a dry riverbed. A pile of rubble had built up against the bank below them.

"Does the river ever flow?"

"Yes, in the rains. That's how this place was discovered. Each one of those stones is a hand axe. You're not allowed in there, but here is one," Jackson drew it from his pocket and pointed out the sharpened edge of the stone. He invited her to handle it. "We think there may have been a factory somewhere upstream, which was washed down here in a flood."

Caroline fingered the object, turning it in her hand. "And this is a sign of early man?"

"Absolutely."

She remembered Charles's parting instructions and looked towards the opposite hills, blue in the distance.

"Is there any other evidence of man in the area?"

"None that we've found."

"Charles told me something about an ancestral cave…"

Jackson regarded her solemnly, and then gazed southwards in the direction of Lake Magadi, hidden behind dark pimples of stunted hills.

"Did he? My father sometimes talked of it. He said we must keep all family traditions alive."

"Would he speak to me? Where can I find him?"

"Ondiek died some time ago."

"You mean *Mzee* Ondiek – Charles's father? I didn't know you were brothers."

"I was from a different mother – the first wife, Simaloi, who was abducted in a raid on the Masai many years ago. She became our tribal sorceress, but has now handed over to my youngest sister, who bears her name."

Caroline studied Jackson's face, recognising the finely

chiselled cheekbones and aristocratic profile of a Masai. She noticed he also had the lithe figure of a warrior.

He led her back up the steep valley side, and twenty minutes later, she bathed her face in cool water. Paul lay asleep in the *banda* and Njeri rested against a tree outside the door.

Caroline interviewed Jackson briefly that afternoon in his office.

"We don't have time to go into the detail you require," he said. "Why don't you visit the National Museum for background material?"

There were dramatic changes in the office when Caroline returned to work.

The partitions had been removed and cars filled the downstairs area. Charles told her that his cousin James had paid the outstanding rent and moved in with his garage workshop. The magazine was reduced to one small office and a Reception room, which they would share with James.

"I'm not sure that I'm going to like this change," Caroline said, realising the reason behind Charles's haste in sending her to Olorgesailie.

"You spend most of your time at the press or out selling space anyway, so we would seldom need to use the office at the same time."

Before she could make further objections, Charles offered to pay her another instalment of commission. Caroline found herself accepting thankfully.

But as James's businesses grew, sharing a telephone became increasingly unworkable. Even when an exchange system was installed, they had nobody to operate it.

Charles approached her.

"I have to go away for a while," he said. "You can stay in the office and answer the phone. There's also the filing to bring up to date."

The advertising copy had been collected for the next issue

and Caroline knew she could work on the editorial while confined to the office. She had hoped to do it at home and spend time with Paul.

"What about the printers?"

"They'll have to do it without you this time. They can send up the galley proofs once they're ready."

"But…"

"I may be seeing my sister. Would you like me to ask her to talk to you about our ancestral cave? Jackson told me you'd shown an interest. You write so well, you could make a good story out of it."

It wasn't every day that Charles complimented her and Caroline had not forgotten the cave.

"That would be nice, but it's hardly a topic for a business magazine."

"I have my contacts. I'm sure we could find someone to publish it."

The office ran smoothly, and one Saturday morning Caroline visited the museum. She was fascinated by the pre-history gallery with its fossil exhibits and representations of early man.

The following weekend she took Paul with her. He enjoyed the bird gallery, with its rows of back-lit glass cabinets and the wonderfully preserved colours of their feathers. He was becoming more of a companion now. Every day she would glimpse a trait of his father, but had no one with whom to share the delights of his development.

She took him into the garden for a picnic and they wandered towards the Snake Park to watch the keepers milking venom from the reptiles. A woman wearing sunglasses strolled along the path towards them, swathed from head to foot in a *kitenge;* she had a scarf coiled round her head. A child, younger than Paul, trailed his fingers along the wall of the snake pit behind her.

Caroline looked again. The woman had taken off her glasses and was wiping them on a corner of material. Caroline could not believe her eyes.

"Teresa! Is that really you?"

Caroline saw panic in the tired eyes.

"What's the matter? How wonderful it is to see you. And you had a boy? I didn't know… Oh, I'm so glad we've found each other!"

She threw her arms round Teresa. But the response was lukewarm.

Teresa replaced her glasses and turned back towards her child. Her shoulders were stooped in the subdued stance of a worn out African *bibi*; in fact, Caroline, looking at her from behind, could easily have mistaken her for one. The only white skin visible was that of the face below the glasses. Even Teresa's sleek black hair was hidden.

Caroline went to drag Paul away from the keepers.

"Come here, Paul! Meet some friends. What's his name, Teresa?"

"Sam."

Caroline nudged Paul forwards.

"They've finished milking the snakes now. Why don't you take Sam to play on the lawn?"

She watched the two boys run off, noticing Sam's wiry black curls rising from a light tan coloured face. She met Teresa's eyes. She didn't need to ask if he was Charles's.

Teresa turned away, hanging her head.

"Wait! Don't go, Teresa. We've only just found each other! I'm working for Charles now, you know."

"Are you?" A flash of fear showed in Teresa's eyes. "He doesn't know – and you mustn't ever tell him. I didn't want this to happen."

"Why ever not?"

"I've made such a mess of my life."

"You haven't heard about *my* life!"

184

They sat on a bench watching their children play on the grass. Teresa insisted on hearing Caroline's story first.

"I'm so sorry about Brian, Caroline. It must have been dreadful for you."

"It feels like a long time ago. But now I want to hear all about you. Where are you living?"

"I won't bore you with my sordid details, they're best forgotten. But I'm happy now. I work part time in the museum Entomology department. I haven't seen Charles since that time at the Thorn Tree and I want it to stay that way."

"Did you know that his brother, Jackson Ondiek, works for the museum? Apparently he is also an Oxford graduate."

"There's a man called Jackson in the pre-history department."

Caroline nodded. "That could be him."

"We met when I first arrived and was introduced round the departments. I've seen him a couple of times since then. He's working at Olorgesaile."

"That's definitely him."

"I had no idea. I've only known him as Jackson."

Teresa looked behind her like a hunted rabbit.

Caroline watched her sadly, trying to understand in a small way how Teresa must be feeling.

Paul and Sam trotted up to them, chattering excitedly.

"Can Sam come and play with me?" asked Paul.

But Teresa dragged him away.

"We'll meet up again next weekend, won't we?" Caroline said, as she fumbled in her handbag for her car keys. "Have you a car, Teresa – or can I give you a lift home?"

"It's all right, we live nearby."

Middle class Indians lived in the area behind the museum, and the slums of Mathare Valley were not far away. Caroline felt a pang of anxiety. But Teresa had survived this far, she told herself, and she had chosen her way of life. Then she thought of Charles. How would it affect their working relationship, knowing what she knew now?

He was in the office on Monday morning.

"I'm glad you're back," she said. "I have to sell more space and the printers have some queries for me."

"But we need somebody to answer the telephone. You can ring the advertisers and I'll deal with the printers. Would you mind staying in the office?"

Caroline had to give way. She tried to settle into her more restricted occupation, but realised that Charles was taking advantage of her. She thought of Teresa, and her resentment grew.

She worked full time in a cubicle, correcting copy, operating the telephone and making appointments for others, with no time to sell space, her sole source of income. This was a far cry from the assistant editorship she had originally applied for. Charles had achieved his status by displaying her during those first months and he had relegated her to the background. She rounded on him one morning after spending a sleepless night with Paul, who was suffering from malaria.

"When will I get the balance of my pay?"

"I've told you before, Caroline, you have first priority in the business and I'll pay you just as soon as I can. Don't worry, I won't let you down."

"I'm not saying you will let me down. I'm just tired of waiting. I'm also worried about the job."

"Oh?"

"When are we going to get a receptionist?"

"Why, Caroline? Is there too much for you to cope with?"

"Not really," she admitted. "But frankly, I resent doing the job of telephonist and filing clerk. It's left me no opportunity to sell space. My commission is my livelihood, and I'm sure you wouldn't deliberately deprive me of that."

"Of course not, Caroline. You're sitting beside a telephone all day and nobody's stopping you from using it."

"You know as well as I do that I need to see new advertisers face to face. Besides, how am I going to interview people for feature stories?"

She had a point, but she also knew that Charles's hands were tied.

"I'll tell you what: I'll pay you a salary to be the receptionist and on top of that will give you commission at a reduced rate. Would you think about it?"

Caroline suspected that James would be sharing the cost of reception duties, and she tightened her lips.

"Not really. I enjoyed working for you at first, Charles, but everything has changed. I can't see a future in it and I have Paul to think of. I'm going to look for another job."

"Please yourself." He shrugged. "But you'll never have another opportunity like this."

"The opportunity has already vanished."

She waited, hoping things might get better. But Charles benefitted hugely by her labours and she had virtually nothing in return. She would not slave so menially for a pittance.

"If I worked as an ordinary secretary, I could earn four times as much as you're giving me. I just can't afford to stay."

Charles had no answer. She suspected that he had not taken her seriously after all. It was hard to walk away from all the money he owed her, but she left a note on his desk giving him a month's notice.

She could understand Charles's way of thinking and the reasons for his actions. She could even see why he found no wrong in using her like he had. After all, it was for the good of his new African business. But didn't he realise that he was doomed to failure by starting without capital? If he tried to create a truly African image and shelved the prospect of making a quick fortune, there might be more hope of success.

Caroline wondered what Brian would think if he were alive. She would have discussed the problems with him. The Africans must make their own way, she would have said. They

187

must create their own national character and direct their own policies. They have many examples to follow from the western world and acknowledged mistakes to avoid. They can tap into advice backed by years of experience.

And then she realised how alone she was.

By marrying Brian and having Paul, her life was chosen. Perhaps a European with a moral and cultural background ingrained by centuries, had no place in the new world the Africans were creating for themselves? However much she would wish to sacrifice for her personal ideals, she must not do so for Paul's sake.

However, if he wanted to identify with this tremendous emergence she knew she would endorse it wholeheartedly and be proud of him.

Charles held up payment of her final salary, and some commission payments from advertisers were outstanding. But Caroline left the office when her notice period expired.

At least she no longer had the burden of keeping Teresa's secret in his presence. She started temporary secretarial work and, after six months, went to see Charles about the money he owed her.

"If you come back you can have your cheque straight away," he said.

CHAPTER 17

It was Saturday again. Weekends were for family gatherings, and here she was, stuck by herself, with nobody to share the delights of Paul's development.

Why should she sit at home and be good while others enjoyed themselves, and why resist Adam's advances?

"You have such a negative approach to life, Caroline," he'd said many times. "So long as Betty doesn't find out, she can't be hurt, can she?"

It made Caroline feel like a spoilsport. After all, he only wanted sex and she found it flattering to be desired. It would be one of those harmless affairs people seemed to regard as a matter of course these days.

She'd met him through the temping agency. Tall, dark, with a broken nose and the rugged good looks of a rugby player, he'd taken her out to lunch and then introduced her to his wife and two children. She and Betty immediately liked each other.

Caroline decided to ring Adam's house. But Betty answered.

"Your party last night was great fun, Betty. Thank you so much for including me. I expect you're both still reeling from the invasion."

"Not at all – everything's back to normal. Adam is just leaving for the office, though goodness knows why he's doing that on a Saturday afternoon. He works too hard."

Caroline hung up. She rang Adam's office three times but nobody answered.

She slept late on Sunday morning. Teresa brought Sam to

play with Paul after church. She never stayed for lunch, but at least she visited fairly frequently, and the boys had become good friends. It saddened Caroline that Teresa never returned her invitations.

After they left, Caroline read for a while in the sun and then went to her desk, which overlooked the garden. Paul was as usual in the servants' quarters. Her neighbours didn't approve of him playing with the African children, but who else could he play with? He spoke fluent Kiswahili, which made her proud. The *totos* always had runny noses and were covered with dirt, but they were company for him.

She watched as the three boys ran to the bottom of the garden. Yellow-haired and jaunty-eyed, Paul picked up an armful of leaves and placed it, businesslike, in a cardboard box. The *totos* toddled after him and copied. The lawn was brown and dusty, the sickly jacaranda had shed its purple blossom amid the carpet of pine needles from nearby firs. Orange from the monkey-puzzle, crimson from hanging orchids and the deep red poinsettia formed a canopy for the three busy little heads, bent in absorption over insects and pretty berries.

Paul snatched up a stick close to the stretching hand of Jacob, his more ponderous friend. There was a scream of rage and the little boy bounced angrily ten yards away and stopped. His cries went unheeded. He turned a sulky back and moaned his way laboriously up the drive between the agapanthus, heavy in blue flower.

At the top, he turned once more to call back. The sudden scratching of a grasshopper diverted him. He stooped to watch it clamber across a dry jungle of blades. He straightened, scrabbled with his toe at the loose stones on the driveway, then ran purposefully back, short-cutting across the flowerbed and the dried-up lawn to where the others were sitting at the foot of a shading neem tree. They were running sand through their fingers onto their clothes, and gleefully over their heads.

Jacob approached, slackening his pace and watching for further signs of hostility. They ignored him, though Paul flashed a wary eye in his direction. He sat down a pace or two away and fingered the sand, but there was no fun with no communication, so he called his brother and they traced their way back between the agapanthus.

Paul followed, his steps gaining purpose as he passed his friends, who bounced in his wake and then turned towards the servants' quarters. Paul scrambled up the front steps.

"Mummy! Mummy!"

His steps pattered past Caroline's door and faded along the passageway. But soon the handle turned and a tousled head peeped round to chortle at his discovery. He held out a hand to show her a tiny scratch and then with a flurry and a flash of heels he was gone.

A yellow butterfly jerked swiftly past her window and a ponderous beetle clambered slowly into a pink rose bloom. But Caroline could not linger further, for it was a full five minutes since Paul had disappeared from sight and she had to find out what new mischief he was brewing.

In the evening they squatted together on a log outside the servants' quarters to enjoy a plate of *posho* and *sukuma wiki* with Onyango and his family. It was tasty, simple fare, and she had encouraged Onyango to serve it up as a side dish at dinner one night, but the paying guests didn't appreciate the plate of boiled maize meal mixed with a spinach-like vegetable, even though she had spiced it for them.

Caroline found a part-time job in the civil service, filling in while a secretary went on maternity leave. She dropped Paul off at school, and on the way to work went to a travel agent to enquire the cost of flying to the coast for Christmas – four hundred shillings. If she went by train, it would cost a hundred and forty shillings.

Then it was time to meet Adam for lunch.

He was late as usual, but he didn't apologise. They went to a Beer Garden but came away because one of his work colleagues arrived, so they lunched at Brunners Hotel instead. Adam talked of office affairs while Caroline leaned back in her chair. She felt lethargic, and also attracted. She must be careful.

"I don't let Betty enjoy herself too much with other men," he told her. "It makes her feel special and wanted. She's a little naïve and I have to shelter and protect her."

"Yes, a woman is sheltered when she's married. It's been a rude awakening for me."

"And you should be thankful to me for protecting you." Adam winked at her.

"Oh, that's what you're doing, is it?"

She felt relieved that he was soon to go on home leave.

A farmer from upcountry approached their table, staring at Adam.

"Hello, Caroline, I've been meaning to ask if you'd like to move back to Nakuru. I need a secretary there and could do with someone like you. Boney sends his love by the way – I saw him last week."

Was he trying to tell her something, or did he want to find out about Adam?

"That's very kind of you," she replied. "But I'm rather committed here at the moment."

After lunch she walked with Adam round the block.

"Let's go to your home for a nice little session together, shall we?"

She did not bother to reply.

"I suppose I won't see you until January?" asked Adam as they approached his office.

"No, and I hope by then your ardour will have cooled."

"The longer you delay the more likely it will happen."

"I wish it would."

She felt her powers of resistance running low. He was so

endearingly open about what he wanted.

Caroline arrived late to work.

"I don't feel like dictating this afternoon; I had a slap-up lunch at Brunners," her boss said, regarding Caroline pointedly.

"Oh – I didn't notice you there!"

"I'm not surprised; you seemed pretty absorbed with each other."

What cheek! But Caroline could not help squirming inside. She took up her pencil. Michael Carling must be twice her age and she had learned that he was working out his contract with the Colonial Service before handing over to an African. He dictated for an hour and when she brought in the letters for signature, he commended her accuracy.

"I have to collect something from Kamiti Prison for one of the Ministers," he said. "They have impressive workshops there. Would you like to come with me?"

He probably regretted his previous remarks, and she had nothing better to do as Paul was going to a friend's house after school.

Kamiti Prison, an austere place with double security locks on its massive doors opening onto a serene courtyard, appeared empty. The prisoners were locked up.

The quality of their work surprised her.

"You can sketch anything you want, and they'll make it," announced the Officer who showed them round. "Dustbins for the City Council, or drinks cabinets for Members of Parliament – you name it, they will make it. They also spray cars. It's a quick and useful service for officials who crash government vehicles."

Caroline smiled. The number of crumpled cars on the road verges was an eyesore, and most of them were the result of incompetence or drink.

"I'm afraid I can't let you see the cells or the execution

chamber," he said in answer to her query. But this is the biggest prison in the country. The eight hundred inmates are locked up at 4.30pm every afternoon. There are five Europeans here, and fifteen condemned men."

He led them towards the chapel, and Caroline examined the handmade pews. There was a peaceful, reverent atmosphere, none of the 'foreboding of doom' she somehow expected. Someone was practising the organ.

"Do you hold regular services?" she asked.

The Officer nodded. "I don't go; I'm an agnostic."

She turned to Carling.

"I'm just a hardened cynic."

They went to a nearby hotel for a drink. Caroline telephoned home to make sure Paul had returned and gave instructions for his supper. Then she arranged for Njeri to stay on and baby-sit. She was enjoying herself.

The barman was an ex-prison officer.

"Do you have any connection with the prisons?" she asked Carling.

"Not now," he replied. "I was in the Kenya Regiment, and used to help screen Mau Mau detainees; we cracked and broke several notorious leaders. But Bob, here, could tell you many a tale."

"You didn't crack all of them!" said Caroline. "I can tell you of one man, Mwangi, an oath administrator. He nearly murdered my friend Teresa. Then after the Emergency he was released and came back to work for my stepfather."

"Is he still there?" Carling asked her.

"No. Boney sacked him when we discovered the truth."

"There were dozens of Mwangis in the detention camps," said Bob. "And thousands of detainees. We used to have a helluva time trying to separate them into groups and make them work. They would break away and then slip back into the crowd." He lifted his mug of beer to his lips. It came away, leaving a froth of white clinging to his moustache. "Once they created an enormous mass of bodies, howling and writhing like a giant mound of wild worms. Whenever we tried to pull someone out, he would slip away and dive back into the depths of the slithering mass. We couldn't hold anybody, their arms and legs were so slippery."

"What happened?"

"They eventually ran out of energy and the pile disintegrated. It wasn't a successful way to make them work."

Bob moved towards a party of Africans who had just teetered in. A couple of British soldiers joined them and then Carling took her back to the office, where she had left her car.

"Would you like to have dinner with me?"

But Caroline wanted to get home.

Carling took her out for morning coffee during a lull in work the following week.

"My wife is in the UK expecting our first child," he said. "That's why you're working for me. She used to be my secretary."

Caroline had heard about his wife through the office grapevine.

"I have an older son," he told her. "I went through a sordid divorce, which I won't bore you with."

Again, he asked her to have dinner with him.

They shared a bottle of wine and her eyelids drooped as she struggled with her mussels. By the time they had finished dessert, Caroline longed to escape into the fresh air. The bill, to her horror, came to more than a hundred shillings but he didn't seem to mind. She supposed he felt lonely without his wife.

After work the following day, he took her to a bar. It was dark and sleazy. The prostitutes were preening themselves and all heads turned whenever the door opened. One of the girls had made an attempt at whitening her face.

"It was quite pleasant when I was here earlier this year,"

Carling apologised.

Caroline wondered what sort of a man he really was.

On the day she left for the coast for Christmas, Caroline invited him to lunch. As he had taken her out a few times, she felt this was the least she could do in return.

Afterwards they lay in the sun listening to records and he played with Paul for a long time.

Caroline started calling him Michael, although she didn't call him anything if she could avoid it. He commanded an aura of superiority. He had a bald patch, which he tried to cover with long strands of straw-coloured hair but it kept flopping over his eyes. She teased him about it.

"You show me no respect," he said, smiling.

"That must be a nice change!" she countered.

She had started writing a column for the local newspaper and he commented on her latest article. Then he asked for her press cuttings book to take home to read.

It was time for her to catch the train. Teresa arrived to take her to the station, but Michael insisted that Caroline went in his car, so Teresa took the boys with the luggage.

"Oh you're *going!*" Carling banged at the side of the coach with a clenched fist to emphasise the last word as the train pulled out.

With relief, she escaped from her complicated Nairobi life.

Paul slept like a lamb, allowing her to read far into the night and enjoy the rhythmic clatter of wheels over the track. There were frequent stops accompanied by the screech and hiss of brakes. She would hear a patter of footsteps on the platform, a low call as the key was transferred, and then a muted whistle. Then the train would lurch forwards and gather speed before the process was repeated.

Brian's Uncle Ed and his Catholic lady friend Meg were on the platform at Mombasa station. Caroline filled her lungs with the salty air, tinged with fish and heavy with humidity. She gathered her bags, pushed Sam in front of her, and wound through the colourful clamour of the vendors and taxi touts to Meg's car. Her neck was damp with perspiration.

The dogs needed a run along the beach, so they went to Nyali and ended up having a swim in the receding tide. She retired to bed with the windows wide open, listening to the rustle of the palms against the shutters. Paul lay sprawled on top of his bedclothes, naked to the waist, his blond hair sleek with sweat.

Meg had an invitation to a cocktail party on an aircraft carrier, due in harbour on Christmas Eve.

They were ferried across in the officer's launch. The *Enterprise* rested in mid-channel, her bridge floodlit. The aircraft crouched on the flight deck like giant insects with wings folded,

Climbing the ladder onto the quarterdeck, Caroline tried to clutch at the billowing material of her circular skirt, wondering what the men in the launch below must be thinking. An impassive officer met her on deck, his arm in stiff salute, but she glimpsed a twinkle in his eye.

She followed Uncle Ed and Meg through endless passages into an air-conditioned room, a relief after the sweaty stillness of the harbour. Then she was swallowed up in a sea of officers in white uniform.

A *Horse's Neck* was thrust into her hand. She tasted it, wrinkling her nose.

"It's brandy and ginger ale."

The man hovering at her shoulder looked younger than the other officers, who tried to outsmart each other in wit and witticism. He inched quietly to her side. He had a nice face.

"Time to go to the flight deck!"

Her most insistent suitor made a point of walking directly behind her to compliment on her figure, her walk, and practically everything else. They were transported upwards on a section of the deck about the size of a small dance floor. As soon as it moved, he flung his arm round her in mock imbalance.

"You're very hot – is it from passion?"

She laughed. "It's probably sunburn."

A warm breeze blew across the flight deck. The floodlights were off and they stood around, waiting for the Retreat. As the band arrived, she heard a voice in her ear.

"I think they're going to start soon. Would you like to stand where you'll be able to see?"

It was the quiet one again. He took her by the arm and found a prime position while the band played 'the Queen'. Caroline had not heard the anthem since Independence and a thrill of patriotic nostalgia went through her. Then they played the Kenya national anthem, its youthful music turning her mind to thoughts of earnest endeavour and lofty hope.

They walked back to the lift, where Uncle Ed and Meg were waiting. She heard Meg inviting some senior officers for Christmas Day so she turned to the quiet one.

"I don't know your name, but would you like to join us on Christmas Day?"

"It's Don – and I'd love to."

She arranged to collect him at noon.

Caroline took Meg's car to the harbour, and waited for twenty minutes before giving up and going home.

Paul had so many presents to open, that he didn't know which one to play with next. The traditional lunch sat heavily in her stomach and Caroline could not muster the enthusiasm to match the festive crowd around her. She thought of Brian. They'd only ever had one Christmas together on the farm when she was pregnant with Paul.

After lunch, everyone decided to go for a swim.

"I won't come with you," she announced. "You can take Paul, but I'm going to have a sleep."

"Sure you'll be okay?" asked Meg, peering deep into her eyes.

Caroline looked at her steadily. "I'm sure," she said. "I just want to be alone for a while."

She dozed on the sofa, then lifted her head at a noise outside and saw a taxi. She went out to find Don on the doorstep.

"You missed a very good Christmas lunch!"

He paid off the taxi. She found him some cold turkey and ham and a mince pie, and poured him a drink. They settled on the sofa while he tucked into the food as if he hadn't eaten for a fortnight. She examined his face, his deep blue eyes, soft profile and cropped, blond hair. He wore shorts and a casual checked shirt. He was so young compared with the other officers and the seasoned men she had met in Nairobi.

"I had to go to a cocktail party on board so I couldn't meet you this morning as planned. I don't know your surname and only vaguely remembered where you were staying. So until now I've been taxiing round the houses looking for a girl called Caroline. Everyone has been very kind but of course they couldn't help me. I'd decided that this would be my last call before giving up."

The others came back for tea and she went upstairs to put Paul to bed. Don came to help her.

"I love children. I have a wife in Southampton. We've been married for five years but haven't had any yet, although we both want them."

Caroline appreciated his honesty, relieved that he was happily married, so she could relax her guard.

"What's her name?"

"Linda – she's a teacher."

"Would you like to go to the drive-in cinema tonight?" Caroline wasn't sure why she suggested this, but she felt refreshed after her afternoon sleep and there would be plenty of willing baby-sitters for Paul.

It was a dreadful film, but she rested her head on the back of the seat with her eyes closed while Don held her hand. Afterwards she drove him back to the harbour. He stayed on in the car, talking and hesitating. Finally, he got out and came round to her window.

"Would you like me to show you over the ship tomorrow?"

"I'd love that."

"Come any time after lunch."

Feeling for him and thinking he's not going to be here for long, and poor thing he must miss home at Christmas time, she put her head out of the window for a brief kiss before driving home.

Don met her at the portside and guided her on board, taking her to the workshops, where he identified the different planes for her. The method of catapulting them off the deck and hooking them back, fascinated her. They wandered towards the bar and were joined by others from the night before.

They talked about getting up a party for New Year's Eve. It would be a grand last fling before *Enterprise* left harbour.

The Chini Club was an exclusive members' club in the shadow of Fort Jesus on the shores of the Old Harbour.

Dinner was silver service under a panoply of stars, which peeped behind the swishing palms. Replete after the full traditional fare, Caroline leaned back in her chair to savour the saline tang of the air. The ruins of Fort Jesus loomed dark and brooding over the gardens. Then the soft lapping of the tide was muted by the sounds of the band, tuning up on the dance floor.

Ladies were in short supply, and it was like being young and carefree all over again.

Don came to sit beside her.

"When is it going to be my turn?"

Caroline felt tired, her toes ached, and her white slippers

had ugly grey splodges over them. The band announced one number before stopping for a rest. Her latest partner had gone to order a bottle of champagne.

Caroline rose, and let Don guide her onto the floor. It was a foxtrot, which transported her into a dream of music and movement. He was the most accomplished dancer she had ever experienced, and all tiredness forgotten, she let him swing her into the rhythm. The others made space for them on the floor and the band extended the music, finally reaching a crescendo as he twirled her with a flourish under his arm.

She threw herself onto the chair, resting her feet on the stone parapet that marked the end of the terrace. Don brought her a drink of fresh orange juice and then topped her glass with champagne. A breeze wafted in from the sea and she raised her face to let it lift her hair, catching the faint odour of fish from the Old Harbour.

They sipped their drinks and Caroline told him about her short life with Brian, and how he had died. Each time she described it she found it easier to bear, but she couldn't control the catch in her throat when she remembered his body lying there in his little blue bathing pants, so vulnerable, so final.

She saw Don brush his face with a finger.

"What a waste, and what a wonderful man Brian must have been," he said.

"I would like go to the cemetery later on to put some flowers on his grave. Would you come with me?"

"I'd love to."

They were the last couple left when the band packed up. Don bought a bottle of wine, which made Caroline feel sleepy. They went into the garden and took a rocky path to the beach. The tide was out and they walked hand in hand, avoiding the crabs and listening to their toes make rubbery noises in the sand.

She gazed out to sea at the twinkling lights of the cattle boat, creeping into Old Harbour. The ruins of Fort Jesus loomed over them. Don turned to kiss her, and their bodies melted together. It began to rain and they ran through the warm tropical cloudburst, arriving soaking wet under the shelter of a flame tree in the garden for another kiss. She felt herself slowly bending over backwards while he towered over her, and then she pushed him away, laughing.

She drove through the empty streets of the town, over Nyali bridge, and stopped at a dark line of shops to waken a vendor and buy a drooping bunch of Barberton daisies.

"There's an urn on Brian's grave," said Caroline. "It will be filled with rain by now so the flowers will soon recover. But let's break off some of this bougainvillea to fill it out."

They wrestled with the thorny strands of papery flowers, which scratched their hands and then drove to the cemetery. The narrow strip of tarmac wound past clumps of banana trees growing between tin shacks. The headlights illuminated the foliage on either side of the road and a bicycle wobbled in the dirt in front of them. She pulled up in the shadows on the edge of the cemetery and pointed out Brian's grave. The marble cross, touched by moon through the palm trees, had tipped slightly. She would have to do something about the subsidence.

She got out of the car and locked it. Caroline stuffed the flowers into the urn, spreading them with her fingers. Then she stood, allowing her eyes to travel up the palm tree to her left, up and up, to the fronds which rustled against the backdrop of stars. Where was Brian now? Could he see her? What must he think of her and Don?

A shout broke the silence and a group of teetering Africans emerged from a shack beside the road, talking loudly. More drunks were slumped on some steps nearby. It would not be sensible to leave the car for too long.

They crossed the bridge to Mombasa Island and drove round the headland past the golf course to park in a lay-by overlooking the ocean.

"I feel so happy and peaceful, Caroline. I never want to do anything to hurt you."

He drew her close.

"Let's take Paul to Diani beach," she said in the morning.

Since Brian's accident, she had often gone swimming in the sea, and now it was time to break the spell by visiting the scene of his death. Don's presence would help her to face it.

It was as she had so vividly recalled in her long nights of loneliness. They negotiated the ragged coral rocks through which she had clambered wildly up towards the beach house, shouting for help because Brian was in difficulties. She had instinctively known he was in difficulties, although she could see him peacefully floating on his back beyond the breakers.

Caroline floundered through the powdery sand after Don, and sank onto the towel he laid out for her. Paul, hidden beneath a large cloth hat, filled his bucket and patted it down.

Don fumbled in the picnic bag for a beer while Caroline stared emptily at the quiet pools made by the receding tide. The sun beat down onto her thin shoulders. The humid air sat heavily around her head.

He sat beside her quaffing his beer. A thin beach shirt protected his fair skin from the sun.

"A drink?" He reached for the half-empty bottle, and a mug.

"Thanks."

She took the mug and sipped at it, hugging her knees. He slid his fingers along the sand and found hers, squeezing gently. They watched Paul digging the foundations of a sand castle, then turned to offer their backs to the sun.

Don started talking. His pleasant voice caressed Caroline, but she scarcely listened to his words, which told of his youth in an Irish village, and of his wife and their tentative plans to adopt a child. His serious eyes considered her, then he rose on his elbows and leaned over, meeting her lips in a brief moment of sweetness.

She settled herself against his shoulder, watching Paul whose tousled head was barely visible in the sand trench he had made.

She took Don back to the ship. The *Enterprise* belched smoke, ready for departure. But they had exchanged addresses, and she concentrated her mind firmly on preparations for her journey home.

On the way to the station, Uncle Ed drove them via the sea front and, with a catch in her throat, she watched the carrier slip her moorings and move through the channel, round turning buoy and out to sea. The decks were lined with white-uniformed men. She wondered which one was Don.

Paul tapped her shoulder from the back seat of the car.

"Will we see him again, Mummy?"

"I don't know, my darling. But we've had a lovely holiday, haven't we?"

CHAPTER 18

Caroline hefted her luggage out of the carriage at Nairobi station and gave it to a porter, then took Paul by the hand to find a taxi.

Onyango welcomed her at home.

"We've missed you, Memsahib!"

"*Jambo,* Onyango. *Habari*?" How is everything?

"*Mzuri,* Memsahib."

Good. All was well, but Caroline paused. There was always something…

"*Lakini…*"

"What's happened now?"

"There's nothing left in the store."

She opened the walk-in cupboard beside the kitchen. She had left more than enough provision for her absence but however loyal, he could never resist temptation. Each day Onyango would have taken a little something and the thefts had accumulated into a large vacuum during the course of her three-week absence.

It was a biblical ethic. If Onyango walked beside a field of maize and felt hungry, he would not hesitate to strip off a cob even if the crop wasn't his, and the neighbour would not begrudge him. But when he took more than needed, trouble would follow.

Onyango earned a pittance by her standards but she wouldn't otherwise have been able to employ him. His life was simple and his needs easily satisfied. She had learned to shut her eyes to the steady loss of tea, sugar, and flour from her

205

kitchen. She had tried buying him maize meal and sugar every week but it made no difference to the state of her store. Whenever the loss grew to unacceptable proportions, she would make him aware that she knew what was happening. Then the thefts would descend to a trickle again – until the next time. It was a way of life.

She took Paul shopping and when they returned, they both slept for three hours, missing lunch. She had not realised how exhausting her holiday had been.

She missed Don. She wanted to tell Teresa about him but something made her stop. Her friend lived in a different world. It made her feel guilty that she could enjoy luxurious holidays while Teresa struggled to survive.

Caroline went back to work for Michael Carling, telling him about her holiday and a bit about Don. Michael was a strange person. He gave her the impression that he knew more about her than she knew herself.

"The one and only time I got emotionally entangled with a girl," he told her, "I had a hard job getting rid of her."

"It's not good to get involved," agreed Caroline.

But she did miss Don.

She worked the whole of the next day. On the way home, she caught a glimpse of Betty and Adam in their car, and waved. Adam rang her and they went to the Beer Garden. Betty knew of these lunch dates now, and she and Caroline would sometimes giggle over the double deception.

She told Adam about Don. He teased her until she let him know that it was only a romantic dream as Don was married. He fell silent. They parted after lunch with no mention of a further rendezvous. Her eyes filled and she tried to shrug off the self-pity before reporting back to work.

In her mind, Michael had the role of a benevolent uncle. His wife had gone back in the UK to have their second child.

"We want to make sure our children are British citizens," he explained. "The only way to do that is for them to be born in

England, which is why she went."

"It must be very hard for you both."

Caroline did not see the need for such elaborate and expensive precautions. Paul had been born in Kenya yet he was also a British citizen by reason of her birth in England. Besides, didn't his wife think it risky leaving Michael behind? She glanced at his profile, which revealed the fine bones of aristocracy. But she did not voice her thoughts.

During a break in dictation, he talked about her tragic circumstances and teased her so much about aircraft carriers, sailors and ports that she started to cry. She wouldn't accept his apologies and left work early. He telephoned to ask if he could come round. In the end, Caroline relented.

She felt very much on the defensive and determined only to talk trivialities. But gradually she allowed herself to thaw and hating herself for being so weak, confessed that she had fallen for Don. Then she told him about Adam.

"Yes, I know all about you and Adam, and the women in Adam's office also know."

Caroline opened her mouth.

"I want you to promise me not to spoil your reputation by lunching with him again. He is a no-good stuck-up ass who is only out for one thing. He is notorious for his affairs."

"Who told you that?"

But Michael would say no more.

"I am not promising you anything," she said.

Before he left, Michael tried to hold her hand, but she disengaged her fingers.

That weekend Paul had a temperature. The doctor diagnosed malaria, even though she'd covered his little limbs every evening while they were at the coast and he had slept under a mosquito net. She forced liquid quinine down his throat four times a day. The poor boy was miserable for three days, and then recovered.

She contacted Betty, who talked about Adam.

"I've tried to divorce him three times already but each time he's gone down on bended knees asking me to stay. Now I'm past caring. He can do what he likes as long as everything stays peaceful. He is most uncommonly jealous and needs to see a psychiatrist."

"Poor Betty. What a life."

Caroline renewed her resolve not to see Adam again and wished she could meet an eligible bachelor.

She invited Michael to a dinner party and he stayed after the others left, encouraging her to bring out her family photograph albums.

The following morning in the office she challenged him.

"'Are your intentions towards me honourable?"

"As honourable as Adam's." Michael glanced at her. "Our relationship will be entirely platonic, if that's what you want."

"That's just fine."

Michael began dictating and then he stopped.

"You hardly consider me as a human being, you know, let alone a man."

Why did he think that? She sensed that he had fallen for her but she didn't want to cause unhappiness in his marriage. On the other hand, they enjoyed each other's company. Torn between what she knew was right and what was happening between them, in her loneliness she composed a poem. Perhaps if he read it, he would understand her feelings.

You are a glowing light amid the dark and stormy sea of my existence;

Your friendship lights my heart, your understanding shoulder 'vites my lonely head,

And when at length the storm clouds disappear, and life is safe, secure and happy once again,

Your gentle guidance and sincere goodwill shall e'er remain a precious memory.

"I wasn't able to work for half an hour after reading it," he told her. "I've looked everywhere for the reference."

She laughed.

"I made it up!"

They went for a curry at the Corner Bar and Michael drank at least six brandies.

"Hadn't you better stop?"

He drained his glass.

"Where shall we go then?"

Caroline drove him to the airport. The new waving base had opened and she watched as a Comet taxied along the runway. A sliver of moon hung near the horizon. Caroline's thoughts turned to Don and the night walks they had enjoyed along Nyali beach.

"What are you thinking?"

She didn't want to tell him but he insisted.

"Don."

He paused, and then moved towards the bar.

She stopped him.

"I don't think you ought to drink any more."

He remained quiet so she continued, "I think we'd better go home."

Poor Michael, she did not mean to be cruel. She took his hand and he squeezed hers hard. She could feel the pent-up emotion in the grasp. He kept his face averted while she watched a VC10 take off. The thundering roar of the engines reverberated deep within her.

They walked out of the airport holding hands, until she drew away.

"A fifty-five-year-old civil servant in an important position shouldn't want to be seen holding hands in public with a girl half his age."

"You *are* a cruel person. But at least you're truthful."

They drove home. He put his arm round her and she laid her head on his shoulder. Then he kissed her. She could feel the intense emotion inside him and his heart was beating fast, but she could only kiss him back on the rebound of his own feelings.

The next afternoon in the office, Michael was in a good mood. They took Paul out for tea and then drove to the escarpment to buy some mushrooms. Michael stayed for supper and Caroline showed him films of her wedding and honeymoon.

She told him she'd received a letter from Don.

"You should not talk about your boyfriends to other men. There is no surer way to frighten them off and it's a sign that you're boasting of your attractions, even if it is subconscious."

"It might be a good thing if I frightened you off. But thank you for telling me that."

She resolved not to talk of her private affairs any more.

"I don't expect you noticed I hardly ever speak about my wife to you."

"I know. Why?"

"I don't like to talk about her because you might bleat it out to anyone who cares to listen."

That was a shock.

"You should either make up your mind to break Don's marriage and marry him," Michael continued. "Or not have anything more to do with him."

She would have to take hold of herself; she realised she was an entirely different person from the girl Brian had married.

"Would you like to come home and have lunch with me to cheer you up?" he asked.

"No, thank you. I don't feel like it."

She needed to think. She was too easily swayed by the last person she met. She despised Adam for wanting her so blatantly, and she did not respect Michael, although she was grateful to him for speaking out. Yet, she felt no guilt concerning Don whom she loved, although he was happily married. It did not make sense.

Life became a routine. Michael took her and Paul out of Nairobi for a drive one weekend. She let her hair stream out of the car window as she savoured the wide-open spaces below the ever-changing clouds and the infinite sky.

They arrived home and she put Paul to bed.

"I feel neither like an uncle or a boss. Do you mind?"

"No."

He took her in his arms and kissed her. "I do love you, Caroline – just a little."

She felt herself soften. He had great will power and although she felt wary, she was beginning to trust him.

She didn't really know what she was doing although she did know that both Don and Michael were temporary episodes. She felt herself responding to Michael's advances. Perhaps time would provide the solution. She enjoyed her outings with him and didn't feel like giving them up. If she tried, he wouldn't understand. He didn't seem to regard their association as long term or serious and wasn't worried about whether he would hurt himself, or even her. She must adjust and try to be more philosophical.

He came to church with her.

"I confess I did rather enjoy it," he said afterwards. "You're coming to work tomorrow, aren't you? Let's have coffee together in town. We'd better go in separate cars though, as tongues are beginning to wag."

How juvenile.

He gave her a signet ring. "I'd like you to wear this for me."

Even more juvenile.

He teased her about her accent and her corn-coloured teeth, but she was quick to retort.

"Why do you bite your nails so much and smooth back your hair in that effeminate way?"

He took it in good part and with great self-control, improved.

Her two paying guests gave notice to leave, and the new man brought his parents over from the UK for a holiday. They arranged to go on a fortnight's safari.

"I have to pay my annual visit to the offices at the coast," said Michael. "Why don't you close up your house while your guests are away and come with me? I could take you and Paul to stay with your relatives in Mombasa."

Caroline thought about it. It would be a good opportunity to give Onyango some overdue leave. She consulted Brian's Uncle Ed, who insisted that Michael stay as well.

They travelled down on the Friday evening, spending the night at Tsavo Inn. She put Paul to bed after dinner and sat with Michael in the porch outside their rooms. The wine and the clear night air, heavy with the scent of frangipani, made her feel languorous. It was the most natural thing in the world to let him lead her into his room. It had to happen, she told herself.

He changed in subtle ways. He became more attentive and attuned to any need, almost before she knew it herself. He and Uncle Ed took an instant liking to each other. Watching them, Caroline realised they were closer in age than she and Michael. On their final evening, they took a motorboat trip round the harbour, chugging quietly among the big ships, which were moored in the central waters. The lights winked and dipped in the swell and wavelets sucked softly at the harbour steps. Caroline remembered the last time she had been here, when *Enterprise* had dominated the scene.

They had drinks with Ed and Meg at the Chini Club, overlooking the moon-washed waters of Old Harbour.

"I wonder what Don is doing now," said Meg. "Have you heard from him at all, Caroline?"

"Not for a while," she answered. "It's actually my turn to write."

Michael sulked for the remainder of the evening.

"There's no point in us loving each other," she protested,

slipping away from his arms when he caught her briefly to say goodnight.

They drove back to Nairobi and Michael stayed on.

"You're literally glowing with radiance," he told her in the office on Monday morning.

His wife had just had a second daughter and Caroline knew about his plans to join them in the UK.

She would wait for time to work it all out. A break now would hurt Michael much more than her, and she would hate to see him hurt.

"Do we really know what we're doing?"

"I haven't heard from Susan for nearly three weeks. Perhaps our marriage has broken up already and that's not entirely due to you."

Everything was so uncertain.

"I'll see how the land lies when I go on home leave next month," he said. "I'll try and get a divorce but I have to move warily in case she refuses to free me."

It seemed incredible to Caroline that, against all her principles, she had got herself mixed up with a married man. She was an idiotic fool.

The time for his leave arrived, and then he told her it was cancelled. Caroline had been steeling herself for the break and the anti-climax unsettled her. She didn't bother to hide her reaction.

"I'm sorry," he said. "I should have gone regardless for our sakes."

So it wasn't the office which had cancelled the leave.

"Well, what's done is done."

Michael wired his wife and she returned home. Caroline met her in the office. Susan looked gaunt, but attractive in an artificial way.

"I have told her there is someone else," Michael said the

213

following day. "But I haven't told her your name and she's asked for time to think about it."

"I hope she won't take too long deciding."

He came to her house at the weekend, when he brought up the Don business all over again. She went to church and spent the afternoon with Paul. Michael arrived for an hour, which passed in a flash.

"My wife is in a hell of a state," he said. "She's stressed and has lost all interest in the baby. She's decided to go to the coast by herself for ten days."

"What about your children?"

"She's leaving them with me and the ayah."

Caroline did not want him to leave her.

"I'll try and come to see you tomorrow afternoon, but please don't expect me."

He had said that many times. She didn't know how she was going to live through the next few months.

"Perhaps we should stop seeing each other? You'd have to get a new secretary and people will talk, but I can't go on like this."

"I'd like you to stay working for me but you can walk out if you can't bear it any longer."

When Michael left, she resented him for going.

She felt guilty, and in a perverse fashion, wanted to help Susan. This was stupid, considering Susan would hate her intensely if she knew she was the cause of her suffering.

"The break at the coast hasn't done Susan any good. She's now swearing at me and threatens to hurt the baby. I got a psychiatrist to talk to her and she's a bit better, but still very odd."

Caroline wondered if Michael was being melodramatic.

"Would it help if I went to see her?"

"You can if you like. I shouldn't think it would do any harm. She still doesn't know who you are."

"I'd like to."

"All right, I'll suggest it."

Apart from making Caroline feel even guiltier, the visit made no difference. Michael told her that Susan was determined to discover the identity of 'the other woman'.

"I gave her a fictitious name, saying you were connected with the motor industry. Susan has telephoned all the car firms in Nairobi!"

Caroline's face swelled up, itching madly. The doctor took an X-ray, diagnosed sinusitis, and prescribed an antibiotic.

"Could it be stress, I wonder?"

"That's also a possibility," answered the doctor.

Michael invited himself for tea.

"Susan has been to her psychiatrist and she wants to try and make a go of our marriage."

This came as no surprise to Caroline.

"It's better we don't meet again," she said. "And I'm going to stop working for you."

She found a job in a garage showroom. In one of the many notes they exchanged, Michael told her that Susan had started working for him again.

Caroline received a telephone call one morning in the office.

"Who is that speaking?" asked a woman's voice.

"It's Caroline Clayton. Can I help you?"

There was a long pause, and the phone clicked down.

Convinced it was Susan, and furious that her whereabouts had been discovered, Caroline took time off to visit Michael's office. She stormed up the stairs and, bypassing reception, tapped on his door before opening it to poke her head round. He had often been interrupted like that by staff, when she worked for him.

Susan was sitting with her back to the door taking notes. Michael's eyes widened when he saw her and then he

215

dismissed Susan to the adjoining office. Caroline half-closed the door, her heart pounding. Luckily Susan had not turned. Michael waved her in.

"Michael, she's just telephoned me at work."

"Why?"

Caroline shrugged. "Did you tell her where I'm working?"

"She must have seen the number somewhere and used it. I'll send her home and then give you a call. You'd better go quickly."

Caroline ran up the corridor. She heard the secretary's door open behind her, but she rounded the corner and sprinted towards the lift. It was full, and there were people waiting. She took several stairs at a time down three stories into the main foyer. The usual crowd of people were milling round the lift doors and on the stairs. She cleared the final four steps in one jump as Susan emerged from the lift and gazed round the foyer. Caroline didn't wait to be recognised, but sped through the main doors and out onto the street.

That was enough. The whole situation was becoming ludicrous, and she made an effort to come to her senses. She told Michael not to telephone her again and refused to reply to his notes.

She could not sleep and was continually tired and irritable, especially with Paul. Was she heading towards a nervous breakdown? She consulted her doctor, who prescribed sleeping pills. But those only deadened her mind and although they gave her a few hours' sleep, the effects would wear off by two o'clock in the morning.

What was going to happen to her? Her future seemed bleak. She was the target of every frustrated married man in the city. Would she spend the rest of her life moving from one to another? Would she ever find someone decent to share her life with?

She couldn't pray any more. Her entreaties were falling on deaf ears and the vicar at the cathedral was too remote to bother with her shameful problems. She cancelled a temping appointment and drove to the Catholic church where Teresa sometimes went. Perhaps the faith she had abandoned would have an answer for her? The courtyard was deserted and the church closed. She loitered in a large parking space, looking through the windows of the priests' offices.

Someone came bounding up the steps, glanced at her and then disappeared briefly into an office before hurrying out again. He was probably in the middle of teaching a class.

"Well, God, I've given you a chance. You obviously don't want to talk to me."

Caroline returned to her car and backed out.

She decided to visit a fortune-teller.

The house was overgrown with creepers and the dismal room full of clutter. A plump figure swathed in brown moved in dim silhouette against the diamond shaped window bars. She motioned Caroline to sit.

"What can I do for you?"

Caroline didn't want to tell her anything. After all, she was the psychic one. The woman produced a pack of cards and shuffled them.

"You're in a difficult relationship?"

"You might call it that, only I haven't seen him for a long time."

"He has a wife?"

Caroline nodded.

She dealt out a few cards and turned them over, one by one.

"I can see you in the cards," the woman told her. "Here he is."

She pointed to the king on Caroline's left.

"And right next to him is his wife."

Yes, the queen of clubs was there.

"You are way over here, separated by all these cards."

The jack of spades lay on the far right of the line.

Then the woman pointed to two cards among several small

ones.

"This five and eight of spades reveals you have a jealous rival. There's no future in your relationship with him. His wife has a very strong hold. I advise you to forget about him."

Caroline pointed to the nine of spades, lying beside the jack in the spread.

"And what does this card mean?

The woman hesitated.

A dark shape leapt onto the woman's lap. Caroline heard a purring sound and the fortune-teller's hand moved to stroke its head. All she could see was a pair of green eyes. She didn't like cats.

"Have you any other concerns? Any fears?"

Caroline stared at her.

"All I want is to find somebody to love me, and be a father to Paul."

The woman nodded.

"I know. The nine of spades shows there's something else, maybe something sinister and disruptive, which you have forgotten about or pushed to the back of your mind. It would be well to prepare yourself…"

Caroline got up from her chair, bruising her thigh against a corner of the table. For some reason, a picture of Mwangi came before her mind's eye, his black eyes glittering with evil intent. She bolted towards the door.

"I don't want to frighten you."

But Caroline had heard enough.

CHAPTER 19

Charles sat at his desk writing an editorial for the next edition of *Growth*, which was late for press. The growl of revving engines and the tinkle of spanners penetrated the closed door of his office, which overlooked James's garage.

His typewriter kept on sticking at the letter 'n'. He pushed the instrument to one side and brought out a lined pad. His pen ran dry. He fumbled inside the desk drawer, which screeched as it lifted off its runnels. It would only open half way but his fingers found the stub of a pencil, which lay in the far corner.

The telephone rang and Charles cursed. Why hadn't his cousin employed a receptionist? He dropped the receiver onto the desk and a barrage of sound invaded the room as he opened the door. Cupping hands round his mouth, he shouted from the top of a rickety flight of steps.

"James – it's for you!"

A mechanic relayed the message. His cousin waved an acknowledgement and then put his head back under the bonnet of a car.

Charles cursed. He eyed the receiver and cursed again. This had happened too many times and he had lost his train of thought.

But this edition of *Growth* was important. The international East African Safari rally was for rich whites in the latest cars, and only one African had managed to penetrate that elite sport. Now he, Charles Omari, would create something for the *wananchi*, the people.

There were millions of bicycles in the country, and he would organise a cycle safari from Nairobi to Lake Victoria. Even if this were to be the last edition of *Growth,* he needed it to launch the idea. The national newspapers would take it up, sponsors flock in, and he would become rich and famous.

Charles told the caller to hold on. He drew the pad and pencil towards him but he couldn't think of another word to write until James came to take the call.

It was a brave last edition. Charles knew the printer would not produce another unless he settled the outstanding bill, but he had no more money.

He flipped through the glossy pages, gloating over the array of advertisements and ignoring the errors that had escaped his notice during proof-reading. He allowed himself a brief thought of Caroline. If she were here, she would be going with him to Germany next month. He'd been offered two free flights to visit their bicycle factory, and the Germans were going to donate fifty machines for the safari as well as pay sponsorship money for prizes.

There was time to spare before his departure for Germany, and he hadn't visited his family since *Mzee* Ondiek had died.

It was a step back in time.

"Welcome, Charles. *Habari?*" How are you?

"*Mzuri.*" Well.

They exchanged a limp handshake. He hardly recognised Simaloi, the girl who had looked after him when his mother, *Mzee* Ondiek's fourth wife, had died giving him birth. A child, tottering uncertainly on skinny legs, peeped from behind her skirt.

"Is this your youngest?"

"Yes. She will follow after me."

"Where's your mother?"

"She's gone to the cave of our ancestors to guard it until her

220

time comes. I am now the tribal sorceress."

Charles knew that Simaloi would also go to the cave towards the end of her life. He longed to know its secrets. If he could break the news and be at the leading edge of its spread around the world, it would be a historic scoop with rich consequences.

Simaloi prepared a meal of *ugali* and goat's meat. He enjoyed a cigarette with his nephews after the meal, listening to the soft munch of cattle chewing the cud in the nearby *boma*. She came to sit beside him.

"We think it's time you took a wife."

Charles had feared this. As a youth in the White Highlands he'd enjoyed the favours of a girl on Boney's farm, but after Teresa and his Oxford lovers he knew he would only find fulfilment with a white woman. He had shelved all thoughts of marriage.

But to his family he was a member of the tribe. He should keep the tradition, they insisted. A beautiful and intelligent girl waited in the neighbouring village; the elders had met with her father. She had been through mission school, and would make a suitable wife for him.

"Who is she?"

"Ruth's father works in the fisheries in Kisumu. Why don't you go and see her? She is sixteen and will bear you many children."

Charles allowed himself to be persuaded to meet Ruth, who was indeed beautiful in the traditional African way. Her wide hips and ample behind were ideal for childbearing and she had a lovely shy smile. But her background made Charles hesitate. He was a Christian, but also a thoroughly modern man, who wanted to make his name and his fortune. He liked his life to be compartmentalised. What had become of Teresa? He'd tried to follow the lead Caroline had given him when she told him of Teresa's adoption, and he had asked Jackson about her, but his brother was uncooperative.

Charles took tea with Ruth's family and the talk turned to bride price.

"Bride price – in this day and age?"

"I don't mean cattle and goats. I have a right to know how you're going to look after Ruth," her father replied. "And her education cost me a lot of money."

Charles saw his opportunity. He would allow the elders to conduct negotiations and agree a dowry in the traditional manner, but he would insist on marrying her outside the Church in a purely tribal ceremony. Then, he thought, he could leave Ruth here and his city life would not be compromised.

The visit to Germany was a success, and a paragraph telling of Kenya's first cycle safari with fifty competitors mounted on imported bicycles appeared on the back page of a national newspaper. Charles paid himself out of the remains of the sponsorship money after handing out the prizes, and prepared for the next year's safari. His magazine died a natural death and he did not go near the printer's offices again.

He arranged another visit to Europe to seek more funding, but first he had to return to his family. Ruth was waiting. They married according to tribal custom and Charles wallowed in the role of new husband, until the time came for him to leave. But he had reckoned without Ruth.

"You're going off without me, Charles?"

"I'll be busy in Germany, and your place is here. Besides," he caressed her faintly bulging stomach, "you don't want to do anything to endanger our child."

The fact of her pregnancy persuaded Ruth against going to Europe, but Charles had no defence against her next demand.

"I am your wife, I am educated. My place is at your side and I will come to Nairobi when you get back."

On Charles's return, he found himself looking forward to seeing her again.

They made a home in a house that had been abandoned by whites in the Nairobi suburbs. It was too big for them and the bare rooms echoed with emptiness, but Ruth's needs were simple. Charles bought a settee and an armchair at an auction. He invested in a new gas cooker and found a second-hand fridge. Then he took her to choose a large double bed. It was good to have a soft full-bodied woman to sleep beside him and he looked forward to filling their home with children. When her time came she called her younger sister to help, and little Maria was born.

The second cycle safari rally was a resounding success. His benefactor again provided machines, and a sponsor from Norway donated a flight to Europe as first prize. Charles made the headlines on the back pages of the national dailies for two days running.

He received a telephone call.

"Is that Charles Omari Ondiek?"

"It is."

"I have seen your picture in the papers. I have something very important to tell you. I cannot discuss it on the phone but what I have to say concerns your future and the future of your family. Meet me in the café next to the Globe Cinema at lunch time today."

"Who are you?"

But the line went dead.

Who was this man – and how did he know the name Charles Omari Ondiek? Charles had dropped the Ondiek from his name years before, to distance himself from his father and put Mwangi off the track.

That intense voice over the crackling line had been vaguely familiar. Charles caught his breath. Could it have been Mwangi? Why had he been so blinded by pride and ambition? Why had he forgotten about the curse against his father and let himself be paraded in the papers for everyone to see?

He knew that Mwangi's curses could not affect him psychologically, but he wasn't so sure about Ruth.

It might not be Mwangi. It could be anyone from his past; it could be someone with genuine good news; maybe someone with knowledge of the ancestral cave? Charles knew he could not ignore the call.

He entered the café, ordered a cup of tea and took a seat in a corner facing the door. He was early. A group of young women came in, their hair in plaits straining against their skulls. They were teetering on high heels and wiggling their bottoms beneath tight mini-dresses. Charles allowed his mind to wander as he studied them.

A man wearing a driver's uniform took the seat opposite. He read the name on the pocket: 'National Museums of Kenya.' Could it be news from Jackson? He hadn't spoken to his brother for some time. Charles looked into black eyes that stared at him with intense hatred.

It was Mwangi.

He scraped his chair backwards.

"I want nothing to do with you," Charles said. "You cannot frighten me."

"You will regret this, Charles Omari Ondiek!"

But Charles walked out, paying for his bill as he went. He could not control the shaking in his body, and he could do no more work that day.

Two healthy daughters now filled their lives and Ruth was about to have their third child. Her sister lived with them, helping with the housework and the children. Charles tolerated her. Although he paid her a pittance, this was her only chance of a job.

He desperately wanted a boy.

The baby was late.

"That must be a good omen," said Ruth. "The others were early babies."

Her waters broke and Charles hurried her to the hospital, run by nuns in Nairobi's industrial area. His first two babies had been born there, and Ruth insisted on going back, even though the Nairobi Hospital was now more convenient for him and far better equipped.

It was a boy, and his joy was unbounded. He didn't know he could be so happy and proud. Charles couldn't wait to come back from the office every day to see his delightfully healthy little son, David.

But he could not hope to earn a good living from running the annual cycle safari. Now that he had a son he must face reality and find a steady income, for David must grow up to be proud of his father.

Charles applied for a vacancy as a reporter with his old newspaper, and it was like old times. He'd always thrived on the thrill of chasing after news, and after a few months, proved his worth in the office.

He returned home to tell Ruth of his promotion to sub-editor, but found her sister wailing loudly in the sitting room. His two daughters were hiding behind the sofa. Charles marched into David's room. Ruth sat on the bed holding the baby at arm's length, her face frozen in shock.

Charles moved forward to take David. The child hung limp in his hands. He looked down; the eyes were glazed and lifeless. He held David close but there was no response. He went to the cot and laid him gently on the mattress, then turned to Ruth.

"What happened?"

She was in a trance.

Charles went again to the cot. It was David, but it was not his David. How had this happened? How could his baby die – his son, his life? He returned to the sitting room. The ululating irritated him but there was no way he could stop it, or get any sense out of the girl. He went back to Ruth and put his arm round her shoulders.

"Please tell me what happened. I beg you…"

Gradually, she relaxed.

"I came to pick him up from his afternoon sleep," she said. "And he was – all floppy."

She looked up at him in terror and breaking from his arms, ran to cower in a corner of the room.

Charles telephoned the doctor.

It was a cot death. What was a cot death? He'd never heard of it before. Why had it happened? There'd been nothing wrong with the baby. He tried to control his anger, but Ruth avoided him. She blamed herself, and he couldn't convince her that his rage was not directed at her. Who was it directed at? He didn't know. He didn't know what to do with himself. He rang his editor.

"Are you going to have a memorial service, Charles?"

Charles had not thought beyond the moment.

"We'd like to arrange it for you, if you will let us. We'll put an ad in the paper. I know it's difficult for you but please give us a picture to go with it."

He sat in the front pew of the Cathedral with Ruth at his side while the two girls fidgeted with the hymnbooks. Silent tears dripped down his cheeks.

The service was solemn and moving, and the support and sympathy of their friends overwhelming. As he and Ruth came down the aisle during the final hymn, a soprano voice soared above the rest. He looked to his left. Caroline, one of only three or four whites in the congregation, was singing her heart out, with Jackson beside her.

"You have a beautiful voice, Caroline," he whispered in her ear as she threw her arms round his neck outside the church. He introduced her to Ruth, and then turned to greet Jackson.

They went to his ancestral home for the burial and the

226

village dissolved into a frenzy of mourning and weeping for several days. When the time came to go back to work, Ruth insisted on staying there with the children.

"It will only be for a while," she said.

He wondered. Something had died between them.

Charles immersed himself in the office and spent long hours in the bars and restaurants of Nairobi, delaying his return to an empty house. He told himself he was gathering material for the paper and some nights he didn't even go home. David's death continued to haunt him.

He met Jackson for a meal in town and remembered Caroline's presence at the funeral.

"I see her from time to time," said Jackson. "She's interested in pre-history. I told her about David, which is why we came to the memorial service together."

"What's she doing?"

"I think she's working as a secretary somewhere. She often brings her son to the museum and meets with a friend who works in the entomology department as a technician." Jackson paused. "Her name is Teresa."

Charles gaped at Jackson in disbelief, but his brother nodded.

Did he want to find Teresa again? His life had changed so much.

"Please don't tell her of your connection with me, Jackson. I need time to think."

But mention of the museum reminded him of Mwangi.

"Do you have a Kikuyu named Mwangi working at the museum?"

Jackson shook his head. "I don't know – it's a common name."

"He's a driver."

"I'll find out if you like. Why?"

Charles shook his head, half ashamed of his thoughts.

"It's of no importance. But if you can let me know…"

Did Mwangi's curse have something to do with David's death? He told himself it was psychological nonsense but the more he thought of it, the less certain he became.

Simaloi would know the truth. Ashamed of himself for the thought, he resolved to go up-country to see how Ruth and the children were doing.

The sorceress dropped the large bundle of sticks suspended from her forehead when Charles arrived. She showed her grief and sympathy with gentle ululations, and the rest of the family crowded close, their voices raised in empathetic chorus. It was good to be surrounded by relatives at such a time. He could understand Ruth's insistence on staying at home, but he hoped to persuade her to come back to Nairobi.

He told Simaloi about Mwangi's threat. She lowered her head when he asked if there might be a connection with David's death, and promised to look at the omens.

"I will have an answer when you return from your visit to Ruth," she said. "My mother exposed his first curse and I helped her prolong *Mzee* Ondiek's life, but Mwangi's magic is powerful. I will do what I can."

Charles drove to Kisumu, on the shores of Lake Victoria. Its vast waters stretched towards an endless horizon. His daughters greeted him with delight, scrambling round him and reaching for the presents he had brought. Ruth's mother emerged from her hut.

"She is still unwell."

Charles entered the dark interior, his eyes taking time to adjust to the smoky gloom. A figure huddled beneath a blanket on a wooden bed, half-visible behind a drab curtain.

"Ruth?"

She moaned. He approached the bed and leaned over, but she curled into a ball, rolling away from his touch. This annoyed him.

"Look at me!"

Obediently she turned over and sat on the edge of the bed. She was so thin. He took her arm to pull her up, and led her to the light of the door. Her skin had a greyish tinge and her eyes were dull.

"What's the matter with you?"

Her mother came forward. "She is still grieving."

"What – after all these months?"

"It takes time."

Perhaps it was time she came home. But she looked in no fit state to carry on as a proud mother and wife of a successful editor. He stayed for a few days. Would he ever be able to coax her back into his world? And, more importantly, she cringed away from any thought of him as a husband.

"It is better she remains here," said her mother. "We'll look after the children and when she is well enough, we'll call you."

He visited Simaloi on his way back to Nairobi.

"The curse is still there," she told him. "It was as you said. It has transferred to you and Teresa."

"Teresa?"

"Yes, that white girl Mwangi wanted to kill and use for the Mau Mau oath against her father. Mwangi is full of hatred – I can see it in the signs. But it is Teresa who is in immediate danger. You should have listened to what he had to say. Maybe you should meet him before you become a target? I don't know if my magic is strong enough to help you."

Charles returned to Nairobi. David had died mysteriously of course, but the doctor had made his scientific diagnosis. And Ruth was only grieving, even though her recovery was far too long. Charles surprised himself for taking all this superstition seriously. That's what came of having a witch for a sister – but to be on the safe side he would avoid any connection with Teresa.

He shut up his house, moved into a flat in town and immersed himself in the frenzy of the newspaper world.

He met Jackson in town from time to time, to keep up with

family news. His brother's wife had a fourth daughter and Charles commiserated with him.

"What has happened to our family that we aren't able to produce sons?"

"I know," replied Jackson. "By the way, there is driver named Mwangi at the museum, but he's left head office to work at one of the regional offices. Want me to find out for you?"

"Don't worry. It's not important."

CHAPTER 20

Caroline turned the car into the school gates. It wrenched her heart to leave Paul there every morning; he was ten years old, and she hardly knew him. But she understood his enthusiasm about their visits to the museum. As he grew further away from her, she was wasting her life on monotonous office work. Why labour to pay for an education that her son did not enjoy? It made no sense.

"How would you like me to teach you at home, Paul?"

"Would that mean I don't have to go to school?"

"Yes". Her motherly instinct made her pull back from complete irresponsibility. "For the time being, anyway."

"I'd like that, Mummy. I hate my teacher, she's so fierce, and always gives me bad marks."

"I might be just as strict, you never know."

Caroline stopped the car and reached into the back seat for his school bag.

"Did you remember to put in your tackies?"

"No. But I don't like running. I always come last."

"What happens if you don't have them?"

"I have to sit on the side with my friend. I don't mind, we always do that."

"No wonder your teacher gets cross with you."

She watched him join his friends, his sturdy figure dwarfed in the crowd. His sun-bleached hair was sticking up in tight curls over his head, like his father's. He had Brian's nose, too. But he didn't share their interest in sport. Although he seemed to have ability, he didn't like the competition. Class work was

231

not difficult for him, although she knew he only tried his hardest for the teachers he liked.

Another thought drifted through her mind, but she put it to one side, to be mulled over and allowed to mature in its own time.

She wrote off to the United States and studied some brochures, and then ordered sample home tuition papers. They were easy enough to follow. The idea of having Paul at home, even if only for a couple of years before going to secondary school, might be worth pursuing.

"Are you still interested in letting me teach you instead of going to school, Paul?" she asked as the end of term drew near.

He hesitated. "Can my friend come too?"

"I don't think his Mummy will want him to give up school. Shall we try it next term, and see how we get on?"

It was a relief not having to worry about school fees, and a delight to walk away from the drudgery of office routine, but she knew that lack of playmates would be a problem for Paul. She invited children to spend afternoons with him, but it was not possible to organise company every day. However, he progressed well under her individual tutelage, and at the end of term wanted to continue the experiment.

But Paul missed his friends.

"Why can't Sam come and have lessons with me?" he asked. "He doesn't go to school. He told me he just plays with his friends."

Caroline smiled. He had voiced her innermost thoughts. She knew Teresa couldn't afford to send Sam to school. That boy deserved better than to spend his life with deprived children. But she would have to choose her moment.

The four of them met at the museum most Saturday mornings, and Teresa knew about her schooling experiment with Paul. Caroline encouraged him to talk about his lessons, and then she sat with Teresa, watching the boys play on the lawn.

"I wonder if you'd let me take Sam as well?" she asked. "Paul misses his friends and it would certainly be easier for me to have two to teach instead of one."

Teresa shook her head. "I teach Sam on my off days, and I have an arrangement with the neighbour when I'm working."

"But Paul needs someone to match himself with, and the boys are so good together. Perhaps we could try it for a couple of months?"

"I don't want to take advantage of you, nor do I want Sam to start something which gives him ideas. I'm serious, Caroline. I can't afford to give him the same chances as Paul. That's why I'm not entirely happy about their friendship. Why do you think I've never asked you home?"

Caroline didn't know what to say. She had never been to the notorious Mathare Valley slums, which were sandwiched between the poor area next to the museum, and the wealthy suburb of Muthaiga. But she had often travelled the road past Wilson Airport, which overlooked the Kibera slums on the other side of the city. The monotonous expanse of rusted iron roofs was a shameful sight beyond the sparkling waters of the Nairobi Dam, where sailors raced their dinghies at weekends.

Once, she had rescued Onyango from the police station there, bailing him out when he was charged with being drunk and disorderly. The narrow tracks between tin shacks were littered with paper and plastic, and the open drains exuded a noxious slime. She'd wound up the windows of her car against the foul odour, shielding herself from the mothers and babies who grovelled in the filth and gawped at her as she drove past.

"I don't want to upset you," was all she said.

Paul and Sam were racing between the bougainvillea bushes, bumping into each other and shouting as they tumbled to the ground. They rolled in a mad mingle of arms and legs down the terraced lawns, gathering dirt and grass clippings on their clothes and in their hair. They were a joy to watch. Paul had a healthy tan, which on a closer look revealed a mass of freckles joined together; Sam was light brown, and his hair black and crinkled.

Teresa sighed.

"I confess that I am ashamed of our room in the city slums where my white skin sticks out like a sore thumb; that's why I cover myself in a *kitenge,* so only my face and hands show. But Sam blends in better than he would in your world. You'd be surprised at the number of children there are like him. What would your paying guests think if you had a half-caste in your house, sharing lessons with Paul?"

"If it bothers them, they can go find somewhere else to live!" Caroline snorted. "The children don't see colour – look for yourself; and neither do I. You know that, Teresa."

"It's not only that."

"I know. You're worried about money. But why deny him? Why not give him this opportunity, especially when it will be so beneficial to everyone? And nobody can ever tell what's going to happen in the future, I can assure you of that."

Caroline thought of Sam's father. Had Jackson told Charles that Teresa was working at the museum? But he probably didn't even know there was a connection. It wasn't fair, a boy needed a father; both boys needed fathers. Perhaps that was why they got on so well together; they were kindred spirits.

"There's no hurry," she said. "Why don't you think about it?"

Her landlord sent Caroline a formal notification the following month. He was going to put up the rent. She didn't blame him, as accommodation was at a premium in Nairobi, but she did not know how she would survive.

A wind of change was in the air.

Boney decided to give his farm back to the government, and take compensation offered by the British for the improvements he had made. Most of his neighbours had left the country, and he told Caroline he was too old to stay battling against the odds when his workers were anxious to take over.

"Let them have it," he said. "They will form a co-operative, and carve up my rolling acres of wheat and barley into small holdings; but it's what they want, and I am now too tired to care."

He retired to a plot on the south coast, taking Ethel with him.

Caroline had to think seriously about her future. She wanted to stay in Kenya, she knew Nairobi, and had made many friends. But her chances of finding a husband were small. It would make sense to own a property instead of paying rent. Many people were leaving Kenya, so it would be the right time to buy.

She took Paul to the coast for a long weekend, to discuss the matter with Boney. He was an outcast from those expatriates who were reconciled to being governed by Africans, and yet unable to condone a mixed relationship. But he and Ethel were content in their tiny shed among the bananas. They sat outside on deckchairs, watching the sea glisten through the casuarina trees. He supported her idea, but couldn't help her financially.

"I need to build ourselves a proper house," he told her. "You never know, you might be pleased to inherit it one day."

Brian's Uncle Ed offered to advance part of Paul's inheritance, and Caroline wrote to Guy and Angela Clayton, now in South Africa. They tried to persuade her to go and live near them, but when she told them that her heart and life belonged to Kenya, they promised their support.

If she bought a large property, she could take in more paying guests.

Caroline negotiated a temporary extension of her lease, and scanned the *For Sale* columns in the newspapers. She registered with several estate agents, and asked Teresa to come with her round several large houses for sale. But they were too

235

expensive, and her extended lease was nearly up.

An agent rang her one afternoon. A new property had come on the market, which would be ideal for her purposes. She didn't even want to view it. Tin roofs had never appealed to her, and two and a half acres of land was excessive. But the agent insisted.

"Just go along and take a look," he said. "You don't have to buy it."

She nearly turned back at the sight of the hideous building. The rough plastered walls were splashed with red soil marks above the flowerbeds, and the roof needed several coats of paint. A makeshift piece of corrugated iron supported by two rickety poles hung over the front porch, and the garden was knee-high in grass.

However, the inside had been recently decorated. This did not disguise the cracks, which Caroline studied avidly. The ceilings were free of leak marks, and she saw evidence of termite treatment on the floorboards. She called in an architect friend who confirmed the stability of the house, and a paying guest climbed into the attic with his penknife to prod the beams and declare that there was no rot.

At least three lodgers could be accommodated in the main house, and a self-contained guest wing, complete with kitchenette, would be suitable for a couple. A dilapidated guesthouse built of corrugated iron hid in the tall grass at the back, but she ignored it.

The owner was in India, and anxious to get rid of this millstone. The price was within her range and the area reasonably safe. Sub-division would even be possible, should the acreage prove too much for her.

Caroline sought advice from friends in the city and persuaded the estate agent to keep other wolves from the trail, while she struggled towards a decision.

Then she applied for a loan.

"Sorry, but we don't issue loans on houses with corrugated

iron roofs."

Forgetting her previous dislike, she exploded in a fit of righteous indignation. The financier listened sympathetically and even ventured to agree with her, but the answer was the same.

Brian's Uncle Ed came up to Nairobi.

"I can pay the deposit," she said to him, thinking of Brian's life insurance money.

After conferring, juggling with inheritance shares and rewriting their wills, Uncle Ed and the Claytons were able to cover the balance between them.

Meanwhile, Caroline had to move out of the rented house. She gave notice to her paying guests and took Paul to stay with Uncle Ed on Mombasa Island. She tried to make him do two hours of lessons a day, but he rebelled.

"I promise I'll work especially hard to catch up. Besides, you need a rest, Mummy."

He said it with such earnestness that Caroline had to laugh. He was growing up – so protective of her in some ways and yet transparently boyish in others. She relented, and lessons were abandoned. It was good to relax in the enervating heat of the coast and store up energy for what she knew would be a stressful time.

Teresa helped her to move.

Her reserves had dwindled. The money she saved from paying rent went straight out again.

She immediately removed the ugly piece of corrugated iron from the porch.

But when the rains came, she realised why it had been placed there. At every downpour, water streamed over the veranda wall, saturating the floorboards and creeping under the front door. Determined not to replace the monstrosity, Caroline examined the guttering and used some sticky black paste to gum up the holes. But while the line of grevillia trees along the side of the house shed leaves over the roof, the gutters did not stand a chance. Moreover, the trees blocked the light from four bedroom windows.

There were two other problem trees in the garden. One undermined the floor of the back veranda, and the second stood dangerously close to the garage.

It was amazing how news travelled. Hardly had Caroline conceived the idea of doing away with the trees, when she was inundated by calls from local contractors. They all professed to know how to go about the job and had wildly differing ideas about price. However, one man spent time explaining to her the problem of the overhead wires, and he hesitated at the proximity of the house to the giant that had lifted the floor.

Caroline fell for his story and gave him the contract. After five minutes' haggling, he dropped his price by a third, but even then she was ashamed to tell Teresa what had been agreed.

Every two days she visited the bank for cash advances, and each afternoon she surveyed the work and discussed plans for the morrow.

After a fortnight of incessant noise from chain saws, there were two enormous piles of firewood on the lawn and wood chippings everywhere. Caroline had not thought about this bonus, but naturally assumed that the firewood was her property. It would be very useful for heating their bathwater in the outside boiler.

She soon learned, however, that the contractor quite definitely knew that it belonged to him.

Rather than be drawn into an argument, she waited while he packed up for the day and then went to the kitchen.

"Onyango, do you want some *kuni*?"

"Yes, Memsahib."

"Well, if we're quick, we'll have enough wood for everyone, and you can take the thin bits for a fence round that patch I've given you for your *shamba*."

Onyango entered into the conspiracy and Caroline called

the gardeners to hide a pile of firewood in her garage. She kept out of the way when the contractor returned with a lorry the following morning and watched through the dining room window while Onyango talked to him.

Paul sat at the table, doing arithmetic exercises. Teresa had left Sam with them while she used Caroline's van to take home a load of firewood. Out of the corner of her eye, Caroline watched Sam look over Paul's shoulder and then sit beside him. The boys conferred together over the problems. She looked out another exercise.

"Here, Sam, I'll give you some sums to do on your own."

She sat him at the opposite end of the table and went back to the window.

The argument between Onyango and the contractor was in full spate, with both men gesticulating urgently. Onyango turned away, but the contractor called him back.

Finally, the men loaded the lorry and disappeared down the driveway.

"Quick, Memsahib!" Onyango called to her. "We must hide some more before he gets back. I've told him he can take whatever we leave behind, and everything must be cleared before the end of the day."

She called the gardeners, who set to with a will, and Teresa went home with a second load.

It was almost six months since she had moved in. The painting of the peeling roof had been her first priority and it still held that position.

She had only been able to give Paul a few hours of lessons each day, and the entrance exam to secondary school loomed.

Teresa often left Sam, who shared Paul's lessons, while she went out on errands for Caroline. Nothing had been said between them, but surely Teresa was not oblivious to what was happening?

Caroline broached the subject again, and the boys helped

wear down Teresa's resistance.

"You can try it for a term," she said. "Don't think I'm ungrateful, but I'm not promising anything."

"You won't regret it," guaranteed Caroline. "But," she warned the boys, "I'm going to draw up strict time tables."

A healthy rivalry developed between them. She took them to the museum, visiting a different gallery each week, and setting exercises on what they had seen. Sam was enthralled by the pre-history gallery with its *Turkana Boy*, a *Homo Erectus* skeleton found by Kamoya Kimeu in the northern district. He would also gaze in awe at the life-sized cave paintings at the entrance to the gallery.

Caroline stood beside him. "Wouldn't it be wonderful if one day we could help discover something like that – and be part of Kenya's history?"

"I'd like that," said Sam. "I'm going to work in the museum, like Mum, when I grow up."

Paul preferred the upstairs gallery, losing himself in wonder at the array of stuffed birds in the beautifully presented showcases.

With Sam having regular lessons, Teresa was able to work full time at the museum, and bought herself a second-hand car. But she never stayed on when picking him up. This insistence on preserving her lowly status irritated Caroline.

One day she demanded that Teresa stay for tea.

"I want to show you something."

"What?"

She led Teresa into the back garden. "I've only recently taken notice of this shack. What do you think I can do about it?"

They regarded the ugly wood and iron building, struggling for space in the long grass between two overgrown fir trees. Faint traces of red could be seen on the roof, and faded green paint was peeling off the corrugated walls in giant flakes.

"It's quite an eyesore, isn't it?"

"Shall we have a look inside? I'll get the key."

The door grated against the concrete floor. There were two bedrooms, and a primitive bathroom with dripping taps. Caroline opened a kitchen cupboard, and cockroaches scuttled into the corner. She stepped outside, brushing cobwebs from her clothes, and reached up to remove a spider from Teresa's hair.

"What do you think?"

"You shouldn't have any difficulty letting it. It's dry, and spacious. With a good clean up and a coat of white paint it could be made quite respectable, especially if you cut the grass and planted flowers."

"Would you like to do it?"

"Me?" said Teresa. "What do you mean?"

"I haven't the time, or the energy anymore," said Caroline. "Would you do it for me? I'll pay for the fixtures."

"How...?"

"I mean, Teresa, would you like to do up this cottage, and come and live here with Sam in return for the improvements?"

Caroline held her breath. She had been as sensitive as she could. She turned away as she glimpsed a tear in the corner of Teresa's eye.

"I must go and check on the boys," she called over her shoulder.

The more she thought about it, the more enthusiastic Caroline became at the prospect of doing up the shack, and putting it on the market. Cheap accommodation was at a premium in Nairobi, and the rent money could go into savings for Paul's secondary education.

She told a gardener to slash the long grass round the building, and gave him a wire brush to scrape the old paint off its outside walls.

Teresa came to collect Sam, and Caroline saw her take

241

notice of the activity. She leaned through the car window.

"The offer still stands, if you want it," she said. "But I can't afford to wait indefinitely."

She held Teresa's eyes, realising she had unwittingly forced her friend into a corner. Teresa smiled, acknowledging the manoeuvre.

"Are you sure?"

Caroline nodded, laughing.

"But I refuse to let you spend any money on it, Caroline," she insisted. "I have my contacts, and I'll pay for everything."

"All right, when are you going to start?"

The shack was transformed into airy white rooms. The concrete floors, painted red, were tastefully covered with local rugs, woven in varying shades of cream and brown, and although the warped window frames would not close properly, they were adorned with bright black and yellow curtains.

It was like old times. Caroline visited Teresa every evening for a chat. She tried to renew the intimacies of their childhood, and talked of finding a couple of horses, so they could ride together again. She even suggested they went to the races. But Teresa did not miss the horses. She had blotted out that part of her life.

"Teaching the children is an admirable thing to do, and you're very good at it, Caroline," Teresa said. "But I know that you don't feel entirely fulfilled. Why don't you join the Museum Society? They're always looking for volunteers."

At first, Caroline helped in the office, and then she became involved with the Council and the awarding of educational grants to students. The Know Kenya Course loomed, and she organised speakers and processed applications from the participants. It was more rewarding than her previous life of taking dictation and typing letters.

She regretted not fulfilling her academic potential, although she wouldn't admit this to others. If she had gone to Oxford, she would never have married Brian, and would not have had Paul. How could she want to wish him away? But her brain was deteriorating through lack of use, and her desires to play a part in developing Africa seemed an impossible dream.

"I think I'll go on the Know Kenya Course, and do the extra Guide's course," she told Teresa. "At least then I will be able to become a Museum Guide."

But there were no places left, so she enrolled for the following year.

Teresa showed her round the Entomology Department, where trays of dead insects were stored in drawers. But Caroline's favourite gallery was pre-history, and she renewed her friendship with Jackson, who worked under Richard Leakey's wife, Maeve. He must harbour many secrets, including those in Charles's ancestral cave, she thought. How wonderful it would be if she could help to expose some treasures for the good of Kenya.

She was talking with Jackson one day, when Teresa passed by.

"You know each other, don't you? Teresa and I were at school together," announced Caroline. "We lost each other for years, and now we're sharing a home with our sons."

Caroline felt a warning nudge in her ribs. Teresa politely acknowledged Jackson, and then turned away. She wondered if Teresa were aware of his connection with Charles. Caroline had promised not to reveal the secret of Sam's father, but the truth was bound to come out one day, and she thought this would be a good thing. Sam needed a father, and Charles did not even know he had a son. She'd felt so sad for him at the loss of his baby.

"How is Charles?" she asked Jackson. "It must be several years since the funeral."

"Yes – that was a strange business… I'm afraid things aren't going well for him personally; his wife left him, you know. She took the girls back to her home village."

"I'm so sorry."

"He's business editor for the newspaper, but is being haunted by ghosts from the past." Jackson paused. "Did you enjoy working on his magazine?"

"I did. I learned so much, and it was great being part of developing Africa. But I couldn't afford to stay. Talking about the past, you remember my asking you about your ancestral cave?"

Jackson gave her a wry look. "I do, but it isn't my secret to reveal, nor is it the time."

Caroline had to be content with that, but she liked Jackson, and went to him whenever she had a query about the pre-history gallery. She looked forward to the next Know Kenya Course.

CHAPTER 21

Sam and Paul had wandered away towards the river. Their latest game was to test each other by identifying the trees using the Latin names, before looking at the plaques for confirmation. They had grown into gangling youngsters, and were in their first term at the local Catholic school for boys.

Caroline had persuaded Teresa to let the school take Sam free of charge.

She saw the boys disappear into the snake park. Paul was fascinated by the reptiles, and liked to watch them being milked of venom. The snake pit was well protected, and the more poisonous ones were behind glass panels, but the boys sometimes distracted the wardens from their tasks and there had been complaints.

A museum van drew up on the driveway behind them. She glanced over her shoulder, to see Jackson. Another car turned into the parking lot, and Charles stepped out. Caroline sucked in her breath. Teresa sat beside her, shielded behind a bush, but the men were only a few yards away.

"Where is he?" Charles's voice carried clearly down the slope. Caroline looked at Teresa, who was staring at the entrance to the snake park. She got up and pushed her bare feet into flip-flops.

"I'm going to make sure the boys aren't interfering with the attendants again," she said. "I won't be long."

"He's in that van," Jackson was saying. "He has to start back to Isiolo before dark. Do you want me to wait for you?"

"Don't worry, I won't be long. Thanks for finding him for

me."

Caroline watched Teresa approach the snake park. Her friend was swathed in a *kitenge*, with a bright scarf entwined round her hair. Nobody would recognise her unless they looked directly at her face, which was so brown, she could be mistaken for an Indian.

She half-turned, meaning to wave a greeting to Charles, but he addressed a driver in museum uniform who had emerged from the van.

"Well? I've found you again, and I want you to explain yourself! Why did you contact me?"

"It is not me who has to do the explaining."

The tones were loud and insolent. The years fell away, and Caroline remembered Teresa's fear. It was Mwangi.

"*Sikia,* listen to me. Your people have caused me much anguish, your father spoilt my oath, and I cannot know peace until I get rid of the family of that man Myers."

"That is absurd," said Charles. "It was years ago. Myers has left the country, and you're still alive, so the Mau Mau oath has not killed you."

"But I have suffered. You don't know what happened in the detention camps, when the prison officers beat us mercilessly, trying to make us work, until we went mad with pain. All the *wazungu* are evil. They must be wiped from Kenya, especially those with connection to the prisons, like your friend Caroline."

She started at the mention of her name.

"What's Caroline got to do with it?"

"Her boyfriend was responsible for the beatings. Why don't you ask her? But my magic is strong. I have forced them apart. She will never find another husband, and her man will lose his wife and his children."

Caroline cowered into the shadow of the bush. What was all that about? How did Mwangi know of her affair with Michael?

"What's all this got to do with me?" asked Charles.

"You are still under my curse. Your baby son has died. That white woman of yours escaped once, but she will be my next victim. Many things will happen before I have finished, which will affect you deeply; you can do nothing about it."

"I won't listen to you. You're just trying to frighten me. This is all nonsense."

Charles marched to his car and slammed the door, spinning the wheels on the gravel as he reversed.

Mwangi stood on the grass verge, looking towards the snake park. Caroline saw Teresa emerge from the entrance. The boys broke from her and ran towards the river. She looked up towards Caroline and her eyes found Mwangi's. Caroline watched as Teresa stood, transfixed, and then started walking slowly up the slope. As she came nearer, Caroline saw the fear in her eyes. She was like a hypnotised rabbit under the spell of a fox. Mwangi stared at her, unrelenting.

"You can't escape me now," he hissed, then turned, including Caroline with an offhand inclination of his head, and drove away.

Teresa did not move.

Caroline cleared her throat. She stood up and put her arm round Teresa.

"You don't believe in that nonsense, do you?"

Teresa shuddered. "That man is evil and I can't escape him."

"Of course you can. You have so far. Come, let's buy the boys an ice cream."

Teresa did not move.

"So far... Caroline, I know my days are numbered."

"Nonsense! Everyone's days are numbered. You're no more special in that department than I am!"

"It's Sam I'm worried about."

"Now you're being ridiculous."

Caroline took her by the hand and led her towards the ice cream van. The boys appeared and enjoyed the treat. But

Teresa remained subdued, and Caroline could not help wondering about Michael. She'd heard that he'd retired from the civil service, received his Golden Handshake from the British Government, and gone to live with his wife in London. Despite their being so close, he had not told her anything about his previous life.

Teresa fell ill. It was a virus, the doctor said, but the effects remained. She became so weak that she stayed in bed for days on end, and had to give up her job at the museum. She showed no interest in food, and when Caroline suggested that at least she could take the boys to school, Teresa shrugged her away.

"I haven't the strength to drive anymore."

"Why don't you come with me, then?"

"Leave me alone. I know I'm going to die. It's better this way. If I die, perhaps the curse will be fulfilled and Sam will be safe."

Caroline knew better than to dismiss Teresa's fears. The proof of Mwangi's hold on her was before her eyes. Her friend's life faded. Teresa refused to go to hospital and nothing Caroline could do or say made any difference.

Caroline insisted that she let the doctor perform tests, but the results were inconclusive, and without admitting her to hospital, all he could do was prescribe plenty of liquid.

"I've seen this happen before to Africans," he told her. "Once they lose the will to live, there is nothing anybody can do, but it's usually the result of a witchdoctor's curse. I've only had it happen to elderly Europeans before, who've lost a loved one and have nothing more to live for. Is there something troubling her?"

Caroline saw no point in enlightening him; it was too complicated and far-fetched.

She watched as Teresa crept out of bed and stumbled towards the bathroom. The flesh fell in loose folds from her body and her limbs stuck out at ungainly angles under the flimsy nightdress.

"Would you like me to call the priest?" she asked.

"No! I'm not that far gone, yet."

Sam lay on his bed in his room, studying. He got up to take Teresa's arm, but she shrugged him off.

"I'm only going to the bathroom," she said with a faint smile. "I can still manage that."

Caroline hadn't seen her smile for months. Perhaps her suggestion to call the priest had done some good.

Sam went back to his books. This environment wasn't healthy for the boy. He had matured considerably over the past months and spent most of the time with his mother. Unless Teresa pulled herself together, she would soon need more intimate care.

The holidays came and went. Caroline noticed that Sam did the washing on his return from school in the evenings. Overnight, the line was full of sheets and underwear. In the mornings before going to school, he would take it all in. Did he think that nobody knew?

Teresa lay curled up in bed facing the wall, when Caroline opened her door.

"What's happening is just not fair on Sam!" she announced. "Do you realise what you're doing to him?"

There was no response from the bed, so Caroline placed a hand on Teresa's shoulder. It was pathetically easy to turn her over. A tear dribbled down her cheek.

"I know." The whisper was so soft that Caroline had to lean down. "It will be better for him when I'm gone."

Caroline chose to ignore that remark.

"I've had to employ another girl," she said. "The workload is getting too heavy for Onyango and I haven't the heart to retire him. Leah's been doing the laundry and general cleaning, but there isn't enough for her to do every day. She can take over your washing."

"I can't let you do that for me, as well as everything else."
Teresa's voice became suddenly stronger.

"I watch Sam struggle with your washing every evening. It's
not good for the boy. He needs a break. Besides, Paul is
missing his company."

Teresa turned back to the wall.

"Let's try it, shall we? I'll tell Leah to come round
tomorrow."

Teresa made no further objection, and before long, Leah
spent most of her time in the cottage.

Caroline noticed bags under Sam's eyes, although the boy
never complained.

"Your mother needs continuous nursing now, Sam. It's more
than you can do."

"I know, Caroline. I've been worried about her. But I am so
clumsy, I just don't know what to do half the time."

"I could easily find a night nurse for her, but she would
need your room. Why don't you move into the main house?
Paul would love to have his old friend back again."

Sam brightened. "I know, and my studies aren't going well
either."

"That's settled, then. I'll find a nurse and you can move out
at the weekend."

The bags disappeared from under Sam's eyes, but Teresa took
another downward plunge. It seemed that all hope had gone.
Now that her son no longer lived with her, she would not even
acknowledge him.

One afternoon, Leah tapped on Caroline's door.

"I think you'd better come, Memsahib."

Teresa lay with her eyes closed. A foul stench invaded the
room. Caroline opened the window, and sat on the bed.

"You'll look after Sam for me, won't you, Caroline?"

The voice was croaky, but surprisingly loud.

"Of course I will, you know that."

"I want you to be his guardian. Please keep him safe for me, safe…from…the curse."

Caroline tried to coax her back to life, but it was fruitless. She called the priest, who said the last rites.

He left, and the front door squeaked as he tried to pull it behind him.

Caroline drew a chair beside the bed; she laid a hand on the counterpane. Teresa lay on her back, eyes closed, breath coming in barely perceptible gasps. Her face was taut and strained.

Then her eyes popped open, wide with fright. Teresa stared past Caroline's shoulder. She half rose in the bed, tangled hair wild about her face, and her mouth opened in a silent scream.

Caroline heard a faint squeak, and a whiff of warm air brushed her arm.

She placed a hand on Teresa's skeletal shoulder, and gently pushed her back into the pillow. But the head was perched forward, rigid in the intensity of its concentration.

"It's him. He's come to get me!"

There was no movement in the face before her. Had she imagined the words?

"Please, Teresa. You'll soon be safe. Trust me!"

Had she said that – or was it a silent prayer?

Her arm felt hot, and Teresa's eyes were focussing nearer and nearer.

Caroline refused to look behind her. She closed her eyes in frantic prayer and forced herself to press gently against Teresa's forehead.

"He can't touch you."

The presence behind her shifted, and Teresa's head fell away from her hand.

Caroline thought she heard the door squeak. Her arm was cool again. But her heart thumped madly. She broke into a sweat, and couldn't control the shaking in her body. It was an age before she calmed down. Could she dare to open her eyes?

Teresa lay against the pillow, yet it was not Teresa. The face had relaxed into a blank vacancy. Caroline closed the lids and gently pulled up the sheet.

She thought she was prepared for Teresa's death. After all, what could be worse than losing a husband? But she had been affected by the death of Charles's baby, even though she hadn't known it when alive.

Now, sitting in the pew beside Sam and Paul with the coffin before her, listening to the prayers, she felt herself losing control. The boys wept beside her. This beginning of the process of healing was a blessed purging.

Caroline met the eyes of the friends who came to shake hands, or offer a hug. Each connection made it easier to bear the grief. In the privacy of the car on the way home, she put her arm round Sam.

"It's all right," she said. "Teresa's at peace, now. She is where she wanted to be. Wasn't the service lovely?"

Teresa had ended her life as a very private woman, how different from the successful racehorse trainer of her younger years.

That evening, Caroline talked about Teresa's racing successes and their rides together on the farm. She saw Sam's eyes widen. He had never known of this side of his mother's life. She could see the questions forming in his mind and wondered how she would answer them. But for now, the grieving must take its course. It would be a long journey for Sam, and she was grateful that her own experience would help her ease him through it.

But she could not banish from her mind the sensation of Mwangi's presence.

PART IV

1978 – 1982

Daniel arap Moi, a member of the Kalenjin tribal community, was Vice President of Kenya from 1967. He succeeded Jomo Kenyatta as President in 1978. The attempted coup of 1982 originated from army barracks in Langata, near Nairobi, and was quickly smothered by the Government.

CHAPTER 22

Jomo Kenyatta was dead.

Caroline listened to the announcement on Voice of Kenya radio at lunchtime on Wednesday 22rd August, 1978.

The President of Kenya had died in his sleep at State House, Mombasa, at 3.30am the day before. At midnight the Attorney General in London at the time, flew to Mombasa in a Royal Air Force plane. The body was taken to Nairobi and Daniel arap Moi sworn in as President of the Republic of Kenya, before the nation could take a breath.

Caroline drove to Westlands shopping centre, which was heaving with subdued activity. People hurried along the pavements, bearing loaves of bread and tetra packs of milk. Cars formed long queues at petrol stations, jamming the streets. Customers crammed the supermarket. She stood behind a large Indian lady waiting to be served, when she felt a tap on her shoulder. It was Charles.

"This is amazing," she exclaimed. "Has everyone gone mad?"

"Haven't you heard that Kenyatta has died?"

"Yes. I caught it on the two o'clock news. I only came to buy some lip salve for Paul and Sam who're off on safari tomorrow. I suppose they'll still go," she glanced round at the static queue. "I think I'll try the chemist instead."

She extracted herself and Charles strode alongside.

"Sam? Is he a friend of Paul's, or do you have two sons now?"

Caroline stopped. "You don't know…"

"Know what?"

They came to the chemist, but it was closed.

"Look – this café is empty. Let's sit here and have a coffee," she said.

Charles hesitated. "I'm on duty, and exciting things are happening."

"You can observe from the café, and we haven't seen each other for ages, Charles. Besides, I've something to tell you."

"Five minutes. Then I must go back into town."

They ordered a coffee each.

"I don't know how to say this, Charles," she paused. "D'you remember Teresa?"

"Teresa?" Charles took a sip of his coffee. "I must confess, I haven't thought of her for a while. Why?"

"She died, two years ago."

He put his cup down, splashing liquid onto the saucer.

Caroline placed a hand on his arm.

"So you finally found her…"

"Yes."

"What happened?"

"She just faded away."

"Mwangi?"

Caroline inclined her head.

"That's what happened to my father…" Charles's voice cracked.

"I know, Charles. Mwangi haunted Teresa. He preyed on her like a – I don't know what – like a cat hypnotising a mouse. Her end was awful. I don't want to think about it."

Caroline shook herself. Many months had passed since she'd let herself remember the circumstances of Teresa's death. But it was about time Charles knew, and she had already said too much to stop now. She looked up. Two youths were running through the market stalls on the other side of the street, pursued by an angry *askari*.

What a time to choose for life-changing revelations.

Charles finished his coffee and leaned over to pick up his camera, his eyes on the upturned baskets the youths had left in their wake. Oranges, mangoes and tomatoes were rolling everywhere, and the outraged shouts of gesticulating *bibis* threatened to drown her words.

"Sam's her son. I said I would look after him."

She watched his face. He had gathered a few more lines round his eyes. The greyish tinge to his skin betrayed his shock.

"But there's something else I must tell you. Teresa made me promise not to, but she's no longer here, and you've a right to know. She used to work at the museum, Charles. That's where I found her. I saw you there once, talking to Jackson and Mwangi. Did you never see her or Sam when you were there? And did Jackson know her connection with you? I've often wondered."

"I've only been there a couple of times. Jackson and I normally meet in town. But, to be honest, he did once tell me she worked there. It was after I'd married Ruth, and I thought I'd better not seek her out. Why? What are you trying to say?"

"It's Sam. He's your son."

Her words stayed in the air, between them.

She searched his face, trying to read his reaction. There was so much more to say.

Then he put his head in his hands.

Caroline fingered her coffee cup. She knew how important it was for an African to produce a son and heir. Her news must be momentous for him, but how much had he really loved Teresa?

Charles looked up, his eyes were dazed.

"But why?"

"Teresa didn't want you to know because she was ashamed, and terrified of Mwangi. She believed that if she disappeared, both you and her unborn baby would be safe from him."

A disturbance in the taxi rank nearby distracted her. A couple of men were arguing and the queue outside the supermarket was disintegrating.

She saw Charles stiffen.

"I must get back to work," he said. "We're in the middle of history, here. And perhaps you'd better go home. There's no knowing what might happen." His hand closed over hers, removing it from his arm. He stood up and brushed his fingers over her shoulder in a brief gesture. "I'll keep in touch."

Caroline did not go home. It might be a foolish thing to do, she knew, but driven by an overpowering sense of history, she wanted to experience what was happening around her.

She crawled along the dual carriageway into the city centre. An eerie silence enveloped the pavements – very different from the frenzy of Westlands, where the only closed shop, in respect of *Mzee*, was the chemist beside the post office.

Outside the railway station, people piled their belongings into over-crowded *matatus*. The pirate taxis were enjoying unprecedented business, as everybody wanted to leave Nairobi. An army helicopter hovered overhead.

She had never known the city so empty. Caroline stopped outside a drycleaner's shop to collect a suit she had taken there earlier in the week, but its doors were closed. Through the window, she saw the manager arguing with an employee. She tapped on the glass.

"Sorry about that." The lady allowed her in, and handed over the suit. "The workers closed the doors immediately we heard the news, but they're too frightened to go home, so I've insisted they complete the orders for the day."

Caroline walked back along the pavement and watched the owner of an Indian textile store open his door and glance furtively up the street before letting in a group of people. And yet, when she cruised down a side street past the former offices of Charles's magazine, the mechanics were busy on the cars as if it were an ordinary working day.

"*Mzee* died in his own bed in his own house. It is *shauri ya mungu* – God's will. Therefore all is well, there will be no trouble." Onyango's wise words greeted her, but she detected a sense of relief in his voice as he welcomed her back home.

He was right. She suspected that Kenyatta had relinquished the reins of governance to his subordinates some time ago, and remained a figurehead. Now, with support from the Attorney General and a capable government to carry on, there was no reason to fear the future.

She experienced a sense of deep gratitude and pride. Kenyatta had so led his country that in the hour of his death Kenya was united as never before.

The days that followed were subdued. Public entertainment and meetings had stopped, but life went on. The newspapers were full of poignant photographs of mourners paying their last respects to *Mzee*.

Caroline joined the queue in the gardens of State House, crammed with people of all races. There was little forward movement. Towards evening, the guards tried to close the gates, and those outside started to agitate. The police failed to pacify them and there were some anxious moments before Daniel arap Moi, the new President, stepped onto the balcony to appeal for calm. He promised that everyone would have a chance to see the body.

Moi was not a pastoralist Kikuyu, like Kenyatta, but a member of the nomadic Tugen tribe from the north, and in his turn, he would appoint a Kikuyu vice-President, to sustain the balance of power in the country. Caroline wondered how long the intelligent and ambitious Kikuyu people would allow themselves to be governed by a man from a different tribe.

The crowd settled. They were counted into groups of thirty and at last, Caroline entered the stateroom. Immersed in a palpable aura of reverence, she filed past the coffin offering silent prayers and thanksgiving for a peaceful transition.

On emerging, Caroline saw that no visible indent had been made on the crowd. A stranger with the leathery, weather-beaten face of an old settler paused beside her.

"Kenyatta was a great man and what he's done to Kenya is a marvel," he said.

She felt proud of her country. It was a blessed thing, this order and calm.

Church on Sunday was full, but when the time came for the sermon, the African minister stood aside for a Hungarian preacher with limited command of the English language. He struggled manfully, but Caroline noted the blank faces of the people around her.

Why ask a foreign priest to eulogise on the qualities of Kenyatta to a mixed congregation who clearly could not understand half of what he said? But at least everyone was united in their hopes for peace and continuation.

There were many rumours.

Mama Ngina, Kenyatta's widow, notorious for her involvement in the illegal ivory trade, had the nickname Mama Ngini, Madam More. Everyone thought she would flee the country to enjoy her ill-gotten gains, yet daily pictures showed her tending the body of her late husband. There were whispers that the new President and his Kikuyu Attorney General had already had a row. But life went on and the new President's directives to stop rumour-mongering were eventually heeded.

Caroline saw Jackson at the museum.

"So…Sam is Charles's son?" he challenged her. "I've often wondered at his parentage. He's grown into an intelligent young man and he's interested in palaeontology." Jackson smiled. "It must run in the family."

She laughed. "I've been encouraging him. Do you blame me? I'm passionate about Kenya's pre-history."

"But are your motives pure, Caroline? Sometimes I wonder whether you haven't got your eye on future fame and fortune."

"What's the harm in dreaming, so long as everybody benefits?"

Jackson appeared to be deep in thought. Perhaps he wanted

to talk about the secrets of their ancestral cave?

"Well, I expect that Charles will want to get to know Sam. Does the boy know about his father?"

"Not yet, Jackson. I need time to break the news. Sam took ages to get over his mother's death. Rightly or wrongly, I didn't tell him about Charles – cowardly of me, maybe, but we'd kept the secret so long and the reasons were so complicated that I hardly knew where to start."

"There's no hurry, Caroline. Let me know when you're ready and I'll inform Charles. We could do something together. After all, he's found a son and I have another nephew."

Caroline's thoughts turned to the arid lands of the south where the ancestral cave was hidden. But Jackson was talking again.

"I have to go to Lake Turkana sometime in the next few months. There's a dig on its eastern shore called Koobi Fora, where exciting things have been discovered. You and Paul should come too, so Sam will feel comfortable. It would be a memorable safari for the boys. What do you say?"

The ancestral cave would have to wait.

"That would be a good idea. Thank you, Jackson."

How would Charles relate to Sam, who had started life in the city slums with an outcast mother of mixed blood, and who was now being brought up by Caroline in the European way? Yet she knew that his pride at having a son after all would not be stifled. He would want to acknowledge Sam. Perhaps they would find their roots together, and with the blood of diverse races coursing through Sam's veins, he would epitomise the new Kenya, a healthy mix of nationalities united in one person.

Caroline gave herself a mental shake and a little smile. It was a long time since she had let herself dream.

But first she had to tell Sam. Her heart quaked at the thought. She looked for an opportunity to catch him alone, but the boys were inseparable and her resolve weakened as the days passed.

On a Sunday evening after church, she prepared a simple supper and cleared the table. Paul helped with the washing up, and then a sudden storm raged outside. The lights went out – a normal occurrence when it rained – so Paul lit some candles and took down the hurricane lamp. Sam came in, complaining at the dark. He took up a log and prodded it into the Dover stove. He'd been in one of his difficult moods all day, and had refused to come to evensong. The grumpiness started in the months following his mother's death, but had become less frequent over the past year, so Caroline was taken by surprise when he jumped back, holding his hand close to his chest.

"Jesus! I've burned myself on the bloody stove."

There was a red weal on his arm.

"Quick! Hold it under the cold tap to cool it down, while I get some ice. It'll be okay. And it's no excuse for any of your Mathare swearing, Sam. I thought you'd got over that years ago!"

She'd coined the phrase when he and Teresa first came to live with her, and it had been a semi-serious joke between them whenever Sam or Teresa slipped into bad habits. His gutter language had returned since Teresa's death.

"It's all very well for you!" he snarled, snatching his arm away as she tried to apply the ice.

Caroline gave him the ice and stepped back, watching, as Sam bathed his arm in silence, his lower lip quivering.

Paul picked up a dishcloth and moved to dry the plates, which were stacked on the draining board, and Sam jerked away from him.

"It's all very well for you," he repeated, his eyes wild with pain. "I might as well go back to the Mathare slums. What's the point of staying here now that my mother is–"

"Sam!"

Paul dropped a glass, which shattered on the concrete floor.

Caroline gave her son a warning look, and moved to take

control.

"We'll deal with that glass later, Paul. And Sam – give me your arm while I wrap it loosely with this clean cloth. I've got something very serious to tell you; something which you should have known years ago." She took up a candle. "Come, let's go into the sitting room. Bring the lamp, Paul, and a soda each from the fridge. I think I'll pour myself a stiff brandy and ginger."

The boys settled on the sofa facing her across the fireplace, Paul's face alive with anticipation, and Sam was less grumpy. They were not often allowed to drink soda.

"There's no easy way to say this, Sam," said Caroline from her favourite armchair. "But it's time you learned about your father."

"My father? Mum told me about him – he just disappeared like so many other dads in Mathare."

His face transformed into a sneer, and Caroline paused to gather her thoughts. She swallowed, and no thoughts came. She prayed for inspiration.

"I know, Sam. Your mother had very good reasons for not telling you the truth, and I promised to keep her secret, both from you and from your father."

"What do you mean?"

"I know your father, Sam. He's a well-respected–"

"Who is he? Why didn't you tell me before? Have I met him without knowing it?" Sam's voice betrayed his anger and hurt.

"No Sam, you haven't met him. And, rightly or wrongly, I have only recently told him about you."

Caroline watched the boy's face as he grappled with this information. Then she turned her eyes away to gaze at the fire. What had they done to him – by what right had she and Teresa kept Sam and Charles apart for all these years? She had respected her friend's decision. But what about her own motives – why had she not revealed the truth earlier?

"Wow!"

It was Paul, his voice soft and wondering. "So you have a father after all, Sam!" He placed a hand on his friend's arm. "You lucky beggar."

Caroline felt her eyes pricking and she turned away to blow her nose. The sight of her orphan son envying his friend reminded her how lonely it was to be a widow. Now, they would probably lose Sam too.

**

Charles put his head in his hands. She wouldn't tell him if it weren't true. Not Caroline. He caught his breath. He had a son. He'd had a son all this time and he hadn't known it.

He thought back to his meetings with Teresa at the races so long ago, and their dinners at the Corner Bar. One night after their meal they parked on The Hill, with the lights of the city spread before them.

They left the car to stand at the barrier while he held her close, breathing in the balmy air. The lawns and miniature lake of Central Park lay below, deserted and greyly shadowed in the intermittent rays of broken streetlights.

He stroked away a silky lock from Teresa's ear and nuzzled her neck. A scent, faintly musk, wafted on the midnight air and a fire stirred in his loins.

A van drew up behind them and three men got out. It was a notorious spot for thuggery, and he pushed Teresa back into the car then ran round to the driver's seat, cursing under his breath. She deserved better than this.

He took her to the Manor Hotel in the nearby Westlands suburbs and told her to wait in the car. Then, holding hands, he led her upstairs to the honeymoon suite, and folded her gently into his arms, holding her pliant body into a mould along the length of him. An answering quiver tensed against him as she arched her back. The most overwhelming sense of love, and giving, and togetherness enveloped him, before an explosion of compulsive fire consumed them both.

There were many other times, each distinct and special, but the first remained the strongest in his memory. Charles wondered which one had resulted in Sam. He would have to find out the boy's birthday. He had a son!

While the turmoil of the country's change of President raged around him, Charles followed lead after lead to record the process for history. The newspaper office remained a hive of bustling activity for weeks, and as the country settled into smoother waves of stability and the weeks turned into months, Charles thought about his son.

Would Sam remind him of Teresa, or would his face be typically African; how pale was his skin; the hair he knew would be black fuzz, for that was often the last feature to disappear in a recessive gene. How would Sam react to a father?

Indeed, what difference would it make to his own life? Charles shied away from the thought as he pictured the environment he worked in, the proud intensity of black Africa, defensive in its attitude to the rest of the world. Would his part in all this be compromised when it became known that his son was half European? He knew his traditional family would not approve. The few Africans who had taken white wives were set apart, marginalised, because they had crossed the invisible barrier where the majority had refused to tread. Teresa had not even been his wife, and Sam was a bastard.

He would never allow that derogatory word to be voiced in his presence. But he could not stop other people's thoughts.

Dear Teresa. Only now did he realise how much he'd loved her. The future would be tough, but he and Sam would stand proud in their emerging country and between them embody the best of both worlds.

But he hadn't even met Sam. It was time. His brother Jackson – thank God for him – would be a willing go-between.

"I think it best you meet on Sam's familiar ground, Charles," Jackson said. "I'll get Caroline to drop him at the museum next Saturday afternoon. She's told him about you, but I warn you, he'll have a lot of questions."

Charles waited on the garden seat overlooking the path to the snake park. He had chosen a short-sleeved blue and white check shirt with open collar to go with his khaki slacks. A brown paper parcel lay at his side. He'd thought long and hard about the gift for his newfound son, and hoped it would be well received.

Jackson waited in the car park to meet Caroline.

Charles heard the car door slam, and the crunch of gravel as it pulled away. He stood up as his brother and his son came into view.

The boy was nearly as tall as his uncle, his skin a chestnut colour, glowing in the sunlight. His full lips betrayed an African heritage, but those eyes – it was as if Teresa were regarding him. Shaped like almonds, their smouldering fire fringed with upward curling lashes regarded him sombrely.

"Sam…"

Charles clasped his son's hand, and felt the positive response. But the eyes were questioning, and wary.

"I'll leave you now," said Jackson. "I have work to do."

Charles gestured towards the nearby kiosk. "Shall we have something to drink? What would you like, Sam?"

"A soda, please."

"Make that two," he said, placing a five-shilling note on the counter in front of the attendant. "Want a glass, Sam?"

"A straw will do, thanks."

The boy stood respectfully beside Charles, sipping at his drink. Charles knew that he would have to take the initiative, and had prepared himself in advance.

"I'm so glad we're meeting at last."

268

Sam looked at him again, with Teresa's eyes. Charles caught his breath.

"You remind me so much of your mother!"

He hadn't meant to say that, but he saw a little smile cross Sam's face, which dimpled exactly like Teresa's.

"Yes – Caroline's always said I have her eyes."

"They were good friends."

"Yes."

"And I expect you have many questions, Sam. I'm not sure I'll be able to answer them all, but I will try. Do you know that my confusion is as great as yours, as I have only recently learned of your existence?"

"Caroline told me."

"So we both have questions, and it might take time to find the answers – if we ever do. But we could search for them together…"

The boy was silent.

"Would you like that?"

Sam looked up at him.

"I think so."

This was not going to be easy, but what else could he expect? At least they had made a start. Charles remembered his gift, and sat on the bench, inviting Sam to join him.

"This is a small token of remembrance of our re-union. I hope you'll like it."

He watched Sam tear open the package, his eyes widening as he drew out a book and examined the cover. "It's a history book of Kenya, written by an African – is he a member of our tribe?"

Charles nodded.

"Oh, thank you so much…"

The boy did not finish his sentence, and Charles smiled with relief that his gift was well received. He motioned him to open the front cover and read the inscription.

To Sam Ondiek,
My beloved firstborn son, on the day we found each other.
Charles Omari Ondiek. 21st April, 1979

"Shall we take a walk down to the river?"

They returned the empty bottles to the kiosk, and strolled through the mature trees to the trickle of water at the boundary of the museum. Charles talked of his relationship to Jackson, and Sam told him the Latin names of the trees around them. Relaxed now, the boy chattered on about the pre-history gallery in the museum.

That smiling dimple appeared with greater frequency, and the time slipped by. Caroline would be coming back within the hour. Before they returned to the car park, Charles stopped to lay his hand on Sam's arm.

"I want to tell you before you go, Sam," he said. "I loved your mother very much. She sacrificed herself for us both. As you read that book, you will know that you and I, and people like us, are the embodiment of hope for a newly emerging Kenyan society, even if it takes more than a generation to accomplish. We owe it to her to keep trying."

He did not tell Sam about the continuing threat of Mwangi's curse. He hoped that with all the deaths, the power of the oath had dissipated. But he could not be sure.

CHAPTER 23

Lake Turkana

"Jackson is arranging a field trip to Lake Turkana, and we're invited to join him, Caroline. Can you get away with the boys?"

Caroline had been wondering what to do with Paul and Sam during the school holidays.

"We'd love to, Charles! And it would be a great way for you and Sam to get to know each other better. When can we go?"

"He is flying up north at the end of the month, but will arrange a lift for us in a museum vehicle as far as Lodwar. We can take a boat across to Koobi Fora on the east side of the lake."

Caroline had completed her compulsory year as a volunteer Museum Guide. She'd heard about Richard Leakey's famous archaeological camp on the shores of the Jade Sea, where only invited guests could go. It was the opportunity of a lifetime.

They travelled northwest through farmlands thirsting for rain, and descended the majestic Marich Pass. Lush, tropical vegetation crowded the track, grand old fig trees blocked the sun and the thick undergrowth allowed tantalising glimpses of the Great Rift Valley, which stretched endlessly northwards.

The Field Studies Centre at the foot of the Pass lay within a circle of simple *bandas* enclosing a dirt-swept dining area. Tall trees studded the site bordered by a wide riverbed, its waters trickling thinly off the escarpment. Caroline humped her backpack into the room she shared with Paul. A washbowl stood on a table beside a jug of river water, with a bar of soap and even a toilet roll on the shelf. The communal showers and pit toilets were to the far left of the compound.

She scanned the trees with her binoculars, and Paul tapped her urgently on the shoulder, pointing towards a giant kingfisher flying across their vision. The leisurely beat of its wings held a straight and purposeful course along the riverbank. Caroline caught her breath and focussed as it dropped softly onto a branch to commence its vigil, the grey spotted feathers blending in perfect camouflage against the rich foliage. It was a 'lifer' for them both – their first.

The resident guide led them on a short bird walk before meeting the others for supper under the stars. She watched the full moon rise, blood red through the trees, as she dunked her bread into an Ethiopian dish of goat meat, swimming in globules of fat.

During the night, her stomach rebelled, and she was forced to brave the distance to the toilets, catching a prospecting reptile in the light of her torch. Her heart lurched. Was it a black mamba? She stamped her feet and struck her stick against a tree to warn off the deadly snake. From the corner of her eye, she noticed a figure in a fez, standing ten yards away. Was it Mwangi? She'd heard he'd been sent to work in the north.

The following morning they explored the nearby Wei Wei valley.

Charles tapped her shoulder as they ambled back.

"Look, Caroline."

She turned to gaze in awe at a rainbow, its multitude of colours ringing the sun in a perfect circle against the dark background of the valley wall.

Charles stood behind her and she could feel his breath against the nape of her neck.

After a salad lunch, Charles and Sam wandered off beside

the river, but she detained Paul.

"Let's leave them, shall we? There's an ethnic walk scheduled later on; I'd like to try it."

The guide made Paul a toothbrush out of a special type of twig and pointed out a variety of medicinal plants as they filed along a narrow winding path, trying to avoid protruding twigs and thorns. He showed Caroline the *acacanthera* bush, which was the source of poison for the arrows of hunter-gatherers, and identified the tracks of a duiker on an area of soft sand.

Trigger-happy Shifta bandits from Somalia were in control of the area, so a police convoy waited for them before dawn the next day. After officious posturing, they lumbered into motion. But when day broke over the desert the line of vehicles disintegrated, each finding its own speed.

The broken tarmac forced their driver to take the corrugated dirt track alongside, and Caroline's head nodded away the kilometres. Hours later, the country transformed into an alien moonscape. Caroline wiped the sweat from her face with her sleeve and adjusted her sunglasses as they drew up for lukewarm refreshments at a local dive in a side street of the sleepy town of Lodwar. Then they followed a faded blue Jade Sea Bus to a discreet papyrus-lined compound where homemade soup and an excellent buffet lunch were served.

The hot liquid was surprisingly refreshing under the blazing sun. Caroline re-filled her water bottle, and made use of a spotless thunderbox, positioned over a deep pit. She hung a makeshift 'Occupied' sign on a twig at the entrance and wondered how she would manage as the only woman on their desert safari.

An open boat waited for them at Kalokol on the sun-stifling shores of Lake Turkana.

"Give me your things."

The skipper extended an arm to Caroline. She didn't want to surrender her camera and binoculars, but the man insisted on putting everything into canvas bags and dumping them into a filthy oil drum in the bow.

"The waves can be rough," he told her. "You don't want to spoil your belongings."

She took a bright blue and yellow life jacket from him and clambered awkwardly over the side. A second boat carrying a group of museum staff with their provisions followed them across the grey waters. Where was the 'jade' so famously promised?

The bow rose above the waves and crashed down, sending up welcome spray to cool her. Nobody spoke during the rough hour-long ride to Central Island.

Caroline saw a pebbly beach in the half-light of late afternoon and the skipper scanned the water's edge before allowing them to disembark. The men lugged the baggage over the stones and up a sand bank towards two meagre bushes. With a minimal attempt at modesty, Caroline changed into her bathing costume.

"Watch out for crocodiles!" shouted the skipper.

Paul and Sam were splashing in the water. She hesitated before plunging in. Slimy wavelets pushed against her, stubbing her toes painfully against the pebbles.

Charles stood on the beach.

"Keep close to the shore!"

The boys had drifted far out and she joined in the chorus commanding them back. She wallowed in the shallows, her eyes skimming the waters, but no crocodiles appeared.

Caroline dried herself and staked her claim to a patch of sand as the sun dipped in a glorious display of oranges, greys and blues. She lay on her back watching the stars prick the night sky, one by one. Satellites darted busily across the sky and a meteorite dived from the heavens. The full moon rose in the east, the stars faded, and supper was served.

Charles placed his mattress next to hers. Remembering his proximity when they were admiring the circular rainbow, she read the signs of his intent. But she didn't want to draw attention by making a fuss.

He leaned across her, brushing shoulders as he pointed. With a gasp of awe, she watched a falling star flare towards the horizon, then turned her back and settled to sleep, conscious of his restless movements beside her. Each time he moved against her, she edged away. In the morning as she rubbed the sleep from her eyes, she saw they were several yards from the others.

"Hey – what've you two been doing, chasing each other over the sand?" laughed Paul, pointing to their sleeping mats when she roused him for breakfast.

She frowned.

"Sorry," Charles mumbled. "I couldn't get to sleep."

They embarked for the eastern part of the island, and Caroline spotted an enormous crocodile lurking with evil intent in the shallows beside the jetty, so they scraped onto a beach thirty yards away. Gigantic rocks towered over them, and an Egyptian vulture soared overhead. The path, which led up to the rim of a crater, was littered with pebbles. Then a small lake appeared, its rim encrusted with pink.

Their guide paused, counting.

"There are three thousand flamingos," he said.

"How did you do that – so quickly?"

"I count a section," he said. "Then I estimate how many sections there are in the whole mass. Then I multiply."

Caroline slid after the others to the crater floor. She stooped to pick up a feather, and examine the webbed feet and curious inverted bill of a carcase, and then laboured up the other side.

Thorns scratched at her legs as she descended towards another crater. Charles waited for her. The boys had gone far ahead. Two circles of murky green water merged into one figure of eight far below. There were no flamingos here. Caroline raised her binoculars and made out the bulk of two large crocodiles lurking deathlike beneath the surface. Paul and Sam emerged onto the shore and waved up to them. They hadn't seen the monsters. She cupped her hands to her mouth to shout a warning.

"Crocodiles!"

The boys signalled an acknowledgement and disappeared into the trees.

Charles took her hand as they turned down the rugged path. She could manage perfectly well with her stick, but didn't want to appear impolite. Her water bottle was empty and he offered her a sip from his. The boys, sensing the homeward run, were out of sight. The long plunge down to lake-level seemed to go on forever. The sandy path degenerated into soft alternatives among tufts of prickly undergrowth, and the sun baked down.

She claimed a place in the meagre shade of a bush beside the campsite and gulped down several mugs of water, before joining the boys in the lake. The soapy wavelets were surprisingly strong, crashing her against the pebbles, but she lingered in the cooling waters until called for a cold lunch.

They broke camp and endured a long ride over rough waters to Koobi Fora. Strong waves crashed over the boat and Caroline appreciated why their equipment had been sealed in containers under heavy canvas. Swathed in a *kitenge*, eyes protected by sunglasses, and a sodden straw hat fastened tightly round her chin, she allowed herself to sway and jolt against Charles as the boat rocked her into a stupor.

Towards evening, crocodiles slid down a sandy beach into the lake, lights twinkled on a gently sloping bank, and Jackson greeted them as they ground onto the shore. Caroline's legs faltered. But she revived after a cool fruit drink and watched the sun set, its ever-changing splashes of colour reflecting on the low clouds.

Jackson joined them round a blazing fire.

"Is there any evidence of early man in these parts?" Caroline asked. "Any collections of artefacts like those you showed me at Olorgesaile?"

"We do find the occasional man-made object, but we concentrate on pre-history here. You need to explore the Rift Valley and around Lake Magadi if you want handaxes and pottery. You should take the boys to Olorgesaile one day, and even to Hyrax Hill near Nakuru."

"Does our tribe have an ancient history?"

Sam asked the question, and Caroline glanced at Charles, wondering if he had primed the boy.

"Every tribe has its history and its secrets, where no white man is allowed."

"But I'm not white, am I."

"No." Jackson laughed. A thoughtful look crossed his face, and Caroline held her breath. "One day, perhaps, when you become an elder, you may inherit the secrets of our tribe. Who knows?"

"Does my father know?" asked Sam, glancing at Charles.

"No. I am the only one, with my sister. All I am going to tell you now is that Simaloi is the guardian of the cave, because my mother, who is your grandmother, has passed away."

Caroline exhaled. So there was a cave.

Jackson took them on a rough journey southwards. As they left the lakeside, herds of Burchell's and the larger, more striking Grevy's zebra lifted their heads. Elegant long-necked gerenuk reached on their hind legs for delicate leaves high in the thorn trees, and stately Oryx shied away, melting into the undergrowth.

There was a wealth of bird life. Caroline scanned the green fig trees and giant acacias, which sucked the moisture from the sand of the dry river beds and pointed out several more 'life-birds' to Paul. The migrants from Europe had arrived and the resident Somali species were new to them.

They topped a gentle rise and headed towards a rocky outcrop in the barren landscape. A strange spectacle of fallen trees appeared, cut into regular chunks as if by giant saws. But

277

as they approached, Caroline saw that the logs were made of stone.

"It's a petrified forest," Jackson told her. "Look – the logs have retained the exact grain of the original wood for millions of years."

"How did they break into such clean pieces?" asked Sam.

"That's due to earth movements, which cracked and broke the fossilised trunks," explained Jackson. "Come over here, and I'll show you some more."

He led them to the outcrop. Great stone roots and vines entwined themselves among fissures of rock. Caroline picked up a stone of fascinating hues, turning it over in her hand to admire the different shades of brown, green and orange.

The birds were quiet in the midday hush. Another hot, rough journey enveloped with dust took them to a low stonewalled building, which nestled in a depression. Its iron roof glinted incongruously in the desert. A warden opened the door and Caroline shuffled gratefully into the shade. When her eyes became accustomed to the dark, she saw an *in situ* fossil elephant of Indian origin, which, she read from notes, had roamed the plains two million years before. Reluctant to go out again into the blazing sun, she lingered to contemplate the immensity of time.

More huts in the undulating terrain harboured the fossil of an enormous tortoise, and a crocodile curled inwards along its tail. As they left for camp, Jackson stopped the car. There, protruding from an insignificant mound of sand, were some hippo's teeth, which had been uncovered only a few months before.

"We'll be sending them for carbon dating soon," he said.

Brilliant carmine bee-eaters escorted them to camp, darting and diving in crimson flashes, and the sea sparkled diamonds in the sunlight, turning into soft jade as it stretched northwards to the Omo River Delta. Caroline breathed deeply, savouring the special moment, and then walked with

Charles back towards the holes in the bank where the bee-eaters nested. She let him take her hand.

"It's been a good trip. Thank you for coming," he said.

"I'll never forget this place. It is utterly wonderful."

His grip tightened.

"Caroline, I don't know how to thank you for what you've done for Sam. He's been telling me about his life with you and Teresa. I'm so proud of him."

She smiled. She too felt proud of Sam, and of Paul. It had been no bother bringing them up together and now that Sam had found his father, she was happy for them both.

But she couldn't help wishing that Paul also had a father.

She tried to release her hand but Charles would not let go.

"You know how I feel about you, Caroline?"

She pulled away.

"Have you forgiven me for letting you down over the magazine?"

She looked up at him. What was there to forgive? He had been disastrously over-optimistic in his business endeavours, and she had expected too much from him.

"Of course, Charles; I put that episode down to life experience ages ago. I think we have both learned much since then!"

He returned her smile. "I'd like you to think about us, Caroline, you and me. Will you?"

She knew what he was trying to say, but didn't feel the time was appropriate. Would it ever be right for her? She'd always thought of him as belonging to Teresa.

CHAPTER 24

Nairobi

Charles turned up the drive and parked near the kitchen. He found Onyango preparing the Sunday lunch.

"Do you ever get a day off?"

Onyango shrugged. "Half a day here, half a day there. I have to work, and am lucky to have a job. The memsahib is a good employer."

"Where is she?"

"You've missed them. They've gone to church."

"I'll wait."

Onyango showed him into the lounge, and Charles fingered through some magazines. He got up to examine the pictures in the dining room. The Rake's Progress. A striking array of red, silver and black renderings, hung in artistic fashion against the emerald green wall; an aesthetically pleasing display, but hardly the subject he would associate with Caroline.

He blamed himself bitterly for the way he'd spoken to her at Koobi Fora. Why hadn't he just taken her in his arms? But she was a deeper character than Teresa. He knew she would disapprove if she heard of his many liaisons. The question of Ruth also remained. He had married her according to tribal custom, but how would Caroline see it?

What had Mwangi said about her – she'd had a boyfriend? He tried to recall Mwangi's words, but could only think of the curse. He, like Caroline, would never be frightened by that nonsense.

A car rumbled up the drive, and Sam entered the room.

"*Jambo,* father."

"Good morning, Sam. I hope you don't mind my coming?"

"Of course not. We saw your car, and you're invited to lunch."

"If it's no problem…"

"I'll tell Onyango."

Sam returned with a beer for Charles. They opened the double doors to the veranda and sat facing the front lawn, divided by an avenue of jacaranda trees.

"You go to church often?"

"Not really, but Caroline likes us to go with her to the Cathedral for Christmas and Easter. She's in the choir."

Charles remembered the day of David's memorial service.

"She has a lovely voice. I heard it once."

Sam laughed. "Yes, she's tried to get us to join the choir."

"Where do you go to school, Sam?"

"Paul and I go to St. Mary's, but he's in a higher class, and is taking exams at the end of the year. He doesn't know what he's going to do after that, but I want to follow Jackson. He said I could work at the museum with him after my A-levels. One day, maybe, I will find the money to go to university."

"Who's been paying for your schooling?"

"I'm not sure."

There was so much he didn't know about his son. Charles wished he had met Sam earlier. He wanted to take the boy to live with him, but he shared a dingy flat in a rough neighbourhood with other bachelors, and his work often took him away for days on end. He couldn't fault the way Teresa had brought him up, and now Caroline had taken over. Would Sam help to bring her closer to him?

"Where are the others?"

"They're at the back somewhere. I think they are leaving us alone together."

281

"She's a very considerate lady."

"She is like a mother to me," Sam shifted in his chair. "Am I going to come and live with you, now?"

"I wouldn't ask it of you, unless you wanted to. My home wouldn't be suitable, but I do have a house in Langata which has been shut up for many years. I had a traditional wife, you know; I don't suppose Caroline has told you?"

Sam shook his head, and Charles told him about Ruth and his half-sisters.

"We had a son, but he died as a baby. It was at his memorial service that I heard Caroline singing. Then Ruth left me and went back to her home, but I must take you to meet your sisters one day."

"So you live alone?"

"I share a flat with other bachelors."

"Would you mind if I stayed with Paul and Caroline?"

"I think it would be better for you if you did, Sam. I must talk to Caroline. I'll have to think of a way to repay her."

But Caroline dismissed his offer.

"Don't worry, Charles," she said as she handed him a cup of coffee on the veranda after lunch. "When Teresa died, the Catholic Fathers said they were happy to have Sam until he passes his A-levels. They have funds available, and he is a model student."

"I'd like to meet them."

"I'm sure they would appreciate it."

Paul approached them.

"Mum, can we borrow your car to go to the sports club? I promise to be careful."

Caroline looked at her watch.

"I'll need it to go to evensong, but you can take it for a couple of hours. The keys are in my handbag."

Charles watched the car turn out of the drive into the traffic.

"I didn't know Paul could drive?"

"The day he turned sixteen he applied for his test, and

282

passed."

"That must be a record!" Charles exclaimed. "Did you have to pay much *chai*?"

"There was absolutely no bribe involved," Caroline declared with a grin. "He earned his licence purely on merit. And he's a good driver; I've no hesitation in letting him use my car."

"And Sam?"

"Sam has to wait another year before he's old enough. I've been letting him drive whenever we visit the Nairobi Game Park, which you can imagine has been rather often."

"I don't expect he's as good as Paul."

"It doesn't come to him naturally. He stalls the engine when he starts. But he'll be fine when the time comes."

"I don't know how to thank you, Caroline."

"Please don't even bother to try," she said. "I love them both. They are so good for each other, and I hope they'll be friends for life."

"Would you let me pay for Sam's keep? I am his father, after all."

"You don't have to. I can afford it now that I have more guests, and Sam is part of the family."

"But…"

"But if you want to…" Caroline shrugged her shoulders.

Charles took her hand.

"Have you thought about what I said at Koobi Fora?" He hesitated. "You're already a family, aren't you? You, and Paul and Sam. It would be so logical to add me, wouldn't it? I'm not saying this very well. But I love you, Caroline. Might you learn to love me, in time?"

At least she hadn't moved her hand. He looked away.

She broke the contact.

"I don't know, Charles."

"I'm prepared to wait, unless there's someone else?"

Caroline turned towards him. "There was someone else, but he's married."

So Mwangi had spoken the truth. But it was none of his business.

"I'm sorry, Caroline. I'll wait – if you'll let me. But in the meantime, please may I pay for Sam's living expenses?"

"If you really feel you want to, Charles, I can understand why."

At least she hadn't rejected him outright.

He drove Sam to the Game Park one Sunday afternoon.

"You can practice in my old rattle-trap," he said. "Unlike Caroline's smart station wagon, you won't have to worry about harming it. She told me you were having difficulty starting? I'll pull over here and you can take over. You might find this clutch easier to use than hers."

He stopped in a lay-by. Small planes were taking off and landing at Wilson Airport behind the boundary fence across the plains where impala, zebra and Thompsons' gazelle grazed. A crooked thorn tree broke the horizon; in it, two crested cranes nudged their beaks. Beyond, the skyline of Nairobi rose in a haze of pollution.

No other cars were visible. The antelopes were grazing peacefully, undisturbed by predators. Nobody was allowed to leave their cars in the middle of the Game Park, but Charles opened the door.

"It's all clear. Quick! Let's change seats."

Charles got out and ran round to the passenger door, while Sam shuffled over the gear lever into the driver's seat.

Sam pulled out, and the car jerked twice before the clutch engaged.

"Well done, my son. Let's try that again."

After several more attempts, Sam finally achieved a faultless start, and Charles sat back, trying to relax as his son negotiated the twists and turns in the narrow track. The car stalled again as he drove up a rocky incline, so Sam practised a handbrake start, making the wheels spin wildly on the loose stones.

A rhino, dozing on a hillock near the road, snorted with alarm.

Sam nudged the car past it, and then stopped to look.

"Keep the engine running, Sam! Don't stall."

The ponderous beast turned towards them.

"I think you'd better drive on, slowly. Faster now."

Charles looked back. The rhino was trotting after them, tossing its head in irritation as they pulled away.

"I started well that time, didn't I, Dad?"

Dusk was falling.

"We'd better turn back."

Charles cringed as the car hit bottom over the speed bumps in the road approaching the main gate. Vehicles crowded behind them in the dash to get out before the six o'clock closure. Sam drew to a halt, straddling the angled lines in the car park, but Charles made him reverse out and try again until the car was accurately parked.

"I need a drink."

Charles led the way to a kiosk, and bought Sam a soda, wishing he could down a cold beer to settle his nerves after the drive. But there was no bar at the Park entrance, and he'd have to wait until he got home.

"What you need now, Sam, is a good long drive on the open road," he said on the way back. "Why don't we go on a day's safari?"

"Where to?"

Charles saw his opportunity. "I have an idea. You remember Jackson talking about an ancestral cave?"

"When we were at Koobi Fora?"

"Yes. I know it's somewhere beyond Lake Magadi, near the Tanzania border. Let's take a picnic and do some exploring."

"But didn't Jackson say it was a sacred place?"

"I don't know its exact location. There's nothing to stop us looking around. When Caroline takes you to the museum, find out if there are any digs down there."

It was a fortnight later, and they were in the Game Park again.

"Been to the museum yet?" Charles asked.

"You were right, Dad. There is a dig near Lake Magadi."

"So we're in luck!"

"Jackson told me it's seasonal, because it floods in the rains. He offered to take us there in the Christmas holidays, but I said you wanted to give me some driving practice. When you're ready to go, he'll give us directions, and a note to the scientist in camp."

"Let's make it a family event, shall we – and see if Caroline and Paul would like to come? I know she is interested in our secret cave."

In the stifling interior of the car, Charles brushed the flies from his face and peered through his sunglasses at the track ahead.

Sam had driven them past the baking salt pans of the Magadi Soda Company, a tiny prick of habitation in the vast isolation of desert sand and dried-up lake, near the Kenya/Tanzania border.

They crossed a tongue of lake and then another before emerging onto a sandbank. Hundreds of flamingos with their attendant spoonbills, storks and waders lined the salt-encrusted water. The rubbery noise of their beaks rose in incessant conversation and an odour of sunburnt feathers and sludgy excreta tainted the air.

Sam struggled to keep the little car going in the soft sand. It was good practice for the boy, and the VW Beetle had enough clearance, but Charles couldn't help wondering what mechanical problems he'd have to deal with when they got back home. He glanced at Caroline – thrown from one side of the back seat to the other as the car bounced over hidden rocks and dipped into small ant bear holes.

"We have to look out for a false baobab on the right somewhere, Dad. Jackson said it was down the first track off the lake after the sandbank."

"False baobab?"

"Yes. It's an enormous termite mound that has grown up round a thorn bush. Apparently, you can see it for miles."

Caroline pointed out some faint tracks, which disappeared into the grass, and Sam plunged the car off the road. An escarpment rose, pale in the distance.

A herdsman leaned on his spear beside a pale pinnacle of earth, which enveloped the thin trunk of an acacia, turning it into one of baobab proportions. The pitted holes and eerie turrets of the great mound betrayed the intense activity of the termites within. Dappled goats cropped at the undergrowth, and lean cattle grazed alongside.

"Is this the way to the museum dig?" Charles asked the man.

"You have a message?"

Charles handed over the letter Sam had received from Jackson.

Sam drove behind the herdsman through the bush, thorns scratching at the paintwork of the car. The camp was deserted.

"Where is everybody?"

"At the dig. But the boss is sick. If you want to visit the site, I can lead you."

The heat closed in and the mid-morning air stilled as they followed their blanketed guide along an erratic path, which disappeared into the scrub. A dry riverbed stretched before them. Two sweat-glistening workers were sifting sand between the banks. Another chipped methodically at a pegged-out square of earth. The fossil of a horned mammal lay on a raised bed of hard sand nearby, and Stone Age hand axes were scattered among a pile of rubble.

"Have you found any hominids yet?" asked Caroline, approaching them.

The men replied with passive shrugs.

Charles studied the distant escarpment. One side had dramatically fallen away as if a giant had bitten out a slice. On the exposed face was a ledge. He raised his binoculars, which revealed a small cave, with one corner glinting whitely in the sun.

"Has anybody explored those hills?" he asked.

"There are no roads."

He lowered his glasses. The key to his ambition could possibly lie on that ledge. He brought out his camera and took a panorama of photographs.

"I feel guilty," said Caroline. "I wonder what Jackson would think if he saw us now?"

Charles took her arm and led her back to the campsite.

"Let's see what the scientist can tell us," he said.

As they approached, a man with lank strands of red hair drooping around his face emerged from the main tent. He weakly swatted at a cloud of bluebottle flies.

"Sorry I wasn't up when you arrived; been suffering from malaria, or dysentery, or a bit of both. Have you seen the dig?"

Caroline nodded.

"Yes thank you. Our boys are still there, talking to the men…"

The man shuffled towards a nearby thorn tree and lurched for the trunk, leaning heavily against it.

"Are you sure you're all right?"

"I'll be fine when I get back to Nairobi. A few weeks at a time in this heat is long enough for me. We've found some hand axes in a layer of volcanic ash and I'm taking away samples for dating. The men are being transferred."

He ended in a bout of coughing.

"What'll happen to the site?"

"We close it down before the rains."

The scientist returned to his tent, while Charles again studied the cave and its vicinity.

"The way is going to be arduous, and the terrain is deceptive," he told Caroline. "We need as many bearings as possible."

"Are you sure we should be planning this without Jackson's knowledge?" she asked. But he ignored her.

Sam and Paul returned from the riverbed.

"I want you to make careful note of that escarpment in the distance, Sam. Here, use my binoculars and see if you can pick out any landmarks between here and there. I have a feeling that dark hole above the ledge might be the key. You should see something bright near it."

"I can see a cave, but there's nothing else."

Charles took back the binoculars, and re-focussed them. "You're right. The flashing thing has gone. Perhaps I've made a mistake. I've taken a panorama of photographs, which we can study when we get home."

He glanced over at Caroline. "What's the harm?" he said, indicating Sam. "It's our family cave, just as much as Jackson's. You need have nothing to do with it."

At their departure, Charles noticed the herdsman hovering in the background. Sam opened the driver's door and a swarm of bluebottles buzzed out at him, one slapping painfully into his eye. He was semi-blinded for the first half of the return journey to the city, so Charles took the wheel.

CHAPTER 25

The Kenya Coast

Family Sunday lunches were becoming a pleasant habit. Caroline poured the coffee while Charles sprawled on the sofa beside Sam. Paul helped himself to a chocolate mint from the mantelpiece.

"What are you going to do for the holidays, boys?" she asked.

Charles looked up.

"I have a week off shortly, why don't we go down to the coast?" He looked at Sam. "You can drive, now that you've got your licence."

"Can't we go to Magadi instead, Dad, and see if we can get to the cave?"

They pored for the umpteenth time over the photographs they had taken of the dig and the escarpment beyond. Charles had ringed a thorn tree and some anthills to use as landmarks.

"There's no way of knowing from the photos how many hills and valleys lie between the dig and the cave," he mused. "Or even the distance between the two. And anthills are unreliable points of reference as they're constantly changing. We need to do more research, but the rains are about to break. We'll have to put it off until the dry season."

"Can Paul come with us to the coast, then?"

"Of course," he turned to Caroline. "Why don't we all go?"

She smiled. Was this a premeditated ruse, she wondered. But half her paying guests were away on holiday, and it would be good to get down to sea level for a change.

"How can I refuse!"

"But we'll go in my car, Caroline. I insist."

Caroline hesitated. "Will it last the journey?"

"Of course, and you know you're never entirely happy for Sam to drive yours. He needs the practice even though he's got a licence."

"How will we all fit in?"

"Easily, Mum," Paul said. "Charles's VW seats four and we needn't take much luggage. Come on – it'll be an adventure!"

"Well, I'll travel down with you," she relented. "But I warn you, I might fly back. I'll ask Uncle Ed if he can find us a beach cottage for a week, shall I?"

The road had recently been repaired and they enjoyed a smooth run with Sam driving the first fifty miles to Hunters' Lodge. Then Paul took over in the heat of the day for the tedious stretch to Mtito Andei, with its giant potholes and treacherous ragged edges of the tarmac.

Caroline cringed in the back seat as petrol tankers and lorries bore down on them along the single strip, forcing them onto the corrugated side tracks. There was no arguing with these monsters and they passed several skeleton cars abandoned in the bush, reminders of what could happen to the unwary.

"You must go slower, Paul. Look for a low ledge to get off the tarmac as soon as a lorry appears in front of you, or you'll destroy the tyres and suspension."

No sooner had Charles said the words, when Caroline felt the car thump heavily in the sand, as if they'd run over something.

"Stop, Paul! We've got a puncture."

He pulled up twenty yards later.

Caroline got out to stretch her legs, while the men examined the damage. The left rear tyre was flat and its sides were in ribbons.

"Sorry, Charles. I didn't realise just twenty yards would do that much damage," said Paul.

"Let's hope we don't get another puncture before we find a garage. I only have one spare tyre."

Caroline sat in the dust on the side of the road while the men changed the wheel.

"I think you should drive on, Charles," she suggested.

"Good idea."

She saw him grit his teeth, willing the little car to survive the forty-mile stretch to Mac's Inn, where he could have a new tyre fitted.

After lunch at the inn, Sam took the wheel and Caroline tried to doze off in the stupor of the early afternoon, her meal heavy in her stomach. But the road had degenerated into diversions. They were enveloped in clouds of dust as trucks sped past, driving blindly in both directions. She couldn't see more than a few feet in front of the car. An impatient driver overtook the slow-moving line.

"Don't you dare follow them," she warned Sam from the back seat.

They topped a rise and the tin roofs of Voi township shimmered in a depression. They were a hundred miles from Mombasa. Fine red dust lingered in the air, tracing the line of road for miles into the distance.

"Would you like me to take over, Sam?"

"It's all right, Dad. I'll carry on to Voi."

The car began to cut out. Several times Sam had to let it roll to a stop, and then start the ignition again.

"It's because of the low altitude," said Charles, his face glum. "We'll have to find a garage to change the timing. I haven't the knowledge or the tools."

"We're on holiday, and it doesn't matter if we arrive late," said Caroline.

"I need a drink. I feel dirty, and this journey is taking too long."

It would be better to stock up for further emergencies, Caroline decided. She bought several bottles of soda and some beer from an Indian *duka* at Voi, and put them in the boot of the car before having tea with the boys in a roadside café while Charles went to look for a mechanic. Two hours later, they left town for the final leg to Mombasa.

"I'll drive now," said Charles. "The last thirty miles will be a nightmare, and it's late."

Caroline sat in the passenger seat squinting into the glaring headlights of approaching traffic. The tankers and lorries were high off the road and even their dipped beams shone brightly into her eyes. There was also the hazard of vehicles with no lights. Charles flicked up his main beam at every break in the traffic to spot the dark shadows looming ahead, but Caroline remained alert, shielding her eyes from the glare ready to shout a warning.

She felt she had lived through a whole week in the space of twelve hours. When they arrived at Uncle Ed's home, she ran in to collect the key to their holiday cottage.

"We can't stop," she explained. "It's too late."

The ferry kept them waiting half an hour before crossing to the south coast, and then Charles negotiated the tracks winding through thick bush towards the beach.

Caroline could hear the crashing of waves on an invisible shore. Only a sliver of moon lit the sky. Their house was in darkness. She walked round the back to the servants' quarters and hammered on the door.

"Nobody's there," she announced on her return. "We'll have to let ourselves in."

There was some milk in the fridge, and a loaf of bread in a bin.

Caroline found linen in a cupboard and made up their beds. Charles would sleep on the sofa. She told Paul and Sam to share the main room, while she collapsed on a sunken mattress in a small bedroom near the kitchen.

She woke early, to discover the boys had gone to the beach. Charles wound a *kikoi* round his midriff, slipped his feet into a pair of flip-flops, and she followed him down the path.

Caroline dived through the waves to join the boys and enjoyed a brisk twenty-yard swim, before turning to float on her back. She noticed Charles paddling in the shallows, and shouted to him.

"Aren't you coming in?"

She came to sit beside him on the sand.

"I can't swim," he told her. "But there's no need to tell the boys."

She trickled sand through her fingers, smiling at him.

"You'll have to admit it eventually," she said.

The boys persuaded Charles to hire a boat to go goggling. Caroline sat with him, watching the fish weave in green shadows through the glass bottom, while the boys enjoyed the wonders of the deep, swimming freely through caverns of coral with their flippers and snorkels.

In the evening, she rested her legs on the veranda wall, a glass of wine at her side and a detective story in her lap, while her men visited the local hotels. She pictured them walking barefoot along the beach, buying a beer at every bar, before tottering home, weaving drunken footprints in the sand.

Late in the night, she was woken by Charles's hoarse whisper.

"Don't tell Caroline!"

"She's let us drink a beer or two on a Sunday before now," she heard Paul arguing.

Caroline smiled to herself, and watched them suffer in the days to come. They no longer joined her for early morning swims. She knew it was part of learning their limits, part of growing up, but she warned Charles not to let them near any prostitutes. She would never forgive him for that.

The car had been parked on top of the driveway in order to make a running start, as the battery had gone flat.

"I'll have to find another one and check the exhaust, as it sounds like a tractor," Charles told her. "I hope it will get us back to Nairobi."

He left them for a morning to take it to a local garage.

"That battery doesn't look new to me," she said when he came back and opened the bonnet for her. "But I expect you had no other choice."

It was time to prepare for the return journey.

"I think I'll leave you to it," said Caroline, and booked a flight home.

***

Before they had gone thirty miles, the noise in the exhaust increased. Charles stopped and looked under the car. The pipe had broken away.

"There's nothing we can do until we reach Voi, so you'd better carry on driving, Sam."

The boys waved energetically at the people they passed, laughing at the attention they attracted. *Bibis* with great piles of fruit balanced in baskets on their heads turned their bodies to watch, full grass skirts swaying under shabby pieces of cloth as they walked. Even the mangy pie dogs cringed away from the clatter.

As they approached a stretch of smooth tarmac, Charles heard a new note in the engine.

"Pull over for a minute," he told Sam, "but don't turn off the ignition."

He opened the bonnet and the knocking noise increased, but he was no mechanic.

He took the wheel for a few miles before the car ground to a halt. He tried to re-start it. Sam and Paul pushed it to the side of the road and Charles waited ten minutes before trying again.

He got out and prodded helplessly at the engine.

"It's not going to start, is it?" Excitement showed in Sam's voice. "Shall we get a lift into Voi and arrange a tow?"

Charles was in a dilemma. He needed to stay with his car, but how would the boys persuade a garage to bring help? Nobody would take them seriously and the price would be extortionate.

"We need help," he said. "Paul, you try and wave down a car. They'd be more likely to stop for a *mzungu*."

"What do you mean?" asked Sam.

"Well," said Charles. "It's a sad fact, but white people seldom stop on the road, because they've been robbed and beaten up too many times. I would always advise a white woman not to stop for someone trying to flag her down, unless it was a policeman, and even then it's risky. There've been cases when thugs have dressed up as the police."

"So that's why Mum never stops to help," mused Paul. "I've often wondered why she hesitates and then drives on when someone is in trouble."

"She's stopped once or twice when I've been with her," Sam argued. "But I guess she's been lucky."

"So now you know."

"What shall we do, Dad?"

"Well, they might stop for another *mzungu*, and a white man is more likely than an African to have a good tow rope. Let Paul try first."

Paul stood out in the road. They were on a new stretch of tarmac and cars whizzed by with no break in speed. Several white faces stared impassively through their windscreens, ignoring his wave. Two Africans stopped and said they would try to find someone to come to their rescue. Then a large Indian family pulled up, tightly crammed into a Mercedes.

Paul explained what had happened and Charles came forward.

"We need to get him to Nairobi before dark."

"I know a garage in Voi," the man said. "I'll get them to send a breakdown. It's the best I can do."

"Could I ask you to telephone his mother in Nairobi?"

"Of course."

Paul gave the man Caroline's telephone number and they watched the car disappear into the distance.

"Let's have something to eat while we're waiting," he said. "I'm hungry."

They had made some sandwiches before leaving, and Sam found the bottles of soda Caroline had left on their downward journey, which had been forgotten in the boot of the car. Charles thought Paul should continue trying to flag down cars, but the boy was tired.

Two hours later a breakdown lorry approached from the direction of Voi. It rolled to a halt and a man in a dirt-smeared turban jumped out.

"Mr Singh has spoken to your mother," he told Paul.

The lorry reversed towards them to hitch the tow.

For ten miles, Charles concentrated fiercely, gripping the steering wheel, his foot constantly hovering over the brake as he tried to keep from crashing into the back of the lorry. He had to be quick to release his foot for fear the short line would snap. When they arrived in Voi, there was a strong smell of rubber and the brakes were smoking. A fierce tension headache spread from the back of his neck, up over his head and across his brow. He bought painkillers but the ache persisted.

There was no hope for his VW Beetle, it would cost too much to repair, the mechanic told him. Charles sighed; the little car had done him well and it was time he got himself another. Their belongings were crammed into the boot.

"You can leave it here while you decide what to do," said the garage owner. "Everything will be safe and I'll lock the key in my office."

Charles had no alternative. He reached under the seat for his camera, locked the car and handed over the key.

"We need to get to Nairobi."

It was late afternoon, the banks were shut and he was running out of cash.

"Perhaps we can hitch a lift?" suggested Sam.

Charles watched the boys go off. The wind caught a newspaper, blowing it across the road. Empty bottles littered the ditch. His head throbbed madly. He broke open two painkillers and swallowed them down before Sam came running back.

"We've found someone going to Mtito Andei," his voice filled with pride. "We can ride in the back of his car. He said it would be easier getting a lift to Nairobi from there, as it is on the main road."

Charles followed to where two men were loading a pickup with fruit and empty drinks crates. They had tied the boxes in three tiers down each side, leaving a small space in the middle, and a gap at the tail of the truck.

Charles stared at it.

"There's no room for us all in there," he pronounced.

"You can sit in the middle with your back to the cab and Paul and I can squeeze up, facing each other at the end. Come on, it won't be all that bad and it's only fifty miles."

The boys looked on it as an adventure. Charles could have done without his headache. He eased himself between the two lines of crates. A sisal basket of mangoes was dumped onto his lap and the boys clambered in to face each other across his feet. The truck sagged on its springs.

"We're too heavy."

"No," the driver assured him. "We normally carry full crates of beer. It will be all right."

They pulled onto the main road. The empty bottles shook in their crates. Charles did not know which was worse, the unceasing clatter and crashing, or his aching head. He rested

298

his face on the basket in his lap and closed his eyes. He could smell the sweetness of the bruised mangoes. His feet were numb under Sam's legs. His bones rattled and shook. Every indrawn breath was choked with invisible particles. At least he couldn't see the clouds of dust which must be swirling round them on the diversions. The piercing headlights of following vehicles blinded him whenever he raised his head to shift position. And it was cold.

The boys shivered as they ran into Mac's Inn to warm themselves at the log fire. Charles enjoyed the peace of blessed silence, before once more succumbing to the agony of his tension headache. He bought some hot soup, but the management would not let him take a bath even though there were few residents in the lounge or dining room.

"You will have to hire a room for the night, if you want to use the facilities."

He lay on a sofa in a corner of the reception area and let his head rest against the arm, hearing Paul announce that he was going to ring Caroline.

"And we'll go to the petrol station opposite to find another lift," added Sam.

Charles grunted, held the shoulder strap of his camera close to his side and closed his eyes.

He stirred. There was a commotion at the reception. Four figures stood near the desk, talking urgently. It looked as if they were soldiers as they had guns; he could see the barrels poking over their shoulders. The lights were dim. He peered at his watch. It was nearly midnight. Where were the boys?

The men were talking.

"Twenty minutes to go now."

"Are the men in the barracks prepared?"

"They know what to do."

"We must act quickly, we have to take control of VOK radio before dawn."

"You're ready?"

"I'm ready."

"You know the password?"

"*Ndio*, I do."

"Let's go, then."

That voice. Would he ever forget that voice? Charles gave an involuntary shiver. But what was Mwangi doing here, now? It sounded as if they were in a conspiracy, but they talked with no effort to keep their voices down. The men moved away into the gardens of the inn. No one else was around.

Charles stood up, clutching his camera, and steadied himself. A folded piece of paper floated to the ground in front of him. He picked it up and put it in his pocket, then followed the men outside. He had to see what Mwangi was doing. His reporter's instinct told him that something serious was about to happen. A saloon car reversed out of the trellised parking bays. It had no lights. It swung away from him, engine roaring, and the wheels spun on the loose gravel. It raced onto the main road towards Nairobi and then the headlights came on. He could hear the whine of its engine as it progressed through the gears and faded into the night.

The Voice of Kenya radio station should be warned. Perhaps there would still be someone in his newspaper office at this time of night?

He had to find a telephone. Going to the switchboard at reception, he lifted the receiver. The line was dead. He ran to the nearby petrol station. The attendant did not have a key to the office, so Charles crossed the highway, waiting while two petrol tankers thundered past, and entered the service station opposite. They were more helpful, but the man shrugged. The line was dead.

"It's always happening – the people steal the copper lines and the telephone service is in a mess. But it was all right three hours ago, when the *mzungu* rang his mother. It must have only just happened."

"Did the *mzungu* have a friend with him? A *nusu-nusu*, a mixed-race boy?"

"Ehhh." The man nodded. "They've gone in a charcoal truck to Nairobi. They should be there by now if it hasn't broken down."

Charles had to find a way to get there quickly. A petrol tanker was about to leave the station. He ran towards it, stumbling over a flowerbed, and stopped the driver. The man shook his head.

"We're not allowed to carry passengers."

Charles banged against the door of the cab. "Don't you know who I am? Charles Omari from the National newspaper. I have to get to Nairobi urgently."

Perhaps money would persuade the driver? He put his hand in his pocket. There were no notes left. A piece of paper drifted to the ground.

"You've dropped something," the driver told him as he engaged gear to roll out of the station.

Charles watched helplessly as the tanker pulled away. He picked up the paper. It was from Sam. The boys had found a lift. They weren't able to wake him up, but they knew he wouldn't like to travel in a charcoal lorry. He mustn't worry as they had been in contact with Caroline.

He turned over the paper. Different writing was scrawled on the other side, in black ink.

YOU KNOW WHO I AM.

Mwangi again; his threats were becoming tedious. Charles read on.

YOUR LIFE IS OVER AND I KNOW WHERE YOUR SON IS.

Charles caught his breath. Mwangi must have read Sam's

message, and now his son was in danger. He had to get to Nairobi. He ran into the shop and roused the cashier for the key to the washrooms, dousing his head with water, and shaking his brain free from the remnants of sleep. The tension headache lurked again at the back of his neck.

He returned the key and spoke urgently to the attendant.

"I am looking for a lift to Nairobi."

"You won't be lucky. The tankers stop on the side at midnight and very few cars come past at this time."

Not a single headlight pricked the darkness. Charles sat on the ground.

He'd almost missed it. The white pickup was pulling away from the petrol pumps when he jerked awake and stood, waving his arms. Two men were in the cab.

"Are you going to Nairobi?"

"Ehhh…"

Charles looked in the back, crammed full with potatoes.

"Can you take me? I'll sit in the back."

The driver shrugged.

"If you wish. I don't know when we will arrive."

He climbed onto the lumpy sacks and moulded his body among the potatoes. It was more comfortable than his ordeal with the empty bottles and much quieter. But two hours later the car stopped.

"We're going for tea. Do you want to come?"

Charles peered round him and shook his head. He didn't want them to go without him and his camera would be safer if he stayed in the car. The men disappeared into a hut. An orange glow showed briefly as the door opened and a hum of voices reached him. He burrowed deep among the sacks for warmth and dozed off.

An hour later, a saloon whined past, its headlights probing the darkness. Was that another carload of conspirators? He felt so helpless.

A large sweep of bare earth lay between the parked car and the ragged lip of the tarmac road. The door of the hut creaked open and the driver appeared, holding a bottle.

"We're going soon."

The car started and Charles lifted himself into a sitting position against the back of the cab. Abandoned cars on the verge drifted past his sleepy gaze. Then he noticed a larger vehicle, awkwardly awry on three wheels. He strained his eyes. It looked as if it had sacks in the back, stuffed at the top with grass. Was it the charcoal lorry?

He thumped hard on the roof of the cab and the car drew to a halt.

"What's the matter?"

"That lorry we just passed – we have to go back!"

"Why?"

"*Sikia*, listen, I'm an important man. I'm a reporter from the National newspaper. I was stranded when you picked me up. My son is in that lorry and you have to take me back!"

"We can leave you here and you can walk."

Charles knew what they were hoping for.

"I won't forget you. I'll give you my address in Nairobi and I'll thank you very generously."

Charles sank back into the pile of potatoes as they turned the car round to pull up near the lorry. He examined the charcoal sacks. Long wisps of grass protruded from the mouths, loosely tied with string. He went to the cab. The driver lay asleep against the steering wheel. Charles shook him roughly.

"You gave a ride to two young men?"

The man yawned. "The *mzungu* and the *nusu-nusu*?"

Charles breathed out a sigh of relief. "Yes, where are they?"

The man shrugged his shoulders. "*Sijui* – I don't know."

"Come on, man! What happened?"

"They went off in a pickup, white, like that one, to Nairobi."

Every second car on Kenya's roads was a white pickup.

"It had writing on the side, it belongs to a garage. That's all I know."

"Thank you!"

Charles ran back. The driver had turned round and revved the engine. He flung himself into the back as it moved off. At least there was still hope.

Dawn broke, and Charles rubbed his eyes. He was stiff with cold. The landscape grew awash with light as the sun began its climb over the gently rolling hills of Ulu. Long waves of brown grass dotted with thorn scrub unfolded behind him, and then they were passing the parched plains of Nairobi Game Park. The Airport turnoff snaked away on the opposite side and the road rose over the hump of a railway bridge.

The car came to an abrupt halt.

Shouts came from the front and Charles sat up to peer over the cab.

"Get out!"

Soldiers in camouflage gesticulated with their guns. The driver and his mate were pulled out of the cab doors.

"Put your hands behind your heads! Lie down there, on the side, face down!"

Charles saw a black saloon on the opposite side of the road. People were standing beside it holding guns.

"You!"

He felt a rough poke on his shoulder.

"Yes, you too! Get out."

He clambered over the side. Cars were drawn up, nose to tail in the road in front of him. Rows of people lay face down on the verge, hands behind their heads. Presiding over them at intervals were soldiers, guns pointing downwards.

"Lie down there!"

He stumbled forwards. One of the men beside the black saloon was walking towards him. He looked familiar.

"Hurry up!"

The driver and his mate lay motionless, their faces flat against the dirt.

"Get down!"

The man reached him. It was Mwangi, pointing his gun. The spiteful eyes bore into him and Charles felt a stab of fear.

"You heard what he said."

He dropped onto his chest, his heart fluttering madly. He thought of Sam. Was he here? He had to warn him. He turned his head and saw Mwangi towering above him.

"Face down!"

He heard the shatter of gunfire and a painful thud ripped into the back of his knee. The sickening ache drove all thought from his head. He retched and clutched at his leg. It was wet. He looked at his hand, it was red with blood.

"Hands behind your head – or I'll shoot you again!"

Charles sank his face into the dirt, tasting the grit, and lifted his hands to fold them behind his head. His nose squashed further into the ground. He could scarcely breathe. What had happened to his leg? He felt a pull at his shoulder strap and his camera was gone, but he knew better than to resist. There was a click and a flash. He couldn't keep awake.

CHAPTER 26

Nairobi

Caroline sat beside the telephone, bemused by the calls she received. It was a wonderful world, when complete strangers went to so much trouble to keep you informed.

First, a Mr Singh from Voi called. He told her about Charles's broken down car.

"It might be a write-off," he said, "but I've sent a breakdown lorry, and your son and his friends are in good spirits."

It was a relief when she heard from Paul to say they'd arrived in Voi, but a worry when she learned from him again about their uncomfortable journey to Mtito Andei.

And then silence, until the call just now – from Europeans this time. They had been waved down as they passed a charcoal lorry on the side of the road. It had a puncture and no spare tyre. The boys had transferred into the back of a pickup.

"They refused our offer of a lift," said the man. "I must admit, they were absolutely black with soot, so would have made an awful mess. But they seemed to be enjoying the adventure; they've got blankets, and drinks, and said you weren't to worry. They'll call you when they get to Nairobi."

She wondered about Charles. Was he with them or not? She'd forgotten to ask.

She dozed off, waking periodically to look at her watch. Half past eleven. They should be here by now.

The phone rang.

"Mum, we're outside the Drive-in Cinema on the Mombasa Road. Did you get our messages?"

"Yes, I did, thank you."

"Can you come and get us?"

The cinema was on the other side of town. Caroline sighed.

"Can't you ask them to drop you in the middle of town?"

"They've gone already. Besides, we didn't have the money to persuade them any further."

"Isn't Charles with you?"

"No, we left him at Mac's Inn. He was so fast asleep we couldn't wake him. Anyway, he wouldn't have liked our transport. I'll tell you all about it when you come."

She laughed.

"I've already heard some of it. All right, stay where you are. I'm coming."

Nairobi was deserted. She locked herself into the car. Some of the lights on the dual carriageway were out, and driving through the industrial area, she switched her headlights to full beam. She caught one or two people in the glare, teetering along the pavement in a drunken stupor.

The boys were waiting for her, black with coal dust, and Paul's teeth shone white through the grime on his face.

Their return journey was strangely empty of traffic.

"It's weird, there's no one around," said Sam, his voice a whisper.

Caroline pressed her foot on the accelerator, and sped back through the roundabouts of Uhuru Highway to the dark suburbs of Westlands.

"You're not allowed to bed until you've both had a good hot bath," she said, handing them each a towel.

Caroline stirred in her sleep as the telephone rang. It was still dark. It continued ringing. She got up, fumbled with the light switch, and went to answer it.

"I'm your Representative from the British High

307

Commission," said a man's voice. "Don't leave home today until you hear it's safe." Caroline hung on to the phone. "There's been a military coup."

"When?" she gasped.

"At midnight last night. It started at Langata Barracks. Voice of Kenya radio station has been taken over."

She stumbled to the radio and turned it on. Loud military music blared back at her.

She sank back onto her bed, head in her hands.

Thank God the boys had come home safely.

The next few days were a haze of uncertainty. Innocent people were gunned down at roadblocks in and around Nairobi, others forced out of their cars, and made to lie face down on the grass for hours, hands behind their heads.

The Government regained control within twenty-four hours, but the city was cut off from the rest of the country for over a week as they tried to isolate the rebels. The aftermath continued with frightening intensity.

At least Charles is safe in Mtito, thought Caroline, as news filtered through that the trouble had been contained within Nairobi.

Things returned to normal, and the boys went back to school.

There was still no news from Charles. Not even the newspaper knew his whereabouts. She went to the mortuary, a mournful place off a large roundabout near the centre of the city. People wandered the corridors like lost souls, looking at her curiously. She was the only white person there. With a great sense of relief, she heard that the bodies recovered from the roadside had been identified, and next of kin informed.

"But there are some from elsewhere who have not been identified. Do you want to see them?"

The attendant shuffled in his flip-flops towards a door, and opened it. Bodies overflowed in haphazard piles from the slabs onto the floor, and Caroline gagged at the putrid smell. But she owed it to herself and to Sam to make sure, and held her breath as she eliminated one lifeless face after the other.

Her car stood baking in the stifling heat, but she gulped hungrily at the fresh air before driving half a mile down the road.

At the main hospital, several people were being treated for gunshot wounds and dehydration. The receptionist showed her a list of admittances, and her heart leapt when she saw the name Ondiek among them. She ran up the ramp to the surgical ward, and approached the bed. But it was not Charles.

Jackson was clearing his desk at the museum, when she sought him out.

"Have you heard from Charles?"

"No. Why?"

"I'm worried. We haven't seen him for a while. He was stranded in Mtito during the coup."

"We've never had regular contact," said Jackson. "But I'll make enquiries. I shouldn't worry too much, though. He might have decided to keep his head down, like me. I'm taking a sabbatical until everything settles. You never know where the rebels might show themselves next, and none of us will be safe until they're rounded up."

"Thank you, Jackson. You make me feel a bit better, I suppose. I'll tell Sam. When are you leaving?"

"At the end of the week." He moved to the window. "There's something soothing about standing in the bush, herding goats, being in touch with my grass roots. And I am needed there in these uncertain times." He turned back to her. "I fully believe that we have the solution to man's beginnings, and our tribal secrets must be protected."

He gestured her towards the door. "We have to take advantage of the knowledge and experience of the western world, but we must never lose the essence of our heritage."

He held her eyes as he opened the door for her.

"I think that you, Caroline, are probably one of the few *wazungu* who appreciate that we must advance in our own way. Only then will we promote a truly African answer to our international identity, and hold our heads up high."

Caroline averted her eyes, honoured and at the same time humbled by Jackson's compliment. It was as if he had rehearsed those words in his mind many times before saying them.

"I'm afraid that Sam is rather keen to learn your secrets," she confessed. "I know he wants to visit Magadi again."

"I'll be in that area for the time being." Jackson returned to his desk, and scribbled on a piece of paper. "When he's ready to come, give him this to show at the museum office. They'll send him in the regular supply vehicle. I'll look out for him."

The days passed, and Caroline's fears for Charles escalated. She thought back to the time she'd kept watch when he and Teresa had met in secret. She'd grown fond of him over the years, but always thought of him as Teresa's. Were her twinges of emotion new feelings, or guilt because she didn't return his love? But he was Sam's father; she must keep searching.

Sam was growing into a handsome lad, very like Teresa in the structure of his face, and those almond eyes were hauntingly beautiful.

Ever since their last escapade from school, they had been hounded by Mwangi, and he certainly had a hand in Teresa's death. She shuddered as she remembered that extraordinary experience. *Mzee* Ondiek, too, had lost the will to live; and then there was Charles's infant son. Could Mwangi have been involved in Charles's disappearance?

Why were her thoughts turning more and more to Mwangi? Could he even have been responsible for Brian's death? Not for the first time she recalled there had been no water in his lungs. He hadn't drowned, and the doctor said the bruise on his head couldn't have been the sole cause of death.

Would the curse evolve onto her – and, worse still, to Sam…and even Paul? She couldn't get the thought out of her mind. This was totally irrational. It was time she sought advice; and not, like before, from a fortune teller.

Caroline parked her car under the grevillea trees bordering a courtyard near St. Mary's church. She removed her sunglasses and wiped an arm against her brow, which dripped with sweat in the midday sun.

The place was deserted. Everyone must be in class. Her steps echoed on the concrete as she approached the wide-open door of the office, but it was empty.

Perhaps she would find a priest in the church? She went to the main entrance and tried the door. It was locked.

A crack of thunder reverberated from the direction of the city. Large splashes dropped onto the concrete, and the fresh smell of wet earth in the flowerbeds invaded her senses. She stood, welcoming the first cool feel of rain on her bare arms. But the torrential cloudburst that followed made her run for cover to the narrow archway of a side door. She tried it, and stepped into the empty church.

Shaking her hair to free the droplets, she walked to the aisle and genuflected before the tabernacle, then knelt in a pew, her clothes dripping water into a puddle on the floor.

Surely she was safe from Mwangi here? She glanced behind her into the shadows, half expecting to experience his ghastly presence once more. She turned to face the altar, chiding herself for being superstitious, and her hand brushed against something on the pew, causing it to fall with a tinkle to the floor.

Her fingers closed round the rosary beads, and a prayer formed in her heart.

Hail Mary, full of grace, the Lord is with thee…

The familiar chant sang through her brain.

Boney had no time for this idol worship, she remembered.

311

But he was wrong. She wasn't worshipping that statue of the Mother of God in its niche in front of her. Biblical scenes flashed through her mind as she pondered over the hardships and agonies Mary must have suffered as a woman and a mother in those long ago days.

How could she get away from that evil man? What had he done with Charles? What more would he do against her, and would he turn his attention to the boys? If only Boney were here…

'Face up to it,' he would have said, as he had when her mother died. She'd done the same after Brian's death. But her situation was different now. Or was it? Perhaps she should confront Mwangi instead of running away from him.

She stayed, head bowed, silently slipping the beads through her fingers, and meditating on the life of Christ until a wave of peace swept over her. It firmed into resolution. Of course she would have to stand up to Mwangi, for he was merely a despicable human being, who had no power over her at all.

The thundering noise of the storm stopped. Caroline went to the door and watched the steam rise from the paved courtyard as the sun beamed down.

Term ended, but there was still no news of Charles.

"I want to know where he is!" Sam shouted. "I've only just found my father, and now he's disappeared. Aren't you worried about him?"

"Of course I am, Sam. We all are. I've done all I can to find him. I even spoke to Jackson before he left for his sabbatical."

Then she remembered the note Jackson had given her before he left. She had put it away in a drawer of her desk.

"Tell you what – why don't you take this note to the museum, and you and Paul can pay Jackson a visit at the dig? Perhaps he will have some news."

But Sam returned in a rage. "When I gave the note to the receptionist," he told Caroline, "she said they were only authorised to take me, not Paul. And anyway, the last visit for the year went yesterday, as the dig is closing down before the rains."

An idea formed in Caroline's mind. "Perhaps we can arrange our own safari," she said. "It would be good to have a break from Nairobi. We'll be able to remember the way, won't we, Sam?"

"Oh yes! After Magadi, you turn away from the lake, then right at the false baobab and follow the tracks to the site." His face dropped. "But we'll need a four-wheel drive vehicle."

"Leave it with me. I'll see if one of my safari friends would let us have one for a week. Tourism has dropped off since the coup, and you never know, we might be lucky."

Caroline contacted several tourist agencies, but they had taken their vehicles off the road for servicing and paid off the drivers. Sam and Paul disappeared one morning, saying they would look for themselves, and came back, grinning broadly.

"We've found a car!"

Caroline was not impressed. "How do you know it's reliable?" she asked. "I'm not going on safari unless I'm satisfied it's not going to break down."

"It's from Vic Preston's service station," Paul said. "You know, the safari rally driver? He has a garage at the back with Land Rovers for hire. Surely you would trust him?"

Caroline hesitated.

Paul nudged her shoulder. "But they can't provide a driver."

"Well, that's that, then. We can't go without a driver."

"But, Mum, surely you can find us one? What about someone from the museum?"

Caroline closed her eyes as the nightmare reappeared. Was this her opportunity? She forced a smile.

"I'll see what I can do."

Was it fair to include the boys in her private vendetta? Would it be safe for them? She chided herself for lack of faith.

It was easy to locate Mwangi. His beady black eyes

glimmered at her from beneath his fez.

"*Ndio*, Memsahib," he said. "There will be no more work for me at the museum until after the rains. I need money, and will look after you very well."

Caroline grimaced, wondering what ulterior motives the man might be harbouring. But she had the advantage of initiating the event, and wasn't she the one with the ulterior motive?

CHAPTER 27

Magadi

Mwangi settled into the wet patch made by his shirt on the back of the car seat. A salty bead of sweat trickled down his cheek and he caught it with his tongue.

A faint track wound away from the soda lake several miles south of Magadi, where large cracks appeared in the sun-baked sand. On the right, a hump of red earth spread from the roots of a twisted thorn tree, dotted by fresh holes and tiny turrets pushed upwards by busy termites. A shadow flitted between the bushes and a cowbell tinkled. It could have been a birdcall. Mwangi glanced over at his passengers, but they hadn't heard it. Their faces were pressed against the windows, peering eyes seeking the false baobab.

He felt a tap on his shoulder.

"Stop here, Mwangi," said Caroline.

The rains had not yet broken, but a thunderstorm lurked ominously to the south. Mwangi stayed in the car while his passengers got out to stretch their legs. He watched them clamber up a nearby sand dune.

Sam was tall and nomadic-looking, but not dark enough to be a true tribesman. It was an insult that such things should happen. The other, Paul, with his fair sun-blotched skin, would be a bonus. But his mind focussed on Caroline.

Mwangi slid a plastic folder from his inside jacket pocket and studied the photograph within. He smiled. The spirits had been kind to him. He would enjoy frightening her with this.

She was at his mercy. And the others he would dispose of soon enough; in his own time.

Then he would be able to live in peace.

They were coming back. Mwangi replaced the photograph, and bent over to feel the reassuring bulk of the gun he'd hidden in a piece of sacking under the driver's seat. It was a relic from the turbulent aftermath of the abortive coup.

Sam opened the rear door of the car.

"Drat those cursed bluebottle flies."

"What flies, Sam?"

"The ones which buzzed into my eyes on the way back last year," he answered. "Don't you remember? When I opened the door they attacked me as they burst out? I could hardly see a thing, let alone landmarks. It was as if somebody had put them there on purpose."

"You mean you can't remember the way?"

"No. Maybe. I don't know. But we can't go back now."

Caroline got in beside Mwangi.

"I don't suppose you know the way to the dig, Mwangi?"

"No, Memsahib. I haven't been here before."

"We'll have to take a chance," said Sam. "There are several termite mounds, but none of them is remotely like the original false baobab. Go left here into the bush, Mwangi."

"How do you know it's the right place, and perhaps the termite mound has collapsed by now," Paul warned, as the vehicle swayed over the rough terrain. "Everything looks different."

Tall grass screened the stunted acacias, and scratched against the doors. Mwangi drew to an abrupt halt as they arrived at the brink of a sand river.

"This must be somewhere near the old dig, I think," said Caroline. "Let's cross the river, and camp on the other side. It's less overgrown."

Obediently, Mwangi inched the car down the sloping bank and it rolled forwards for a few yards, then ground to a halt.

He engaged four-wheel drive and revved the engine, spinning the wheels, but they only settled in deeper. The car was immersed above its axles in the sand river. He held his palms upwards, exaggerating the shrug of his shoulders.

"I need to walk back to Magadi and get a tow."

Caroline shook her head. "You must help us make camp first, Mwangi."

He cleared the ground for his passengers to pitch their tents, and then prepared a fire. Sam and Paul headed up the sand river to explore. As Caroline fussed over the provisions in the area she had set aside for the kitchen, he seized the opportunity.

Her back was to him, but before he could extract the photo from inside his jacket, she turned.

"Mwangi, I want to talk to you."

The steely penetration of her deep blue eyes belied the softness of her voice.

She spoke in English. "I know you can understand me, and my Swahili is not as good as your English. I want to know why you hate us so much?"

Mwangi remained silent. He wasn't going to talk to this white woman in her own language. And what could she understand about the African people, anyway? Now that he'd dealt with Charles, he just wanted to be rid of her.

"It can't still be connected with the Mau Mau thirty years ago, surely? I can understand your hatred of Dudley Myers. I didn't like him either. But he's long gone, and the people of Kenya have for years been asked to forgive and pull together. *Harambee*, you know."

Caroline gave a little smile as she repeated the late President Kenyatta's famous buzzword.

Mwangi did not want to be drawn by her friendly approach. But he couldn't stop himself.

"You don't know anything!" he retorted. "It is the oath that kills. It has nothing to do with *Harambee*."

He ended the word with a sneer as he allowed his naked hatred to consume him. He noticed her recoil from him, and his hand went towards his inner pocket.

"The Mau Mau oath, Mwangi?"

"Yes, I swore I would use the daughter's dead body to bind their servants in an oath to kill her family. That old man Ondiek speared me in the forest before I could fulfil my task. I got rid of him easily. Then I was redeemed by the daughter's death, which I caused with the power of my curse."

Mwangi watched Caroline, and he saw her face change as her mind grappled with his words.

Again, he groped inside his jacket.

"Teresa? You say you killed her because she was Myers's daughter, and through her death you have fulfilled your oath?"

"Yes," said Mwangi, his lips turning into a snarl. "Even though she died in your house. My powers are great."

"I don't doubt your powers over Teresa."

Caroline's meek answer was a joy to his ears.

"But I had unfinished business – Ondiek's son Charles escaped me for many years," he continued. "I've done away with him now."

His fingers closed over the photograph in his pocket.

"You don't understand..." Caroline's gentle voice interrupted his gloating thoughts.

Mwangi turned on her. "I know everything!" he shouted into her face.

But she did not cower away from him. Instead, her eyes looked through him, and her voice became stronger.

"You don't know, Mwangi. You don't know that Teresa was not Dudley Myers's blood relative."

"What do you mean?"

Although he made his voice loud and challenging, the fear welled in bitter waves over him. He caught his breath, and swallowed down the bile.

"Her father was a coolie working on the railway, and Dudley

Myers adopted her. So, your act of redemption was all for nothing."

Mwangi felt Caroline's eyes focussing on him, but his mind became an inner turmoil. If what she said were true, then he was still cursed.

He knew it was true, because Caroline had spoken, and he could sense the spirit in her. How could this happen to him?

His mouth went dry, he brushed away the beads of sweat gathering on his brow, and his heart pounded.

The storm was nearly upon them. The youths had returned from their exploration, and were standing on the opposite bank. Mwangi looked across at Sam silhouetted against the swirling black clouds. He had taken off his shirt and the disappearing sun caught his glistening skin in a golden bar of light.

The old terror and despair took hold. Charles's boy: that was the only way to shake off the curse. He ran for the car.

A tear in the sacking caught on the gear stick, and Mwangi pulled at it, ripping it further. It took him a few more moments to extract the gun, and then he slammed the car door behind him.

He saw Caroline clambering up the opposite bank, gesturing towards the boys, and raised the gun.

A flash of fork lightning lit the sky. Ngai, his God, replied instantly with a crack of thunder that shook the ground. As the lowering cloud enveloped him, the first hard drops bulleted down, creating pock marks in the sand. Mwangi cringed, curling in on himself as a furious hail of bullets smacked into him, pounding his head and stinging his limbs. He fired haphazardly at the invisible foe, and then straightened, rubbing his tender skin. There were no wounds. Little stones jumped in the dirt around him and settled, creating a spreading mat of whiteness. He bent down to feel them, wincing under their continuing assault on his back.

The stones were freezing cold. Never in his life had he

experienced such a thing.

He had to find shelter. He dropped the gun and ran for the car, weaving erratically and covering his head with his arms as the hail battered down.

The battering, the warders battering and battering him. He twisted away. They couldn't grab his body, slippery with sweat and blood. He felt a clutch at his ankle, pulling hard. He kicked himself free, and dived back into the heaving mass of humanity, which writhed about him.

He wrenched open the door of the car and flung himself across the seat, to shut out the pandemonium. The noise on the metal roof was deafening. He slipped into the foot well, limbs curling awkwardly round the gear lever as he cowered, covering his ears with his arms.

He burrowed deeper and deeper into the slithering mound of arms and legs and bodies, but all the while piercing ululations of terror pounded his ears. His mouth was open, but he could not hear his own scream. They didn't stop. Nothing could stop the batons, beating and beating, until the whole moving mountain of flesh writhed into exhaustion, and collapsed, and they pulled it apart, to recover the dead.

A second roar, more disturbing than the howl of the Mau Mau, filled his world, moving, rocking, spinning. He was flung from side to side, bruising painfully against the gear lever. His head bumped on the roof, his nose banged the windscreen; water everywhere. He couldn't breathe...

***

Caroline threw herself under a tangle of thorns, shouting to the boys to follow her.

She heard a massive roar. An avalanche of foaming water and loose debris rushed down the donga, leaping metres high as it tumbled past them. Between the prickly branches, she watched the pounding, angry waves sweep down, inches below her. The opposite bank burst, and the level dropped as water spread through the surrounding scrub, wrecking their campsite.

They were on the wrong side of the river and there was no sign of the car. The wait-a-bit thorns scratched at her bare legs and arms as she fought her way downstream, followed by the boys. She saw the car toppled against a boulder, half submerged in the rapids. Murky waters were greedily sucking out its contents, and Mwangi had disappeared.

Caroline stepped into the water, but it tugged urgently at her legs. She jumped back.

"We can't do anything now. The current's too strong. We'll have to wait."

"What for?"

"For the river to go down."

"How long will that be?"

Caroline turned to meet her son's eyes. A line of freckles across his cheekbones interrupted the angry pink where the sun had burned his skin. "I don't know, Paul. Could be twenty-four hours…"

They walked on. Sam rescued a can of vegetables that had washed up on their side, and Paul found a saturated box of teabags. Caroline snatched down a towel, caught on a branch, and already dry in the hot aftermath of the storm, and made her son drape it over his head to form a shadow for his face.

After several hours, the flash flood slackened pace and the level dropped, leaving a steady flowing stream cluttered with debris. Caroline followed the boys back to where the Land Rover lay firmly wedged on its side between two boulders, the river lapping through it.

"We'll have to get help to move it," said Paul. "I wonder what's happened to the driver."

Sam waded into the water.

"The current's not too bad now, and it's not that deep, either. I think I can cross here."

"Be careful!"

As the water reached his armpits he caught hold of some driftwood, jammed against a boulder. He steadied himself, and then slipped. Caroline watched him tumble down a rapid and disappear from sight. Her hand covered the scream that rose from her mouth.

She rushed into the river. The current swirled against her legs as she struggled to keep her balance. It was no good. She had to turn back.

"I'll go," said Paul.

"No – wait." Caroline barred his way with outstretched arms. "Let's go further downstream, so we can see what's happened to him."

They had to fight their way through the bush inland for fifty yards before they found a rock overlooking the rapids.

***

Jackson stood on one foot, the afternoon sun glinting on his spear as he watched the subsiding waters. He waded into the river to wrench open the driver's door. The vehicle creaked, shifted slightly, and settled. A body lay wedged against the opposite door. The eyes were open, and he recognised the face. He searched the sodden clothing and withdrew a folder, concealing it under the blanket knotted at his shoulder.

When figures emerged on the far bank of the river, he melted into the undergrowth.

A shout echoed from the opposite back, and he saw Caroline on a rock overlooking the rapids. A swirling whirlpool sucked in floating debris at her feet. Sam was thrashing violently in the water, dangerously close to the vortex.

Bare-chested and waist-high in the waters, Jackson braced himself against the raging torrent and reached with the shaft of his spear across the pool. Sam grabbed at it. Standing firm, Jackson drew him in, inch by inch.

"Thank God you were there!"

The wind took Caroline's voice, and the roar of the waters smothered the sound. Jackson looked up as she cupped her hands over her mouth.

"Is he all right?"

"Yes, but you stay there," he commanded.

He steered Sam to the riverbank. The boy was shivering.

"He needs to keep warm!" Caroline shouted.

Jackson turned to speak to Sam, who disappeared in the direction of the campsite.

An hour later, Jackson helped Caroline and Paul wade through the tugging torrent. But he would not let them near the vehicle.

"You don't want to see what's in there," he said, throwing Caroline a meaningful glance. "I'm afraid your driver has been unlucky."

Caroline closed her eyes for a brief moment.

"Is he...?"

Jackson nodded. "We're well rid of him."

But Mwangi was still there; his body was in the Land Rover.

Jackson stood guard while another storm raged later in the evening, and Caroline came to him twice in the night.

"I can't sleep," she said as they listened to the rushing waters. He knew she was grappling in her mind with the spiritual forces around them.

In the morning, no trace remained of the vehicle or the body.

"Shouldn't we go looking for it?" asked Paul.

"Leave it," said Jackson. "There's nothing anyone can do.

The museum will have to write off the vehicle, and Mwangi's body won't last long."

Vultures would tear into the remains, and hyenas would slink away with severed limbs.

It was time for them to go.

"You have a long walk in front of you," Jackson told Caroline. "You should leave before the sun gets too high. Keep your right side to it. Climb sand dunes on the way, to look for the salt pans of Lake Magadi, and get your bearings. The men at the soda company will help you to Nairobi."

"Aren't you coming with us?"

"No, Sam, I'm still on leave. And I have work to do here."

"What work?"

Jackson met Caroline's eye, and then he looked past her shoulder towards the escarpment.

"Perhaps I'll tell you one day, Sam," Jackson said. "Maybe I will show you where our ancestors are sleeping; and you can help in the work I am doing. But now is not the time."

A white glimmer flashed on the escarpment to the east. Jackson watched Caroline and the boys disappear towards the soda lake, then he worked his way upstream to find a safe river crossing. He loped towards the skyline in easy strides, zigzagging over the rough terrain. Sometimes the distant scarp disappeared behind a folded hill or an eroded bank, but he headed for high ground, picked it up again, and renewed his steady run.

As the afternoon waned, he inched up a rock fissure, then, catlike, clambered across a ledge, feeling for familiar foot and handholds until the dark yawn of the cave engulfed him.

The sorceress greeted him, clad in faded cotton rags, the tools of her trade scattered round her. A goat's foot lay at the cave mouth, pointing towards the distant remains of the campsite. The mirror shard she had used for signalling lay propped against the rock.

"You did well to destroy the termite mound which marked the way," she chuckled. "It confused the *wazungu*, and the gods are surely with us, for the storm has taken the car, and they have a long way to walk."

"They are not all *wazungu*, sister," chided the tribesman. "One has our family blood in his veins. But you are more right than you know, for in that car was the cause of a generation of suffering. His body is now washed away and will become food for the hyenas."

"Ehhh – the curse is broken at last," Simaloi touched his arm and smiled up at him, "and we can rest in peace."

Jackson entered the cave and, from a leather briefcase leaning against the rock, he pulled a pair of binoculars. He scanned the distant river. The roof of the vehicle, washed up some miles downstream, leapt closely before his eyes. There was no sign of Caroline and the boys.

"Yes, sister, the cradle of our ancestors will now lie undisturbed. Our country must not become a stamping ground for the greedy until we are sure we can have our say. And our people must be guaranteed their land."

A faint wheeze and a cough sounded from the depths of the cave, and Simaloi stirred beside him.

"He's improving," she said in answer to Jackson's raised eyebrows. "But he is still very sleepy. My herbs and potions are taking effect, but it will be a long time."

"The pneumonia hasn't helped," said Jackson. "How is his leg?"

"Not good."

"We'll give him some more of the *dawa* I got from the doctor at the Mission Hospital which rescued him. Did you know it was where his children were born?"

Jackson knew that Simaloi didn't believe in the white man's medicine, but they agreed it was necessary to use every possible means to further their brother's recovery.

He replaced the binoculars and, picking up a fluorescent

torch, approached the pallet where Charles slept.

After gently brushing away the beads of sweat from his brother's forehead, Jackson shone his torch into a large inner chamber of the cave. He tucked his blanket behind his knees, folded his ochred limbs in a single lithe movement, and squatted at the rock face.

He dusted out the corner he'd marked many years before, and uncovered faint scratchings on the surface. The etching of stick men dancing above a buffalo never failed to quicken his heart. He brushed some more, to disclose a spear protruding from the animal's side. He opened his briefcase to extract the materials he had brought with him to trace and preserve his discovery.

The rock face stretched for over twenty feet. There was no knowing what other treasures would be revealed. The work of a lifetime lay before him.

EPILOGUE

There is a path leading down to the beach, a white sandy path, dotted with prickles and pine needles under the casuarina trees.

Caroline picks her way barefoot down the gentle undulations of the terraces, toes scrunching in pain as her soles encounter the spiky cones. She doesn't like wearing her sandals, because then she has to leave them on the shore, a temptation for passing *totos*. Around her, three Alsatian dogs race in circles, chasing each other. They thunder across the short grass and gallop up to her.

"Down, Tawny. Down!" Her voice is angry.

A red line drips from a scratch on her thigh, and she pushes the puppy away. Her skin is paper-thin. She picks up a stick and throws it. Tawny wins the scramble and proudly paces up to her, stick in mouth, but refuses to surrender it. Caroline gives up and lifts her binoculars to search the bushes where a white-browed coucal has made its gentle bubbling call. She catches it, lurking among the leaves, its soft brown silhouette briefly showing against the breakers.

The tide is on the turn. It is early morning and hers are the only footprints on the beach. Waves languorously lap in huge folds, breaking against the rising sand. This is the time she likes best, when the sea is glassy, and her arms slice the water leaving her head sticking up like a turtle's, with no danger of being splashed. She has always hated getting her face wet.

She lifts her legs to float chin on chest in the salt-heavy water, and gazes back at the shore. The palm fronds are

327

golden-tipped, catching the first rays of sun; a dark cliff broods out of the waves to the north. This was where she last saw Brian, so long ago. Her eyes prick with tears, but she is at peace, now.

Along the beach, the dogs bark as they scuffle after crabs, charging over her wrap and binoculars. She shouts at them, wading through the waters, her loose-skinned limbs wrinkled, her belly softly sagging under the bright blue swimsuit.

She recovers the *kikoi*, shaking out the sand, and inspects her binoculars, wiping them carefully with a corner of the material. Then she hangs them over her head and strides southward in the wake of the dogs, who bark and cavort towards a distant figure.

They draw closer. The dogs yap their greetings, tumbling over a Jack Russell terrier, and sniffing noses with a golden Rhodesian Ridgeback.

The animals run circles round each other as Caroline approaches Michael, who turns to match her strides, walking briskly, stopping from time to time to remark on a rare starfish, or turn over a piece of coral to surprise a crab. The treasures of the coast are not as rich as they used to be. Butterfly shells and leopard cowries now recline on the shelves of overseas tourists. But the sun is the same. It warms their backs, which are tanned to a leathery glow. They turn, squinting into its brightness, and quicken their steps. Caroline waves briefly as Michael calls goodbye at the path to his cottage.

"See you this evening!"

She stops and listens, lifting her binoculars, then creeps towards a patch of scrub. A bright flash of yellow quivers deep among the leaves of a high flame tree; the bird frisks briefly to an outer branch. Caroline catches her breath at the beauty of the golden oriole, its throat opened in glorious song. The ecstasy lingers as she walks away into the sun.

Ethel has laid the breakfast table, freshly squeezed orange juice and toast without butter. Caroline swallows a blood pressure tablet, wipes her mouth and heads for the shower.

"What do we need today, Ethel?"

"Bread, and more bananas, Caroline. And don't forget the dry ice."

Her old car coughs into action. She reverses into the deep sand banking the driveway, and edges onto the tarmac road, giving way to a delivery van. Heat radiates through the car. This is the part of the day she likes the least. She'll be getting a new car soon, with air conditioning. Perhaps that will make a difference.

The *duka* down the road is now a modern supermarket, but the tellers are the same friendly Indians. Caroline wanders round the lines of shelves, picking out cans of beer and a bottle of wine. The boys are due to arrive tomorrow; she still thinks of them as boys.

A friend is browsing the next aisle and they share a cool drink together on the patio, then she gets into her car, almost too hot to touch, to fetch some dry ice.

By the time she arrives home, there is a wet patch of sweat on the seat, and her blouse is sticking to her back. Ethel unpacks while Caroline downs a glass of water and goes for another shower. She envies Ethel's ability to absorb the heat without seeming to suffer. Lunch is a simple salad with a glass of shandy, and then she carries a camp chair to the spreading macadamia tree half way to the beach.

The dogs plod after her, and flop down, tails wiping sand onto her feet. Her binoculars dangle from an arm of the chair; she puts on her sunglasses, adjusts her straw hat and opens a novel.

But her ears are attuned, and with every call or rustle, she lifts the binoculars to surprise yet another marvel of nature. A swarm of bees hum towards a nearby mimosa. Translucent crabs, their eyes on stalks, creep sideways from their holes, and scamper back at the merest lifting of a finger, raising puffs of sand. A chameleon, green, black and brown, makes a movement, then freezes, to progress in slow stages along a dry twig towards a fly, busily preening its wings. Caroline's eyelids droop, and the paperback slips from her lap.

The wind has picked up and the sun finds a gap in the leaves. Her nose is burning red, and she glances at her watch. She is almost late.

The school nestles at the end of an avenue of jacarandas, their flowers making a purple carpet on the drive. Caroline parks in the shade beside the roundabout, whose centre is a riot of bougainvillea bushes, reds, all shades of purple, and whites in blazing contrast. A low fringe of Christ-thorn lines the drive, its delicate blood red flowers lost amid the profusion of colour.

She springs up the steps between whitewashed columns and turns into the quadrangle to enter a classroom. Sister Reilly has closed her bible. The children, perched on benches, swing their bare feet under long wooden tables, chatting quietly. Little Emily, her head stretched into lines of tight plaits which taper into a bunch at the nape of her neck, smiles at Caroline, her brown eyes wide with delight. She's wearing a faded blue check dress today, far too big for her. Her arms are invisible, and little hands protrude from the puffed sleeves. She is Caroline's protégé, as her mother, Ethel's granddaughter, has died of AIDS. Ethel told her once that Emily's mother was Charles's daughter, causing Caroline to wonder at the intricacies of African life. Her mind returns to the fateful aftermath of the coup, and to Jackson's disclosure when he returned from his sabbatical.

"The day I rescued Sam from the river, I took a couple of things from Mwangi's pocket before his body was washed away," Jackson had told her. "One was his driving licence. The

330

other was this."

He handed Caroline a sealed plastic folder. She turned it over, and a colour image of Charles stared back at her. It was definitely Charles. He was on his back, eyes closed, arms flopping around his head as if he had been turned over. His right leg below the knee was black with what could have been encrusted blood. It projected at an unnatural angle away from his body.

Her heart raced as she studied the photograph. He might not be dead.

There's no more time for reminiscence.

The baby class now numbers over forty, and the nuns can't take any more. Sister Reilly nods serenely at Caroline and, composed for prayer, slips out of the classroom. The children are round and bonny. You would never have thought they were AIDS orphans.

Their eager faces lift as she delves into her bag for jelly babies, then she distributes foolscap paper, used side face down, and passes out crayons. She turns to sketch a chicken on the whiteboard.

"What am I drawing?"

"Kuku – kuku!"

A chorus of voices call out in delight, as they take their crayons and try to copy. It's no use giving them pictures of leopard or lion – they've never seen one. She writes the word 'kuku' on the board and goes round the class, helping them with the letters. Next, it's a goat, but this time she doesn't let them say the Kiswahili word. Emily, bless her soul, pipes up, waving a hand in the air: "Goat! Goat!"

Twenty minutes pass, and it's time for a drink and a biscuit before the orphans wander, hand in hand down faint paths through the bush. Their dormitories are cool thatched rondavels surrounding a patch of bare earth. Here, the boys kick at a football, and the girls stand in a circle, throwing an old tennis ball.

Sister Reilly reappears and chivvies them to wash their hands under a tap before going to the kitchen where she has prepared a pot of *posho* and *sukuma wiki*. They line up with their bowls and accept dollops of the maize meal mixed with spinach-like leaves; it is the cheapest obtainable vegetable when the week's allowance barely stretches the distance. This time a goat has been slaughtered, and gristly lumps of meat swim in thin gravy. One piece is allocated to each child as they sit on the bare earth to slurp up the food with their fingers.

It is pleasantly cool as Caroline drives back to the five-acre plot she inherited from Boney. She allows her hair to ripple in the rush of air from the open car window, and draws up beside the ten thousand gallon rainwater tank, screened behind vibrant bougainvillea bushes. The gutters need cleaning again, and the one over the back door is detached from its drainpipe. She must remember to ask Michael to contact the new handyman in the area.

The sun casts long shadows over the beach, and she changes into a pair of shorts, picks up a *kikoi* to wrap round her shoulders, and chooses a long stick, one of many propped beside the veranda steps, useful when prodding the sea bed for new discoveries, or to keep balance when negotiating rock pools. Latterly, she has used it to lean on as she eases her back after plodding through the sands left stodgy by a receding tide.

The dogs emerge from their stupor, stretch from end to end and shake themselves. With a final flick of their tails, they trot after Caroline down the path to the beach. Tawny starts running in circles, and soon they are all enjoying the game of 'fetch'.

Michael is waiting for her, hatless, on the beach. He is almost bald now – a few thin strands of white hair wisp over his brow, and he flicks them away with his fingers. Their feet sink into the stiffly clinging sand, leaving deep prints as they turn northward this time, to skirt the coral cliffs and paddle

332

among the rock pools. The thunder of the waters beyond the reef, a kilometre away, shifts a tone.

"Tide's turning," Caroline mutters, as they quicken their steps to round the point and stride along the wide sands of the beach. Groups of walkers in twos and threes are silhouetted against the sand. They meet and pass, calling their dogs to heel, sometimes stopping to talk. The holiday season is upon them, when children and grandchildren emerge from the palms, gripping buckets and spades to make castles with moats to meet the incoming tide. Hotels, hidden behind thick foliage, are awakening.

There are disadvantages to living in such an idyllic place, but the residents have learned to adjust their habits during peak seasons. They sacrifice their multiple mile daily walks to avoid the tourists, and drop in on each other for coffee or sundowners instead, exchanging gossip, walking round gardens, taking cuttings and tearing up roots to proliferate exotic tropical treasures.

Caroline and Michael lengthen their strides and go about the serious business of daily exercise. The trippers are behind them. There is no breath to spare for talking. The dogs forage in the undergrowth above the tide line, leaving their marks on others' territories, sniffing noses with strangers, and running to catch up.

Caroline breaks into a jog for a hundred yards, then stops, puffing heavily, and throws herself onto the sand. The dogs lick her face, and flop against her as Michael removes a handkerchief from his pocket, places it in an indentation in the sand, and carefully sits down.

They watch the incoming tide. She casts a sidelong glance at him. She can see every rib in his tanned body. The skin hangs loosely under his arms and thighs, but she knows he is still tough. They've both come a long way, he with his broken marriage, and herself nearly the cause of a second. He is now a respectable widower, but Caroline remembers him as an irresponsible profligate who cannot control his passions. She wonders again how many children he has fathered, with how many different women. She cannot believe his repeated assurances that he only has a son with his first wife and two daughters with his second.

Amazingly, after a period in London, he is now back, retired to the same tiny corner of the world where Boney built his refuge with Ethel. Is it really a coincidence? She wouldn't put it past Michael to manipulate even that. He shifts his gaze to interrupt her thoughts.

"No, I'll never admit to more than three children, my dear; and I assure you, I had no idea that you take your annual holiday along the very same beach where I bought my retirement home. I just had to come back. Do you blame me?"

She laughs. It is uncanny, the way they are so much in tune. His hand creeps along the sand between them, and finds hers. A faint thrill surprises her. At her age... She laughs again, shifting slightly so their hands fall apart, and looks him in the eye.

"None of your nonsense, Michael – I'm a grown girl now. This is not the naïve secretary you picked up all those years ago!"

He looks away.

She didn't mean to hurt him, but she won't fall into the old trap of apologising and trying to make up again. Not anymore. But there is one question she's always wanted to ask.

"You were always vague about what you did before I met you. Did you have any connection with prison camps and Mau Mau detainees?"

"Not in person. But I did help devise a technique – which went dramatically wrong – of forcing obstinate prisoners to work. We would separate them into small groups of three or four, guarded by warders to prevent them from joining up. Sometimes the prisoners would get away, and huddle together in a large mass. Did you ever hear about the Hola Massacre?"

"No."

"People died, and it was hushed up. Even the name of the place was changed. It was said that the incident helped to precipitate Independence. We weren't proud of it, but we were only doing our job. Why do you ask?"

Caroline gazes out at the ocean.

She remembers what the prison officer told her in the bar, about a slithering mass of Mau Mau forming themselves into a writhing heap of humanity, ten feet high. They must have been terrified out of their minds by the clubbing of the warders. Mwangi could have been one of them. Now she knows what he meant when she overheard him talking to Charles at the museum. His prediction has come true, for Michael is now a widower, and she has never re-married.

Did Charles die in the attempted coup, or did he disappear to live another life, like Teresa? It was all so long ago.

The beach has reduced by half, and is no longer bathed in sunlight. Waves are gathering momentum, but it is only a neap tide, so they don't have to worry about the headland on the way home.

Boney's old home is now hers, although Ethel will live there for the rest of her life.

Caroline's life scrolls before her. The paths she has taken were littered with choices and consequences. Looking back, she sees them now; but in the throes of living, blinded by the moment, how she thrashed about, sometimes wildly, sometimes helplessly; sometimes remembering to cry out for help, sometimes not.

Most of all, she realises that however much she wants to be an integral part of this country that she loves, she can never really belong. Her contribution is confined to humble charities, but what wonderful satisfaction she gets from little Emily.

The sky has darkened. Michael stands and dusts his handkerchief against his shorts, then offers Caroline a hand up. They turn to retrace their steps along the sand. The brief African twilight gives way to star-spangled night, and the half-moon is rising as they pick their way among the crabs.

THE END

GLOSSARY

askari	guard
bandas	round huts
bibis	pronounced 'bee-bees', wives
boma	livestock enclosure
bwana	of Arabic origin, used as a respectful form of address for a man
chai	literally 'tea'. Another word for bribe.
chang'aa	an illegal alcoholic drink, distilled from grains, which is very potent
Chini Club	literally 'the Club down below', the Mombasa Club on the shores of the old harbour, exclusive to Europeans
Coup	The coup of 1982, attempted by disaffected politicians, was quickly smothered by the Government under President Daniel arap Moi. After the Coup, Kenya became a one-party state.
Daniel arap Moi	A member of the Kalenjin tribal community. He was Vice President of Kenya in 1967, and succeeded the Kikuyu Jomo Kenyatta as President from 1978-2002. In turn, Moi's Vice-President was a member of the Kikuyu tribe.
Dawa	medicine
duka	small wayside shop
habari	how is everything, or how are you?
Harambee	We will all pull together. The slogan of President Jomo Kenyatta when he came to power at Independence in 1963. Included in this invitation were people of all races, in an effort to foster reconciliation.

Hola Massacre	A dark moment in Kenya's history in 1959, when hard core detainees in Hola prison camp got out of hand and were beaten by local warders in the absence of officers, who had devised a divide and rule technique to force the prisoners to work. Eleven died. The name of the place was changed, and the event hastened the granting of Independence.
Independence	The Mau Mau rebellion precipitated the granting of Independence to Kenya in 1963. There was a major exodus of settler farmers in the run up to Independence, as they took advantage of the British Government's compensation program for improvements to the land, which had been allocated to them in the early 1900's.
jambo	greetings
Jomo Kenyatta	A member of the Kikuyu tribe, he was Kenya's first President. He went to mission school, and after furthering his education in England and Russia, he returned to Kenya to play an active part in politics. He was arrested in 1952 for implication in the Mau Mau movement, and finally released in 1961. During his term of office, Kenya was a two-party Republic.
jua kali	literally 'hot sun', refers to businesses open to the elements
KPR	Kenya Police Reserve, formed in 1948 to support the regular police
kanzu	long white robe worn by African house servants
kikapu	pronounced 'kee-kaa-poo', a commonly used soft basket made of woven straw

kikoi	a colourful length of cotton, fringed at each end, often worn round the waist
Kikuyu	farming people of Bantu origin, the largest ethnic group in Kenya, who started the Mau Mau rebellion of the 1950's
kitenge	length of colourful multipurpose cotton
Kukes	White settler slang for their Kikuyu labourers. The Mau Mau belonged to the Kikuyu tribe.
kuni	firewood
kwaheri	goodbye
lakini	but, or however
Masai	pronounced Maaa-sai. A powerful semi-nomadic warrior tribe of Nilotic origin, whose lives centre round the herding of cattle. Traditional enemy of the Kikuyu.
matatus	pronounced 'maa-taa-toos', local taxis, usually minibuses, which were crammed with as many people as possible
Mathare	The name given to notorious slums on the outskirts of Nairobi, bordering on the exclusive suburb of Muthaiga
Mau Mau	Liberation fighters against the white farmers during the 1950's, which led to Kenya's Independence in 1963.
memsahib	originating from India, colonial title of respect for white women
Mzee	to rhyme loosely with 'day', this is the respectful Kiswahili word for 'old man'
mzungu	a white man
mzuri	well, or good
ndio	yes
ngini	more
nusu-nusu	literally half-half. A person who is half one race, half another.

Ondiek	pronounced 'On-dee-eck'. Charles Omari Ondiek is a member of the agricultural Kisii tribe. Of Bantu origin, the Kisii occupied fertile land along the shores of Lake Victoria, and frequently battled against the neighbouring Masai.
posho	porridge made with maize meal
rungu	traditional weapon comprising a stick with a heavy knob on the end
shambas	farmland, small holdings
shauri ya mungu	God's will
sijui	pronounced 'si-jew-ee', I don't know
sikia	listen
simba	lion
sufuria	metal cooking pot
sukuma wiki	literally 'pushing the week', a hardy vegetable, which tastes like spinach, eaten when there is nothing left of the weekly wage
swara	antelope
syce	Arabic origin, common word for a groom
Tanganyika	A sovereign state in East Africa, south of Kenya, until 1964 when it joined with Zanzibar and the name was changed to Tanzania
thahu	Pronounced 'Thaa – hoo', curse
totos	Pronounced 'toe-toes', children
wananchi	ordinary people
watu	people
wazungu	white people

Fantastic Books
Great Authors

Meet our authors and discover our exciting range:

- Gripping Thrillers
- Cosy Mysteries
- Romantic Chick-Lit
- Fascinating Historicals
- Exciting Fantasy
- Young Adult and Children's Adventures

Visit us at:
www.crookedcatbooks.com

Join us on facebook:
www.facebook.com/crookedcatpublishing

2526286R00209

Printed in Germany
by Amazon Distribution
GmbH, Leipzig